Whirlwind of the Lord

To order additional copies of *Whirlwind of the Lord,* by Margaret White-Thiele, call **1-800-765-6955.**

Visit us at www.rhpa.org
for more information on Review and Herald products.

*The fascinating true story
of Sarepta Myrenda Irish Henry*

Whirlwind of the Lord

MARGARET WHITE-THIELE

REVIEW AND HERALD® PUBLISHING ASSOCIATION
HAGERSTOWN, MD 21740

This book was
Edited by Jeannette R. Johnson
Designed by Patricia S. Wegh
Cover illustration by Joel Spector
Typeset: 12/15 Bembo

PRINTED IN U.S.A.

02 01 00 99 98   5 4 3 2 1

R&H Cataloging Service
White-Thiele, Margaret Rossiter
        The whirlwind of the Lord: the story
of Mrs. S.M.I. Henry.
        1. Henry, Sarepta Myrenda Irish, 1839-1900. I. Title.
                        [B]

ISBN 0-8280-1398-5

In hope and blessed memory

DEDICATION

The story of this woman of lofty purpose, outstanding ability, and rare experience in public work has been written in the hope that it may be an inspiration to the young people of today, and may keep in blessed memory for the older generation the significance and scope of Mrs. Henry's contribution to the Advent cause.

—Margaret Rossiter White-Thiele

*The fascinating true story
of Sarepta Myrenda Irish Henry,
crusader for temperance*

In appreciation

ACKNOWLEDGMENT

The material of this book is a fabric woven from many threads. Most of them were drawn, directly or indirectly, from *My Mother's Life,* written by Mary Henry Rossiter. Some of them came from the published works of Mrs. Henry, now out of print and difficult to obtain. Members of the Henry family, some of whom still live on the old homestead at East Homer, New York, supplied letters and reminiscences. Mrs. Grace Mace, of Takoma Park, Maryland, who was Mrs. Henry's secretary during her later years, had many interesting stories to recall from her memories of her association and travels. To Henry Brown, who first made the suggestion to begin this project, and who has kept it alive when difficulties arose, as well as to all those who have contributed in the preparation of this book, my earnest appreciation.

—*Margaret Rossiter White-Thiele*

ACKNOWLEDGMENT

CONTENTS

Dedication
From the Author to the Reader

FROM THE AUTHOR
TO THE READER

*T*his is the true story of one whose life reached out and touched countless thousands of people, not in influence only, but in personal contact and soul-saving work; who pioneered in the organization of one of the greatest forces for good in the country. Her work is a challenge to the mothers of today who must face the same problems in their homes, in their communities, and in the nation. The challenge is the same as that made to American womanhood by Peter Marshall, former chaplain of the Senate:

"The modern challenge to motherhood is the eternal challenge—that of being godly women.
The very phrase sounds strange in our ears. We never hear it now.

"We hear about every other kind of women—
beautiful women,
smart women,
sophisticated women,
career women,
talented women,
divorced women,

but so seldom do we hear of a godly woman—or of a godly man either, for that matter. . . .

"The world has enough women who know how to hold their cocktails
who have lost all their illusions
and their faith.
The world has enough women who know how to be smart.
It needs women who are willing to be simple.
The world has enough women who know how to be brilliant.
It needs some who will be brave.

"The world has enough women who are popular.
It needs more who are pure.
We need women, and men too, who would rather be morally right than socially correct."⋆

Sarepta Myrenda Irish Henry, affectionately called Smi by Frances Willard, was a godly woman. She lived with a single purpose, to follow the guidance of God in her life. She was of the stuff that reformers are made, and of those few in the world to whom have been given an absorbing passion for souls. Such as these are hard for ordinary mortals with ordinary inclinations to self-indulgence to understand. But they are a binding influence in the world. The records of history are accented with their heroic figures.

The trend today is to exalt and exploit the superficial feminine qualities. The admiration of young people is daily directed in countless ways to the importance of beautiful hair, clear skin, an alluring smile, and a well-proportioned figure, instead of to the charm of cheerfulness, the premium of patience, and the pride of purity. We need more models for the garment of holiness and fewer for the creations of the dictators of fashion. When our young women are stirred to emulate a Jane Addams or a Frances Willard or an Ellen White rather than some star of stage or screen, then our divorce courts will be empty and our homes for juvenile delinquents go out of business.

—*Margaret Rossiter White-Thiele*

---

*Peter Marshall, *Mr. Jones, Meet the Master* (New York: Fleming H. Revell Company), pp. 154, 155.

Part One

THE SEEDS
OF TRUTH

*A*nd thou shalt love the Lord thy God with all thine heart, and with all thy soul, and with all thy might. And these words, which I command thee this day, shall be in thine heart: and thou shalt teach them diligently unto thy children, and shalt talk of them when thou sittest in thine house, and when thou walkest by the way, and when thou liest down, and when thou risest up" (Deut. 6:5-7).

Chapter One

ON THE
WESTERN TRAIL

*I*t wasn't really a road at all, only a widened trail, not many years removed from the quick tread of the moccasined feet of the red men. But it was at least a clearing through the woods, and there were no fallen trees or impassable boulders to obstruct progress. This much was owing to the new ruling of the Pennsylvania Legislature that each county should be responsible for the maintenance of its own roads, to convenience the increasing number of wheels that were rolling westward. But at times it took discernment to discover a road at all, and a mariner's sense of direction had to substitute for signs and guideposts.

The square carriage behind the team of gray horses mounted the crest of the hill with difficulty. It was as streamlined as a full-rigged sailing ship, and just about as steady, for the road held unseen pits under layers of dust, as well as outcropping rock and the remains of old stumps. All day the riders had lurched and swayed in uncertain rhythm, sometimes hardly keeping their seats, which were perched atop the carriage bed with utter disregard for the principles of air flow and wind resistance.

But the family of four did not mind the bumping and jolting and shaking and swaying. This was the first day of the big adventure, the 800-mile trek was to lead them from the grandeur of the Pennsylvania hills down through the gradually flattening country of Ohio, along the shores of Lake Erie, beside the sand dunes of Lake Michigan, into the prairie land of Illinois.

"How long will it be, Father, before we reach the main turnpike to Erie?" asked Hylas, a sturdy lad of 14, sitting beside his mother on the rear seat.

"That is hard to say," his father answered without turning in the seat, "but, God willing, and with favorable weather, we should be out of the woods of Pennsylvania within a week."

As they came up over the hill a delightful panorama of wooded hills spread out below them. The maples, hemlocks, oaks, and elms each contributed a different shade of green to the unending ridges. There was hardly a break in the virgin forests—hardly a spot where a man could plant a field or pasture his cattle. In fact, looking down, as they did now, they could not see a house or a barn or any sign of habitation within range of their vision.

But far ahead on the little strip of road, which appeared now and then as a slender brown cut in the green as it unwound itself down the side of the mountain, was a tiny moving speck. Hylas braced himself and stood unsteadily in the wagon box to peer ahead.

"There it is again!" he cried eagerly. "I can see now—it is a wagon and a single team of horses. See, Sara, just going behind the trees down there! I wish we could catch up with them! 'Twould be jolly fun to see who they are and where they are going. Can't we go a little faster, Father?"

"Doubtless in due process of time we may come up with them, my son, but on this downgrade it will be our care to restrain our speed rather than to give rein. If we should move faster than our brakes would hold—"

"Horatio! What would we do then?" the mother asked in a tone of alarm.

"We might have to chain the wheels, if it gets too steep; but don't worry, we'll be careful." Horatio Irish turned slightly in his seat and smiled reassuringly at his wife. His strong angular face with

18

the intense black eyes might have been harsh had it not been softened by the kindly lines etched by an abiding spirit of goodwill and an expression of deep spirituality.

"I do wish we could turn south and travel the Cumberland highway," Hylas said, looking up from the map he was studying. "Certainly it is by far the best road, and there must be a lot of interesting things to see that way, all kinds of traffic, and we'd meet travelers from the Far West, and—"

"The only thing is," the father put in mildly, "it is not the best route to our destination."

The decision Horatio Irish had made that spring of 1843, to sever the ties of kindred and comfortable living in the home of his forefathers at Albion, Pennsylvania, and move his entire family nearly 1,000 miles to a frontier village, was not the whim of a roving spirit or the youthful craving for adventure.

By disposition he was studious and fond of special research, and would have been content to continue with his family in tender intimacy and comfort, holding the respected place in a community where the name of Irish had long been held in honorary esteem. But he was a man of deep religious purpose, whose daily actions were submitted to the guidance of God, and whose heart was always open to the whisperings of the Spirit, so that when at last he heard within what he considered the imperative voice of God bidding him go to the then Far West and preach the gospel to the pioneers and Indians, there was only one thing to do.

With his family assembled around him in the austere but comfortable surroundings of the high-ceilinged parlor in the old home, he told them of his purpose. He had already confided in his wife and received her assent. She knew full well the implications of such an undertaking with two young children, but she stood by her husband, as she always had, with full courage and confidence.

The decision was far harder on those who would be left behind. But the blood of the pioneers was in their veins, and it was not in their nature to complain or to make a show of emotion. One of the family virtues was to allow each individual the right of choice and to encourage independent thinking and action. "Every tub must stand on its own bottom" was an oft-quoted family proverb. And so, when the day came to go out from their own land and their own kindred, like Abraham of old, they went happily and gladly, while the hearts of those who waved them off were filled with pride and love and hope.

Little Sara had been the favorite of her uncle, her mother's brother, and she long remembered this pale man who drew her tenderly to his side and talked in such a serious and quiet way.

On the day of departure Grandma Irish took her little granddaughter into her lap and held her close.

"Sarepta Myrenda," she said solemnly, calling her by the full name as she did only on special occasions, "you are going on a long journey, and this may be hard on you at times. You may be in danger of Indians, or wild rough men, or animals, but if you trust in Jesus, He will take care of you. Here is something I want you to take with you, not to remember me by, but to be a comfort and joy to you wherever you go." And she put into the child's hand a plump little old-fashioned Bible, strongly and securely bound in calfskin.

And Sara, sitting close to her father on the front seat of the carriage as they jogged over the bumpy road, clutched the precious gift to her bosom and longed for the time when she would be able to read it herself.

It was pleasant riding, hour after hour in the bosom of her family, observing the fresh foliage on the wood-covered hills, watching for sparkling streams coming down from the hillsides, and listening to the deep voice of her father as he discoursed of the things of God revealed in nature and the Word. Sometimes she did not understand, for she was only 4, but mostly the lessons were simple and homely.

> "The trees of the Lord are full of sap;
> The cedars of Lebanon, which he hath planted;
> Where the birds make their nests—"

He made it sound like poetry with his musical voice. She was constantly amazed at his knowledge of the Bible and the beautiful things he had to tell.

To Mr. Irish every chestnut tree and every sycamore, every cascading waterfall or distant mountain peak, suggested some verse of Scripture or lesson in Old Testament history to share with the family. These thoughts were not hammered into them in a pedantic or dogmatic way, but were brought forth as treasures from a rich and spiritual mind, the very breath of his soul.

There was a feeling of family unity and solidarity, which was never so strong as through the long hours when the family sat together, sharing their pleasures and thoughts as well as the inescapable hard seats. This first day of many they were to spend on the journey was a happy one.

The sun was hidden behind the hills when they found a spot off the road favorable for the first camp. A small stream in a fern-lined ravine provided both water and music, and a level floor of grassy turf was selected for the site of the tent. To jump off the hard carriage seats and begin making camp was a welcome change from sitting all day. Hylas unhitched the horses and then helped his father with the tent. The heavy carriage poles were removed from under the carriage bed; the canvas was spread over the frame and fastened tightly to small wooden stakes.

Sara helped her mother gather wood and brush, and soon a fire was crackling merrily, and they brought forth the good things to eat that had been prepared in advance for the first few days of the journey. A savory stew was hung on a tripod over the fire to warm while the beds were made up in the tent. Soon all was in readiness for the darkness that would erelong overtake them.

The firelight brought out the glow of happiness on the four faces as they were gathered around the cloth spread with the many good things. The neighbors had been kind and brought many delicacies to add to the provisions for the trip. The first day in and out-of-doors had doubled their appetites. Sara sat close to her father, her large dark eyes luminous with enjoyment, and her small thin face a dainty miniature of his bold features. Hylas was fire tender, and was hardly still a minute, jumping up and down between every mouthful of food to poke the fire or add fuel. Mrs. Irish, a large matronly figure, with a broad motherly face and a passive expression, ministered to the needs of her family with such quiet unobtrusiveness that in a less-appreciative family her work might have been accepted as unconsciously as the sunshine and air.

When everyone else was tucked under the covers, Mrs. Irish carefully covered the fire, so that there would be a mass of coals for getting the early breakfast.

Sleeping on the ground was not a hardship but a privilege, and for those who were willing to try it there were special rewards from Dame Nature in the pine-scented air, the hum of cicadas, and the sound of running water. The first effect of the full tide of fresh air that filled their lungs was exhilarating, almost too much so for sleep; but suddenly—not one of them could tell how or when it happened—they each dropped off into a dreamless slumber.

The delight of choosing a spot to camp and of sleeping so close to nature was not to decrease as the days went by, and the little map was marked with a record of their campfires.

The meeting of fellow travelers, some on horseback, some in covered wagons, some in lighter carriages like their own, was infrequent enough to be the occasion of considerable interest, if not excitement. To Hylas and Sara they were the big events of the day, and the children's eyes and ears were sharp to detect the first sound or motion on the road ahead.

Very rarely did anyone pass without stopping to exchange a greeting or make an inquiry about road conditions. In this way it was possible to get information about bridges or ferries or trading posts along the route.

One evening when they were looking for a place to spend the night, they came to an opening in the trees and a cove between two hillocks where a camp had already been made. Their eyes quickly took in the details of the situation. A dilapidated ragged tent was clinging wearily to one end of a small wagon covered with dirty and travel-worn canvas. A horse tethered nearby pricked up its ears and eyed the newcomers with apparent curiosity. A second horse, lying with its head on the grass, paid no attention. A few ragged garments drying on the bushes and a number of miscellaneous items of household equipment indicated longer occupancy than an overnight camp, but finally they saw a man seated on a block of wood some distance from the wagon. He had his head in his hands, and his shoulders were hunched in a dejected attitude. He seemed oblivious to the arrival of visitors.

Mr. Irish drew up the reins, and the carriage came to a stop at one side of the road. Obviously there was trouble here. It was quite possible that any intrusion would not be welcome. But his natural instincts overcame the momentary hesitation arising from this thought, and giving the reins to Hylas, he jumped down from the carriage seat. The man turned his head slightly, showing a dissipated, flushed face and an expression of despair mingled with shame.

"Do you need any help?" Mr. Irish asked pleasantly. "Looks as if you've got a sick horse there." He continued to walk toward the camp.

The man swore a volley of foul oaths. "There's nothing you can do," he made plain. "Get going, and get out!"

A tall black-haired girl appeared from the wagon, and behind her came two little girls in ragged gray dresses, smirking and giggling like two little elves.

"What do you want?" she said brusquely. Her dark eyes snapped defiantly, and her expression hardened as though she was used to scorn and contempt and dared not hope for anything else. Her features were strong and even; happiness could have made them beautiful.

"We want nothing but to learn if you need help. Saw your horse there, and thought maybe you had been forced off the road longer than you had supplies for. This is a lonely place to be stuck in, with no help near or—"

"It's not far enough to keep Pa from the bottle though," the girl said bitterly. "We're never far enough for that."

Mrs. Irish had gotten down from the carriage, and joined Mr. Irish, and little Sara was running over to make the acquaintance of the two little girls, who grinned shyly and clung together self-consciously.

"You're wasting your time to come here," the girl insisted. "There ain't nothing you can do. It's time we Fletchers gave up trying to be

23

folks or go anywhere or get anywhere. There's no use pretending any longer." In spite of her stiff exterior she was near the verge of tears.

By kindly patience and tact the Irishes gradually broke down the wall of distrust and suspicion, and the whole story came tumbling out. They had left Chicago 31 days before, hoping to rid themselves of associations that had brought Mr. Fletcher to a condition where he was no longer the mainstay of the family, but a burden and a hindrance. Things had gone along well at first, and he had let drink alone. But gradually the troubles of the trip had mounted, and difficulties had arisen.

"First one of the horses gave out two weeks ago yesterday, so we couldn't go on. There he is, not able to travel yet. We've just been lying here all this time, and then Hartley—that's my brother—got in with some fellows in the town two miles back and got drunk and disorderly and is on the stone pile working out a fine. Of course, we hadn't money to pay fines with. Father was going to take $10 to pay it, and I told him he shouldn't. Let the boy work it out till the horse gets well anyhow. If he's let out, he'll go right on as bad as before, and we'll have another and bigger one to pay. If he is left to break stone till he pays his fine, he may learn something."

Mr. Fletcher had risen and was coming toward them.

"It will take 20 days," he said, "at 50 cents a day, and—"

"No," the girl said positively, "I say let him stay till we can go on. Then we can pay what's left. Nobody knows when that horse can walk, maybe a month yet."

"What's the matter with the horse?" asked Mr. Irish, turning to look at the animal.

"Wasn't of much account anyhow," the man said. "Jest broke all to pieces on a Sunday, at the top of that hill, and wouldn't budge."

"Sunday! Were you traveling on Sunday?"

"Of course! We ain't no Christians."

"Christians or not, it's all the same to horses that work seven days a week. You should have at least given the horse a day off."

"We couldn't afford to lay by for any such sentimental nonsense," Fletcher growled doggedly.

24

"Well, if you choose to defy the good law that God wrote in the legs of a horse, as well as in the brain of a man, you deserve to be worsted; that's all I have to say about it. You see what you've made by driving these horses so many days running."

"Don't see what reasons you had to expect me to stop for Sunday. I don't believe in any religious tomfoolery. I believe in practical things."

"I'm not talking religion but common sense," said Mr. Irish, "but you're in a fair way to learn that religion, including faith in God's law for man and beast and machinery, is about the most practical thing I know of. Even you wouldn't stand it to keep going."

"Well, I wish we'd never left Chicago, and thought of coming back East again; we've had nothing but trouble."

"Stop wishing like a baby; get up like a man; get rid of that used-up team in part payment for a fresh span, and start ahead; and after this remember the right of horseflesh and wagon wheels."

"I've no money to patch up a team with," said Fletcher sullenly.

"Well, then, we must help you out. But I must have it distinctly understood that if you drive my horses, you let them rest one day in seven."

Mrs. Irish looked aghast at her husband, but he did not notice her. He went over to study the sick animal and to figure on the value of the team. Fletcher was astonished out of his sullenness by this turn of affairs, and the girl stood with silent shamefaced surprise. The matter-of-fact way that this visitor discussed the terms of the loan he would make without requiring any security from such a poor risk as her father appeared to be revealed a quality of character that she had never encountered before.

Mr. Irish told Hylas to unhitch the horses, and they made their camp near the Fletchers for the night. Mrs. Irish went to work with Bessie to prepare dinner for the entire party. Within the wagon they found Mrs. Fletcher ill and discouraged, a woman of evident grace and refinement, who was grateful and cheered by the strangers who were so generously giving them aid.

At this dinner, which was eaten together, the little Fletchers

25

heard a blessing asked for the first time. With wonder and suppressed mirth they made expressive grimaces at each other while Mr. Irish offered thanks, and made a fervent prayer for the blessing of the heavenly Father on this family in all their trouble and endeavor. Bessie's face forgot to be scornful. The prayer from the lips that had offered such timely help in their distress must at least be respected.

The next day Mr. Irish and Mr. Fletcher went together to the nearest town, returning in the afternoon with a farmer and a good strong span of horses. After looking the disabled animal over, the farmer concluded that he could get a horse out of the wreck after a few weeks at pasture; and a trade was agreed upon. Mr. Irish paid the balance, asking only a signed note from Fletcher payable in six months as security on the team. Hartley had been rescued from the stone pile by the payment of his fine, so the family could continue their journey without further delay. The several days he had spent breaking stone had made small impression on him; indeed, he seemed rather to look upon it in the light of a good joke, a pleasant bit of adventure.

Fletcher was too sullen by nature to make a show of gratitude, but there was just a hint of it as the two families parted, going in opposite directions. Mrs. Fletcher seemed to have acquired a more hopeful attitude, Bessie's face had lost its bitter expression, and the two small sisters smirked and giggled and waved their hands at Sara as the team pulled out of sight.

Chapter Two

THE NEW HOME
ON THE FRONTIER

*T*he loungers on the boardwalk in front of the general store in the frontier town of Pecatonica, Illinois, stopped in the middle of their talk as the square carriage drawn by the gray horses came up the rutted dusty street and slowed to a stop. A few doors down the street the faint rhythmic whine of a cheap banjo could be heard behind the door of one of the false-front shacks. Otherwise, life in the sleepy little town seemed to be suspended for the hot afternoon.

Sam Cleburn nudged old Jake Thorne, who was staring curiously at the newcomers. He sucked in his cheeks and spat the tobacco juice from his mouth before he could speak, then said under his breath, "Wal, I'll be switched if it don't look like a parson. Hain't seen the likes o' him for a coon's age. But I tell ye, I kin spot 'em like they's wearin' a halo. Wonder what he's a comin' to this forsaken hole in the mud fer."

Mr. Irish handed the reins to Hylas and stepped down from the carriage seat. His black frock coat, white linen and tie, and tall dignity caused the few passersby to slow and turn and listen as he addressed a few questions to the slouching Sam and Jake.

"Can you tell me what accommodations are available to travelers in this vicinity?" he asked politely.

Sam and Jake looked as nonplussed as though he had been speaking a foreign language. Instead of answering, they looked at each other with puzzled expressions. Tom Bossick, the manager, proprietor, and clerk of the general store, who had been standing in the doorway and watching the strangers, stepped forward and injected himself into the conversation. Taking advantage of the moment of hesitation, he inquired, "Be ye lookin' fer a place to live, or jest want beds for the night? If ye's jest lookin' fer a place fer the night, ole lady Shaw as lives a piece up the road sometimes has rooms fer a takin' folkses in. She's a right nice lady, she is, and will cook as good victuals as ye'll find anywhere."

"Thank you, my friend. Now can you tell me if there is a church in town and where it is? This being a Wednesday evening, we thought we might join with the believers—" Bossick rudely interrupted him.

"Church? Did you hear what he says?" he asked in a tone of amused astonishment. "Church? No, sir. There ain't a church within a hundred miles o' here as I knows of. We're kind of a wild lot, I reckon—ranchers, homesteaders, and what not. Five saloons and no church. We have a school though. Ya betcha. Goin' to git our kids eddicated. And really, we're not such bad 'uns on the whole. Better stay with us, Mister, and pitch yer tent nearby. You'll find we're real people, and maybe we'll find ye be too."

"I believe you're right. This is just the place I have been looking for," Horatio Irish said firmly, to the surprise of everyone, and turning, stepped up into the seat beside Hylas and drove off down the road in the direction of the home of "ole lady Shaw."

The cottage the young missionary built with his own hands in the midst of the prairie was surrounded by wild and lawless people and scattered Indian villages. To preach the gospel to these people, many of whom were highwaymen and robbers, was the purpose and occupation of the tireless "parson," who soon earned the love and respect of his neighbors. As time went on, his influence and mission spread out in a gradually widening arc to cover a multitude of interests in a wide territory.

Mrs. Irish left the preaching to her husband and busied herself with making a home out of a crude cabin.

Horatio Irish had known how to pick his wife. He knew it wasn't corsets or fandangles that made the woman. He wanted a home girl, and he got her. The skills and handicrafts that were necessary to maintain a home in those days were many and varied. The mother tended the fires as well as the loom; she made her own soap and milked the cow, if she had one. She baked her own bread, made her own butter, nursed her own babies, and raised her own wool, which she carded and wove into cloth and made into clothes for the family, even the men. She cooked over an open hearth, unless she were lucky enough to possess one of the newfangled iron stoves, which revolutionized interior decorating and cookbooks about the middle of the nineteenth century. But most women of that time were loath to admit that any stove stew could equal the kind that bubbled as it hung from a crane over a slow hearth fire, or that any bread or beans could match the flavor of those that came from the fireplace pit or oven.

The small cottage on the prairie was mostly kitchen, with a loft above for sleeping. Most of the activities of daily life were performed in the kitchen. It was the office, the chapel, the milk room, and the nursery, as well as the culinary department; so it was natural that it should be the biggest and most important room in the household.

One Sunday morning soon after they had moved into the little cabin, Sarepta and her mother were busy about the kitchen putting it in order when they looked out the window and saw their first visitors arriving. Indians! A large company of them in colorful robes and mounted on ponies were approaching the house.

Mrs. Irish stood petrified as she watched the group dismounting and coming toward the door. Mr. Irish had gone to conduct a preaching service some miles away, and Hylas was sick with the ague in the loft above. What should she do? The dusky visitors were all carrying guns, and to her terrified mind were intent on plunder and killing. She turned deathly white and dropped into a chair.

But Sara noticed that the Indians stacked their guns beside the gate before coming to the house and that there were women among them, and in her friendly way she opened the door and smiled a shy welcome. The chief, resplendent in colorful blankets and headdress, entered first with his wife, who had upon her back a board on which was strapped a little papoose. The others followed and found seats beside the fireplace, looking queerly at Mrs. Irish, who was still unable to overcome her fear and showed it to her guests.

The squaw lifted the board from her back and brought the papoose around to her lap, where the small girl could see him better. Sara was delighted with the charming baby, and held the little hand in hers while she noticed every detail of the clothing and wrappings. Over the baby's head, fastened to the board, was a bent splint bow strung with brass thimbles. The squaw, observing the white girl's eyes upon this queer arrangement, shook the bow, making all the thimbles jingle. The face of the Indian baby broke into smiles, and Sara could not resist the impulse to lean over and plant a kiss on the small cheek.

Unconsciously she had done the right thing to please the entire company, for they smiled and nodded, and the chief then took off his garter of wampum, made of crimson and yellow yarn and ornamented with white beads, and tied it about Sara's neck. No gift that she ever received in later life did she prize more than this piece of wampum, which she preserved among her lifelong treasures.

Sara, happy with the beautiful beads around her neck, looked over at her mother, who was still unable to rise from the chair, and expected some assistance in showing appreciation and doing the honors of the house. But Mrs. Irish was still in the grip of uncontrollable fear of her strange visitors. All the stories of the cruelty and savagery of their race and the history of destruction and brutality that she had listened to from childhood could not be wiped out in a moment.

Sara had not known fear, and she felt she must do something to honor her guests. Across the room on a shelf were piled the loaves of crusty homemade bread, baked the day before in preparation for Sunday. She was not used to cutting bread, but she went over and took out the knife and attempted to slice it as she had seen her mother do. Her small hands were awkward with the knife, and the chief, now her friend for life, came to the rescue and drew a sharp knife from his belt and cut the bread into large lumps and passed them around to the company.

The Indians ate and chattered and dropped food on the floor, and were obviously enjoying themselves. The chief looked around the room and seemed to be expecting someone.

"Big chief—he no here?" he finally asked in broken English. "We like see preacher man. Him tell about Great Spirit—no?"

Sara explained that her father had gone away and would not return for some time. Hearing this, the Indians peacefully retired, mounted their ponies, and rode away.

What Mrs. Irish did not realize was that they were in more danger from some of their White neighbors than they were from the Indians. There were continual feuds and contentions over land and squatter regulations and disputes that Mr. Irish was often unwittingly called upon to arbitrate.

The influence of this man of God reached out far beyond the immediate neighborhood. Many of those who had not heard the gospel for years, since they had come into the wilds of the West, came long distances to hear him preach. One thing the preacher claimed as his special right—the first three-days use of every new barn built in the country, before it was appropriated to its designed purpose.

The mow would be stacked with hay for sleeping purposes, and then he would call a three-day meeting for worship. The people would come 20, 30, and 40 miles; camp in their wagons or sleep in the barn. The great threshing floor was the auditorium. A program of services was presented from early morning until late at night, very much like a camp meeting.

The people were stirred by the eloquence of the plain Word of God as it poured from the heart of this earnest man of faith and prayer. They were proud of his cultured language and gentle manners; they were comforted by his words in times of sorrow and trouble. Here he spent the years of his health and strength, never sparing himself, never resting, fighting against sin and disease and ignorance, overcoming obstacles that seemed insurmountable. For the first year of his work he received just 25 cents in money. What else he received, and how his family got along, and how the bills were paid, and who paid for the shoes are details that are omitted from the family records.

Typhoid fever weakened his strong constitution, but it did not stop him. As time went on, his work carried him on extended trips into the north and west. The square carriage and the dapple-gray horses traveled uncounted miles across the prairies, along the water courses, under the shadow of the Missouri bluffs, and to the lead mines along the Mississippi. They made long trips over the marshes that later grew into the city of Chicago and its suburbs. Sometimes the water over the tall prairie grass was up to the hub of the carriage wheels, and the horses' feet would swish, swish through it hour after hour.

That inner compulsion—that "woe is me if I preach not the gospel" fire that burned within him far beyond his physical strength—led him on and on to answer the calls that came to him more and more.

Whatever the weather, wherever the call, Sarepta was the constant cheering presence beside him on the hard seat of the carriage. Her younger sister, Paulina, did not care for the hardships and inconveniences that were inseparable from such tours. Hylas was needed at home until he reached the age when he went away to school; so it was Sarepta who sat beside her father while he prepared his studies, who early learned to drive the team, who sat through countless cottage meetings, hearing her father speak to motley groups of reverent listeners.

One day in early fall Sarepta sat beside her father as usual as they drove along hour after hour, following a meandering road through rather desolate country. They were in the lead-mining district near the Mississippi, for Mr. Irish had found an interest in spiritual things among some of the humble laborers, and he was spending some weeks among them. He had the same experience as Jesus in discovering that "the common people heard him gladly."

The road could be called a road only by the necessity of mentioning it at all. At that time there were no state-supported turnpikes, no national highways, no grading, no oiling, no road signs. The roads traversed by the regular stages were slightly better than the trails that connected towns or villages, but even the best roads and turnpikes were difficult to maintain against the action of time and weather.

The road passed around stumps, over rocks, and sometimes it was necessary to go for miles on a corduroy paving of felled trees that prevented the tires from sinking into the sand or mire. They had made poor progress, and the day was beginning to be chilly.

When the wind began to blow and Mr. Irish felt a few drops of rain strike him, he stopped and put on the side curtains that somewhat ineffectually protected them from the weather.

Sara greeted this necessity with enthusiasm. "I love to ride in the rain with the side curtains on," she said. "It makes me feel so cozy in here. I play that I'm in a little house and the fire is burning in the fireplace. I hope it rains real hard."

"Are you sure you're not cold?" her father asked solicitously, as he tucked a blanket around her, and saw the water leaking through in spite of everything.

"Oh, no," she said, although her teeth chattered as she spoke.

She was sound asleep when they got to the cabin. She wakened sufficiently to realize that a strange woman was taking her out of the carriage and carrying her into a room that was full of people. The next morning she just faintly remembered being tucked into bed and knowing that there were people sitting all around, even on her bed, and then she went off to sleep again while listening to her father's preaching.

The sun was shining when she woke up, but she felt chilly and uncomfortable. Her father was already dressed to go and was standing, hat in hand, talking with a plain-faced, sober woman.

"It's plain to be seen the little girl is not well, although, I'm sure, sir, it's not anything serious, but ye'd better leave her here with me, sir, whiles you go yore way. You say as how you'll be comin' back this way in a week's time, an' you can get 'er then. I've a keered fer lots of young 'uns, an' I'll tek good care o' her, sir."

Sara's eyes grew large as she realized that her father was going to go on without her, but her devotion to her father, even at the age of 6, was such that she would not do anything to disturb him or hinder his work. So she remained tearless and silent as he went out the door and left her for the first time alone among strangers.

They were humble, kindly people, but their background for living was utterly different from that to which Sara was accustomed.

When they sat down to the evening meal of cornmeal mush and milk, the man of the house served the little girl and his wife, and then began to spoon up his cereal. The child sat still.

Presently the hostess said, "Why don't you eat your supper? Aren't you hungry?"

"Yes, but we're not ready yet," the child answered; "we haven't asked the blessing."

The man stopped eating and looked at his wife. Finally he said, rather gruffly, "Well, don't wait for that, because we don't have any blessing at our table."

"Oh, dear!" cried Sara. "Aren't you afraid to eat? Why don't you have a blessing?"

The man hesitated a moment, then said in a low voice, "Because we're not Christians."

Sara was puzzled, but after thinking about this for a little, she declared, "Well, if you can't, I can. I never did such a thing in my life, but we can't eat till we've had a blessing." Then folding her hands she softly said a prayer.

The miner was strangely affected by the innocent words of the little girl and her saying of the familiar grace. He could not eat, and soon left the table. After a while he returned and took her into his lap, and told her that when he was young he had been a good man, but after coming to this mining region he had grown bad, and he could not ask the blessing because it would not be honest.

"But," Sara insisted, "do people have to be good before they ask God anything?" And thus she challenged a concept that has kept many an unhappy person from seeking God.

During the remainder of her stay with these people, Sara not only asked the blessing before each meal but brought out her little red Bible and conducted worship, as was done in her own home. It was as natural to her as the air she breathed, and she was unconscious of doing anything unusual. Years later, when she was a grown woman, she received a letter from this man saying that the family altar she had established when she was with them had never been broken up.

Chapter Three

ONE WAY OF
TEACHING SCHOOL

*E*very truth," said Horatio Irish, "has its roots in Genesis, grows its trunk and branches through the historical books, blossoms in the Gospels, and drops its fruit in Revelation."

More than any other of his children, Sarepta inherited her father's deeply religious nature, and shared his interest in the spiritual welfare of others. She was his constant companion at home, and accompanied him on his long itineraries through many states, sitting quietly while he prepared a sermon or visiting with him as they rode across the prairies, drinking deeply of his knowledge of the Bible. From him she received her entire education until she was 15 years of age. The little calfskin Bible was her chief textbook.

Mr. Irish was eminently ingenious in making the Bible a textbook for every subject. At first he taught her to read and spell simple words from its pages. The processes of counting, the names of figures learned from the divisions of chapters, and the first lessons in notation, numeration, multiplication, and division were all taught from its sacred pages.

It was no haphazard instruction that the child received in this way. Lessons were arranged by topics to correspond to her everyday surroundings and experiences. She would be assigned to find every passage of Scripture wherein occurred the names of certain articles in the room: the furniture, as bed, chair, table; the parts of the house or articles of her own clothing; cooking utensils; familiar animals; parts of harness for the horse; the different types of vehicles. Later, as her knowledge increased, her father would take these passages of Scripture, carefully note the findings she had listed, and bring out lessons of lasting interest from the homely texts.

One study on "the voice of many waters" grew out of their contemplation of a beautiful spring, where they had stopped for a drink on one of their many trips.

"Where does the water come from, Father?"—a natural question asked by many a child. "The water keeps coming, and coming, and running away in brooks, and I should think it would run dry after a while. Where does it come from?"

A common question, indeed. But not many a father would answer his child as did Mr. Irish. In simple language he explained that God had given a law to the streams by which they were constantly giving and constantly receiving. He told how the waters are constantly circling around the world, changing from the surface to the depths of the sea. He described the various forms the water would take, the rain and dew and snow and hail. He showed how the same water would ascend to the clouds, and descend in the rain many times, at length finding its way to the secret places of the earth, from which it would flow out again as in this sparkling spring.

"The very drops in your hand, Sarepta, may have been in China or in Jordan or in Galilee."

"Father, do you think they might have been in the waters when Jesus said, 'Peace, be still'?"

The study of waters continued for days. Mr. Irish led his small daughter to a larger comprehension of what was meant in the phrase "the voice of many waters." She listed in her little notebook all the waters she could think of: the dew and the rain, snow, frost, and hail; springs, rivers, lakes, oceans, cascades, and cataracts; the waters under the earth; heavenly waters. Then she made a study of each type, and studied the references in the Bible to these various forms of water.

Discussion of these beautiful passages with one possessed of her father's spiritual insight, coupled with a love and understanding of nature, was a unique education for this growing girl.

"For the seed shall be prosperous; the vine shall give her fruit, and the ground shall give her increase, and the heavens shall give their dew; and I will cause the remnant of this people to possess all things" (Zech. 8:12). From Sarepta's study of dew she learned of the times when it had been a blessing to Jacob, to Joseph, and to Israel, and when it had been withheld as a curse. She learned how the dew was used as a figure to represent the sweet influence of the Spirit of God upon the heart, making it as the garden of the Lord. "I will be as the dew unto Israel: he shall grow as the lily, and cast forth his roots as Lebanon" (Hosea 14:5).

These studies molded the life and thoughts of the growing girl, so that as she would perform some simple household task, singing happily as she wiped the tea things, or swept the kitchen, she would think of the speech that "shall distil as the dew," or the doctrine that "shall drop as the rain."

The use of the concordance was as much a part of daily routine to this girl of 10 or more as the reading of comics was to a child of the mid-twentieth century.

When their adventures in learning took them to other books, the living Word was not laid aside, but was in constant use to guide in the study, like a compass charting the way so that there would be no deviation from the truth of God. In this way Sarepta's faith grew sturdy.

Chapter Four

MR. IRISH'S INSURANCE PAYS DIVIDENDS

*T*here came a day when the giant constitution that had endured years of nomadic life, long rides in all kinds of weather, and constant exposure finally broke down. It was on one of their trips through the villages of Wisconsin, when Sara was about 13 years old.

She awoke suddenly that morning, hearing the insistent drip, drip of the rain outside the window of the small country inn where they were staying. Her mother was standing beside the bed, looking down at her sorrowfully, with troubled countenance and reddened eyes.

"Mama, what is it?" Sara cried, sitting up quickly.

"Your father. He is very sick. He will not be able to go on anymore. We haven't any money, not even enough to continue staying at this hotel. I don't know what we are going to do." She sank into a chair, and bowed her head on the bed and wept.

Sara jumped out of bed, and still in her long white gown, slipped out of the room. She stopped suddenly in the doorway of her father's room at sight of his pale, gaunt face, but he smiled as he saw her and cheerfully extended his hand.

"Father, you are ill," she gasped, "and I didn't know! What is it? Mother is so worried." Her tears began to fall.

He held her hands and reassured her.

"I have never doubted my heavenly Father's care, and I do not now. We have served Him faithfully, and He will provide. Do not worry, my child." It was impossible, after that, for Sara to understand her mother's distress and concern.

Just how Mr. Irish's illness was known in the community the record does not tell, but later that same day a beautiful, well-dressed woman of obvious culture and means came to the hotel and insisted on the Irishes going to her home, where the sick man could have the care he needed.

"You must not refuse," she said. "You have given freely of your time and talent in benevolent service to God, and now we want to do something for you and for God." It was impossible to refuse what seemed to this man of faith such a positive evidence of God's care for His children.

And so this pleasant home and garden became a hospitable shelter to the invalid and his family for more than a year. For weeks his life hung in the balance, and then gradually Mr. Irish was able to be about a little. The friends of his host came under the spell of his magnetic personality, and the home circle was broadened and blessed by his presence.

One evening their guest for dinner was a gentleman well known in business circles as a very practical and prosperous man, but an avowed agnostic, if not an atheist. He was immediately attracted to Mr. Irish, and entered into a long conversation in which they shared many mutual interests, and he learned something of Mr. Irish's background and experience. Glancing over to Mrs. Irish and Sarepta, who were sitting beside the oil lamp with their mending, he remarked, "And I suppose, Mr. Irish, that you have in former years been able to make a comfortable provision for your little family, so that they are taken care of in any event?"

"Oh, yes," replied Mr. Irish, with a bland and confident voice, "I have made ample provision for them."

Mrs. Irish looked up quickly, and her bewildered expression surprised a questioning look in the man's face.

Catching his wife's eyes with a smile, Mr. Irish continued, "You, sir, would not think my provision for my family substantial, but I assure you it is more substantial than any ordinary business. A long time ago I made a contract with Him who holds all things and all events in His hands—Him to whom belong all the gold and silver and the cattle upon a thousand hills. I purposed to give Him the undivided service and loyalty of my heart and life. He in return promised to provide all necessary things for me and mine. I have, to the best of my ability, kept my part of the contract, and He will keep His. Because I have done the best I could for God, I know that He will do the best He can for me and my family."

The visitor had listened sympathetically but dubiously.

"That is a beautiful theory," he said, "but I fear it will not materially stand between you and want."

"On the contrary," returned the other, "it has substantially stood between us and want. You see how it was. When I was taken sick in this village and was unable to look after myself or family, my rich Father sent one of my sisters to the rescue, and we were brought to this home, which is my Father's home, and here we are invited to share without stint or measure in all the comforts it affords."

"But," said the businessman, "these people are unusual. There are very few like them in this wicked world."

"Yes," agreed Mr. Irish, "but there are enough. I do not believe that if I were able to work, or if any of us should sit down in idleness and wait for God to provide, that He would do any such thing. He will not do the work He has given us to do. But He will take care of us when we need Him most. If I did not know this to be true, I would have no security for this life or confidence in that which is to come."

The guest in the home that night took with him such a profound impression of this man's faith that it subsequently led to his own acceptance of Christ.

Although Mr. Irish never regained his former health and strength, and was ever afterward an invalid, his work for God continued to the end of his life, as he was able to give counsel and inspiration to those who came to him for help.

One day his hostess answered the knock at her door and found a stranger inquiring for the sick man. She led the gentleman into the room where Mr. Irish was reclining on a couch, quietly studying, with his daughter by his side.

"Mr. Irish, I presume," the visitor said, shaking his hand. "You do not know me, but I have come to see you by request of some of your friends at Pecatonica."

"From Pecatonica? Well, you have come a long way, and we are certainly glad to see you, and are eager to hear the news from our friends there. Do be seated and make us a long visit."

"I have brought you a special message from the community there. Here," he said, feeling in his pockets and pulling out a paper, which he handed to Mr. Irish, "this will convey their wishes and state the proposition better than I can."

As Horatio Irish read the paper a radiance and a glow suffused his face.

Since the years when he had done pioneer service among them, the people had paid for their farms, and many had become well-to-do. The children had grown up and settled about the old homesteads. A flourishing village had sprung up in the center of the territory over which he had traveled so long, and had become the terminus of a stretching line of railroad. The people had not forgotten their former pastor and friend, who had shared the dangers and hardships of pioneer life, and had given freely of his time and love, and asked nothing in return.

Now they had sent this messenger with the written request for Mr. Irish to return with him to his old hometown. He should be well taken care of, the journey made as easy as possible, and he should select the most desirable location in the village for a home. The citizens would build the cottage and pay him a pastor's salary from that day for as long as he lived. He would not be expected to do any service except to marry their children, if he were able to receive them at his bedside, or to bury their dead if he should recover sufficiently to do so.

As he read the list of names signed at the close of the paper—

Sam Cleburn, Jake Thorne, Tom Bossick—he remembered incidents connected with each person, seasons of prayer and victories won, or moments of crisis and tragedy when he had tried to bring comfort from the Word. There was that time when gangrene had set in on Jim Dallon's leg after it had been crushed under a cart wheel. There had been hours of helpless watching beside the cursing, rebellious man, hours in which it seemed that the pain was his own, that his presence was a failure, for it was impossible to save the man from agony or to give him comfort that would reconcile him to a life of disfigurement. Then he remembered the sorrowful face of Sally Tompkins and the night she was ready to run away or take her own life rather than endure the scorn and reproaches of her family, whose very harshness and misunderstanding had been the cause of her weakness. One by one these people whom he had loved and helped came into his mind. And a great joy filled his heart, not only because they wanted him to come back to them, but because it was a confirmation of his faith and a vindication of his years of labor.

The messenger assured Mrs. Irish that he had come prepared to take Mr. Irish with him, and every provision for his comfort and safety had been made. Three months later the family followed and moved into the new parsonage home, built, paid for, and furnished by the loyal parishioners of Pecatonica.

Chapter Five

EMERSON
AND CALVINISM

*B*ut life on the prairie was not for Hylas Irish. While Sara was sharing her father's travels and studies and simple way of life, Hylas was far down the road toward a different pattern of living and thinking. After the first few years at Pecatonica the young lad had gone East to complete his education, and by the year 1854 had become a promising young lawyer in Philadelphia. He married an accomplished young woman and established his residence on one of the quiet tree-lined streets. The opportunities for advancement along cultural and intellectual lines suited his temperament exactly. In fact, he was so pleased with the advantages of the big city that he wanted his favorite sister to share them.

He had always possessed a special fondness for Sara and a recognition of her unusual traits of personality and character. In the summer of 1854 he returned to Illinois for a brief visit, determined to pry Sara loose from her restricted surroundings.

"But I say that Sara is not getting the right kind of education. She needs to expand her horizons a little. She spends too much time indoors, and is getting pale and stoop-shouldered."

Hylas was standing with his back to the fire, facing his father, who was lying on the couch. Mrs. Irish, Sarepta, and Paulina were all working on a quilt together. Mr. Irish had said very little, letting Hylas do most of the talking, but something in his quiet manner, so well known to his children, made Hylas feel he was not convinced. This was a daring charge to make in a family in which parental authority was held in such awe.

"I am able to provide a good education for her now, and it isn't fair to keep her here shut up in a sickroom so much of the time. Let her come back with me, and Lillian and I will put her through a stiff line of study so she will be ready to enter Mount Holyoke Seminary by the first of the year."

Sara listened quietly while her brother argued determinedly with her father. This prospect was very alluring to the ambitious girl of 15, who possessed an intense thirst for knowledge and an ambition for a broader education.

While her brother and father discussed the question, she suddenly realized that her brother's plan would mean separation from her father, and knew the pain this would mean not only to her but to him.

"No," she said. "I think I will stay here."

Her protests were waived aside. "But you can't go through life always clinging to Father," her brother insisted. And Mr. Irish, finally convinced that it would be for Sara's benefit, immediately subjugated his personal feelings in the matter.

Before Sara hardly realized it, her trunks had been packed by her practical mother, and she was seated on the coach for her first trip on a railway train. It was the smoke-and-cinders type of train, the engine being dominated by a potbellied smokestack, and the coaches looking like a string of horseless stagecoaches. But it was a great advance over previous modes of transportation, and it was a thrill to Sara and Hylas to travel back across the very same territory they had covered with their square carriage so many years before.

"Just think," said Hylas as they looked through the smoke-begrimed windows of the dusty coach, "only five years ago this would not have been possible. We would have had to go by stage. In 1850 there were only 100 miles of railroad in all Illinois. Soon the Illinois

Central will complete a great system of tracks, and there is a project before Congress right now to construct a line all the way to the Pacific. What a wonderful thing that will be! The railroad will be the making of this country.

"It surely is a wonderful age we are living in now," he continued. "We have so many things our grandparents never dreamed of. Take this new reaper of McCormick's for instance, invented just a few years ago. It enables two men to do the work of 10. Already it is being manufactured by the thousands, and it will revolutionize farming. And the cylinder press—it's been four years now since our Philadelphia *Ledger* was first printed by steam. A wonderful thing! I've heard that someone has invented a machine that will sew cloth, a sewing machine. You women ought to be interested in that."

Philadelphia in 1854 was the financial and cultural metropolis of the country, a sprawling city of half a million population. Stately homes were being constructed with columned porticoes and large surrounding gardens, and were lived in by people who had time to think about art, and literature, and music, and who were discussing the writings of Emerson, Thoreau, and Alcott, and reading the poetry of Longfellow and Whittier. It was a long way from Pecatonica and its absorption in mere survival through droughts and wind, grasshoppers, dust, and mud.

The topic that was often on the lips of people both East and West that year, and for many years to come, was the burning question of abolition and slavery. The publication of *Uncle Tom's Cabin*, by Harriet Beecher Stowe, two years before had stirred up the fires of hatred and suspicion between the North and South, which had been smoldering for decades. The seeds of civil war were germinating.

Franklin Pierce was in the White House, trying to justify his unqualified support of the Compromise of 1850, and seeking to appease the group who demanded that Congress prohibit the expansion of slavery into the new territories of the United States.

Stephen A. Douglas was chairman of the Senate Committee on Territories, and was championing the doctrine of popular sovereignty and the creation of new territory. Kansas was a burning issue.

In Crimea the Russians had just been driven back into Sebastopol, and Tennyson had written his famous "Charge of the Light Brigade." In the Far East, Commodore Perry had visited Japan with the largest fleet the United States had ever assembled in Asiatic waters.

The year 1854 was also significant for the birth of the Republican Party, beginning in a mass meeting in Ripon, Wisconsin, and growing first to state organizations, and later, national. In this way the opposition to the expansion of slavery into the new territories achieved a united front.

It was a stirring year for Sarepta to spend with her brother in a new and different environment. But her preparation for Mount Holyoke received a strange and unexpected setback.

"What that girl needs," confided Lillian to her husband one evening, "is not more book knowledge, but a little more discipline and practical experience in the home. Why, I would never have dreamed that a 15-year-old girl could be so ignorant about the simplest things, like caring for her own room and clothes. She would never think of picking up a dustcloth or straightening up the parlor when it is disarranged."

"Well, don't we have servants for that sort of thing?" Hylas asked, hardly looking up from the paper he was reading.

"Yes, of course, but don't you think she should be taught that life is something more than dreaming and writing verses? She likes to sit by the hour with a pad of paper and a pencil, and her head in the clouds, writing and erasing, happily unconscious of anything else to do."

Hylas was unwilling to admit fault in the sister who had been his darling and pet, but the verse writing was one thing for which he had had little sympathy, remembering how his mother would stand by Sara's bed at night and hold a candle while she wrote down the lines that kept her from sleeping. So he quickly agreed with his wife on this point.

"Maybe you are right. She has been with her father constantly, and Mother has never required much of her in the house. Do what you think best, and we'll let down on the studies for a while."

Lillian was a pattern of housewifely efficiency. The next day she presented her young sister-in-law with a written schedule.

"Sarepta, my dear," she said firmly, "Hylas and I both feel that it is time you should know more about domestic affairs, and should learn to bear your share of the household responsibilities. I have made out a little program of duties for you and hours for everything, so that your time will be spent to the best advantage. I want you to take care of the library and your own room, sweeping, dusting, tidying. Every week you must polish all the silver and clean out the china closet. On Wednesday afternoon you will sit down with me and bring your workbasket, and we will go over all your clothing fresh from the laundry, and examine buttons, tapes, and ribbons, and repair anything that needs mending."

And Sarepta, with that desire to go the "second mile" that characterized her through life, also learned to sew, and made a beautiful linen shirt for her brother, carefully counting three threads of linen to the stitch, on the fine tucks of the bosom.

Her time for reading was strictly regimented. Never was she permitted to read anything by herself. By present-day standards this would have been an unmitigated hardship, a cause for rebellion especially for a girl whose nature was sensitive to everything that was joyous and beautiful in nature, to every shade of feeling in the hearts of those surrounding her, who could see romance in everyday happenings, whose mind craved enrichment through the sharing of human experiences. This guidance had been the rule of her own household, but had been handled so wisely that she had not thought of it as a restriction until now.

Lillian selected her books, and required her to sit beside her in the afternoons and read 10 pages aloud, no more or less, from some substantial volume such as Hume's *History of England* or Gibbon's *Decline and Fall of the Roman Empire*. She was required to write a synopsis of each book that she read. Never by any chance was there a book of romance or any so-called light reading of the day.

Reading was not intended, her father had taught her, to be a channel for escape, by which the eye, running faster and faster, pulled the mind along without thinking, like a wheel rolling down-hill without brakes. Reading was for instruction, not entertainment. It must serve a definite objective; otherwise it was a waste of time. One must never read without reflection, time for the mind to digest and absorb.

This attitude toward reading was perfectly consistent with the way of life of a people who never relaxed from the conviction that their lives should serve a useful purpose, and that time was a gift of God. This sense of obligation seemed to rest heavier on the people of that era than today, when instead of asking, "Will it be a help to me?" they say, "What harm is it?" The lines of Longfellow, "Not enjoyment, and not sorrow, is our destined end or way; but to act, that each tomorrow find us farther than today," were accepted at their face value.

Sarepta Irish had a large capacity for enjoyment and for living, and such a keen appreciation of knowledge that it is doubtful whether she felt any deprivation at the time, aside from the separation from her father, which became increasingly poignant as the days went by.

Hylas, whose brilliant mind and abilities later enabled him to serve the government as a foreign diplomat, and then as chief of the Bureau of Engraving and Printing during Garfield's administration, was more liberal in his views than his father. His reading branched out and sampled some of the new theories and philosophies that were the talk of the professional circles in Philadelphia at that time.

These and the news of the day he brought home for discussion in the evening as he sat with his wife and sister beside the lamp on the round table in the parlor.

In Plymouth, Massachusetts, crowds were flocking to the church to hear the eloquent Henry Ward Beecher, eminent on two continents as a pulpiteer without a peer, and his discourses were given wide newspaper publicity. He was an ardent abolitionist, a first-rate showman in the pulpit, a dyed-in-the-wool Calvinist, the son of the great Lyman Beecher, and the brother of the now-famous Harriet Beecher Stowe.

Hylas Irish, although opposed to slavery, was also opposed to emotionalism and religious fervor, and preferred the quiet philosophy of Emerson.

"I note that Emerson calls the Calvinistic theology a blight that stifled every creative impulse in New England, and he maintains 'that there was not a book, a speech, a conversation, a thought, in the whole state of Massachusetts between the years of 1790 and 1820'! I wonder what Mr. Beecher thinks of that."

Lillian was bending down at the mending in her lap, and hardly looked up. Sarepta's fingers continued to fly on the sock she was knitting. But her eyes were alive with interest. Although a member of the Methodist Church, she had been taught the Word, and was not familiar with the differences in the creeds of the denominations.

"What is the matter with Calvinism? What does Emerson have against it?" she asked.

A slight expression of impatience crossed Hylas' face.

"Too much preoccupation with sin and total depravity, and the helplessness of mankind in the face of it. You know, I can see Emerson's viewpoint. That kind of thinking is definitely opposed to progress and developing self-reliance."

Sarepta found her brother's ideas stimulating. Such thoughts as he presented she turned over and over in her mind, examining each facet, and comparing them with the things she had been taught by her father.

"I've been thinking quite a bit along a line that is going to change the thinking of a great many people," he said one evening. "An English scientist named Darwin and a great many other thinking people are advancing the theory of evolution, and it seems to me they have considerable evidence to support their ideas."

"Evolution?" inquired Lillian. "That means a process of change, does it not? Tell us what you mean."

"Well, this teaching shows that man has gradually been progressing upward," Hylas explained. "By a comparison of different forms of life Darwin has discovered that one species has developed from a lower form, that even today this process is going on, though

49

quite imperceptibly, of course. Life is changing, improving, by the process of evolution."

"You mean that there was a time when there were only lower forms of life, and gradually they changed into higher forms like animals and men?" asked Sarepta in amazement.

"Yes, that's the general idea. It's a wonderful story of progress and adaptation, taking long periods of years."

"But that doesn't agree with the Bible story of Creation," Sarepta concluded quickly.

"Now, Sara," Hylas' voice was very tolerant, "we are going to have to modify some of our conceptions of truth that have been based on interpretations of Scripture that were limited by our ignorance of science. It doesn't necessarily deny the Creator to see the impossibility of a six-day creation."

"But if God said it took six days—"

"But you know that the Bible was written a long time ago; and before it was ever put into writing, these stories were handed down from mouth to mouth. Sometimes figures were used that were not intended to be taken literally. You remember it says that with God a day is as a thousand years. The days of creation could have been 1,000-year periods. It doesn't really matter just how one thinks of them."

But it mattered to Sara. She wished for her father to reassure her that what she had always taken for truth was truth. She pondered these and other discussions with her brother, and for the first time in her life felt doubt and uncertainty. If the story of Creation was only a figure of speech, and men had appeared upon the earth only after millions of years of change and progress, there never could have been any fall! Sin, instead of entering the world through the disobedience of Adam, must, then, be considered a natural condition that could only be eradicated by countless more ages of progress. As the full significance of this line of reasoning dawned upon her, leading to the logical conclusion that without the fall of man there would have been no need of a Saviour, Sara felt bewildered and overwhelmed with questions and fears.

Her longing for her father increased and occupied her heart with a consuming anxiety. She tried to disguise her feelings from her brother and his wife, for she knew how desirous they were of her preparing for higher education at Mount Holyoke, and she felt grateful for the interest and care they had given her. She was filled with a tremendous conflict between her own plan for education and her growing need for her father.

"Have you noticed Sara lately?" Lillian asked her husband one evening after the girl had retired.

"Not especially; why?"

"She is not her former self at all, but seems terribly disturbed about something. She hardly eats a thing, and is pale and sad."

"That's strange," said Hylas, alarmed. "I wonder what could be the matter with her."

Days of anxiety followed when it became apparent that their sister was definitely failing. Finally a letter from their mother arrived, requesting Sara to come home, stating that her father felt his life was short, and that though he had tried to endure his daughter's absence, he could no longer bear it. It was with great reluctance and bitter disappointment that Hylas yielded his cherished hopes and himself took Sarepta home to her father. Their reunion after an absence of 13 months was an occasion of inexpressible joy to both, deepened, perhaps, by the hovering presence of the great shadow.

Anxious to demonstrate her newly acquired skill in household arts, and convinced thoroughly of the importance of a knowledge of domestic science to every girl, Sara devoted a great deal of time at first to helping her mother with the cooking and cleaning.

But Mr. Irish had other plans for her.

"Let Paulina give your mother what assistance she needs," he said. "She is stronger anyway. I do not have long to accomplish my mission, and that is to train you in Bible truth. There is no time to spare."

And so "I was left to grow up," Sara wrote in her diary, "knowing nothing at all about keeping a home, except what I had learned from my brother's wife. Doubtless I should have been stronger in body if I had done the housework, but still I should not have been qualified for the life that afterward came to me."

Now that she was able to reestablish her old intimate talks with her father, she opened her heart with all its new doubts and uncertainties. With great sympathy, tenderness, and understanding he discussed with her all the lines of speculation that had been awakened in her mind, from the origin of evil to the reason that it was permitted to continue unpunished throughout so many centuries.

"There is no truth more fundamental and undeniable, as taught in the Bible," he told her, "than that God is our heavenly Father, and our relation to Him is in every sense that of beloved children. God is not simply a great presence, a great intelligence, a first cause of all things.

"That He has a personal love for us as individuals is shown from Genesis to Revelation. He walked with Adam in the garden in the cool of the day; and in the last book of the Bible He gives the invitation, 'Behold, I stand at the door, and knock; if any man hear my voice, and open the door, I will come in to him, and will sup with him, and he with me.'

"Any system of truth or philosophy that denies the person of God or Christ is not founded upon the Bible."

By this experience Sara's faith was firmly reestablished. She had learned one thing, and that was that she must know for herself, and must be independent of the influences around her. Not even her father's faith was sufficient for her now. Gladly would she receive the treasures of his mind and heart, but she must study and think, and decide for herself.

In harmony with this decision she told her father one day that she had decided she would like to join some other church than the one she had been born into.

"Suppose I had not been born and reared in the Methodist Church," she said. "What would be my convictions? I must be free from even unconscious prejudice."

Her father sympathized with this idea, saying, "I wish you to be intelligent in your choice of a church home. You must be able to give a reason for your church preference."

There followed then a study of creeds and confessions of faith and of church books of all denominations. Mr. Irish so faithfully presented the principles, doctrines, and methods of each denomination in turn, and seemed to place himself upon the side of the church they were studying that when Sara finally decided to remain in the Methodist Church, she did so on her own conviction and choice.

Chapter Six

WHAT? NO HOOPS?

The little cottage that had been built for the Irishes by the love of their fellow townspeople gradually became engulfed by the growing town, and the corner where it stood became too noisy for the invalid. So the property was sold, and a new house was built on a few acres of land a mile and a half from the village. This was known as the Parsonage Farm.

This quiet spot was soon invaded by the controversy regarding slavery, which was increasing in excitement, and was absorbing the attention of Congress, the newspapers, and every legislature in the land. The Irishes were intense patriots and followed closely all discussion of this national problem. Sara was an excellent reader, and it was her habit to read the congressional documents, which were teeming with arguments pro and con, aloud to the family and any neighbors who came to join them.

The townspeople held Mr. Irish's opinion in esteem, and such was the interest that frequently large groups would assemble after the arrival of the mails to discuss the latest news. The little sitting room became a sort of auditorium or town hall where opinions were exchanged. The distance from town was no obstacle.

One day Mr. Irish returned from town and startled the group by announcing, "I shall become a criminal upon the first opportunity!"

He then informed them of the passage of the Fugitive Slave Law, which he denounced as a crime in itself. "If there ever comes to me an opportunity to help any poor victim of the American curse, I will not hesitate to do all in my power to do so."

These intense events emphasized the need for intelligent understanding of civic and national affairs, and Mr. Irish recognized as never before the advantage of a better education for Sara than his failing strength would enable him to give her. Thirty miles away was the Rock River Seminary, at Mount Morris, Illinois, a small but growing Methodist institution for men and women. Mr. Irish favored coeducation, which was at that time an innovation for many schools. Arrangement was made for Sara to live in the home of Barton Cartwright, a Methodist minister who had moved near the seminary for the purpose of educating his own children.

Ellen Cartwright, Sara's roommate, was a thorough extrovert, a wholesome, popular, breezy young woman; and her room, not far from the campus, was often the scene of a flutter of feminine activity.

One evening, soon after Sarepta's arrival at the seminary, a group of girls had gathered at Ellen's to put the last-minute touches on their costumes before attending a school social. It was a cool, brisk evening in the early spring of 1859. Only a few patches of snow remained on the boardwalks, and a faint green veil was showing in the tips of the trees.

Ellen had obtained a few extra candles from her father's study to increase the light in the small room. Here, amid the flutter of ribbons, the scent of cologne, the treble of light lively voices, the girls laughed and joked and teased one another. Sara, sitting quietly at one side, her hands in her lap, was enjoying the occasion immensely. Her previous experiences had not given her much opportunity for association with girls of her own age.

An oval, gilt-framed mirror on the wall was like a frame for the group of sweet girlish faces reflected therein as they amiably jockeyed for position as curls were adjusted, strands were smoothed, and cheeks were pinched to a rosy glow.

The conversation on this occasion did not include such topics as the Lincoln-Douglas debates, or whether Congress would pass on the Pacific Railroad project, or whether the Homestead Act had a chance, or what would be the benefit to the country of oil recently struck in Pennsylvania, or whether John Brown was a saint or a sinner. Nor was there mention of topics that were of current interest in the literary field—whether Harriet Beecher Stowe's new book *The Minister's Wooing* was equal to *Adam Bede*, recent best-seller of the English writer George Eliot.

No, more important right now was the problem of whether the bows were set too high on Jennie's billowing skirts, or whether a rose ribbon or blue looked better on Isabel's sprigged muslin, and what Amy would do without an appropriate evening wrap. These questions were only incidental, however, to the main theme of the discussion, which was whether Stanley Maxson would attend the social or not, and if not, why not!

"He usually comes and looks in at the door for a minute with a look of disdain on his handsome face and then goes away," complained Isabel, the golden-blond girl with the cornflower-blue eyes. "But tonight, maybe—" and she looked approvingly at the smiling beauty in the mirror.

"Anyone home?" a sweet voice called outside the door after a light rap.

"Oh, that's Mabel. Come on in," called Ellen. Mabel's skirts completely filled the doorway as she swept in carrying a large, square, white box.

"Look, girls," she said, "Bishop Vincent sent some flowers from the greenhouse for us to make into nosegays!"

The girls clustered around while she pulled off the strings and wrappings and opened the box. Fragrant mignonette and pansies, rosebuds and ferns, brought squeals of delight that would have rewarded Bishop Vincent if he could have heard.

"The old dear, he's always thinking of something like that," said Ellen. "Now come, girls, and pick what you want to go with your dresses. O Mabel, have you met Miss Irish? She's going to be my roommate. Am I not lucky? She's the poetess, you know, the one who writes for the *Ladies' Repository*."

"You mean Sara is Lina Linwood? Ohhh—" and Mabel, obviously quite impressed, gave Sara a long glance.

Sara had been happily a part of the group, her heart drawn out in friendliness to these charming girls, but quite unobservant of the fashion and colors of their dresses. As she rose now to help in the arranging of the flowers, there was an apparent marked contrast in the lines of her figure and those of the other girls. Isabel glanced at her sharply, her eye traveling steadily from the white linen collar down the slim outlines of the plain dark dress hanging limply at her sides.

"Are you ready to go, Miss Irish?" she asked pointedly. "You're not going like that, are you?"

Sara had not realized that she was the only one in the group who was not wearing hoops under yards and yards of skirts ornately decorated in the fashion of the time. She quickly glanced down at her own plain dress, but smiled back unabashed.

"Why, certainly, do you think anyone will care? Will it matter to anyone else? It doesn't to me."

The other girls looked at one another in embarrassed silence. They were used to Isabel's cutting statements. Ellen Cartwright's hearty voice broke the awkward moment.

"Come on. Let's go. I think Sarepta looks fine. Maybe she will set a new style."

On this particular occasion Stanley Maxson did more than just look in the door and then disappear. He came in and participated in the games and the spelling match, and listened to the readings, causing many eyes to turn in his direction and many hearts to beat a little faster.

"Who is the new girl?" he whispered to Ellen. "The one with the cameo face and the classic features?"

"Oh, haven't you met Sarepta? She's my new roommate. Come on. I'll introduce you."

Sarepta had been conspicuous, but not because of her un-hooped skirts. Her animated face, although not qualifying as beautiful, had a charm and personality that were more than beauty. Her hair, smooth as black satin, was swept away from the straight white

part, and drawn to the roll low at the back of her neck with un-
pretending severity. Only a face of striking features would benefit
by such a coiffure. The high forehead, wide-apart eyes, pointed
nose, and a certain piquancy of feature did not need a frame of
curls to set them off.

"I've been wanting to ask you something all evening," Stanley
Maxson said, taking a seat beside her.

"You have? What's that?" There were no fluttering eyelashes,
no coy looks, no admission of flattery. She showed only a frank interest free from self-consciousness.

"What were you thinking about when you were sitting here by
yourself a few minutes ago? You had an expression like the *Mona
Lisa*, and you know no one has ever been able to explain what she
was thinking about."

Without the slightest embarrassment Sarepta told him.

"I was just thinking how fortunate I am to be here attending a
Christian school. I guess the expression you saw must have been one
of great satisfaction," she said, smiling.

"I wish I felt that way about it," he said, as a look of discontent
came over his face. "As for me, I didn't want to come here at all.
Only came to please my parents, but I would have preferred to go
to a good boys' school."

"You don't approve of coeducation, then?"

"No, frankly, I don't. What good is it going to do all these girls?
They'll just get married anyway, and go to keeping house, and they
should get what education they need at girls' schools. Now really,
what do you think it will do for you?"

"Oh, I'm planning on being a missionary, and I'm sure there is
just as much reason for a girl to have an education as for a boy."

Stanley smiled a rather condescending smile. But whether he ap-
proved of coeducation or not, he spent the rest of the evening with
Sarepta, enjoying the novelty of the girl who could talk about serious things intelligently. He accompanied her to the cottage, walking
slowly along the slippery boardwalk.

Soon after Sarepta entered her room, Ellen came bouncing in

exclaiming, "Where is the witch? Where is she? I want to find the witch that brought down Mr. Proudhead!"

Sara merely looked at her in astonishment without a word.

"You should have heard what Isabel said! She is simply furious! But Jennie and Mabel said to tell you they're glad that Mr. Maxson is conquered at last."

"What nonsense are you talking?" Sara exclaimed impatiently. "He simply sat down and talked to me, as any other gentleman might have done."

"That's just it," laughed Ellen. "That's what amuses us, to see him do just as any other gentleman might have done under the circumstances. He has never done so before."

Chapter Seven

THE HEART OF
THE TORNADO

*I*t was the last week in May 1859. Spring had burst into bloom in a flash of purple irises, red peonies, yellow tulips, and fragrant lilacs, and a twinkle of feathery green leaves on all the trees and bushes. Sara's step along the boardwalk under the elms was light and lively, reflecting the happy thoughts that filled her mind. Commencement was only a few weeks away, and President Harlow had asked her to write a poem to be read at the closing exercises. She still had not given her consent, the bogy of having to deliver it personally before the audience frightening her somewhat; but already her mind was leaping along to the task, thinking of subjects and opening lines. She loved to write, and had already become a regular contributor to the *Ladies' Repository* and other periodicals. (The first money she had earned in this way had been spent for three stout pairs of shoes for the family.)

Thus preoccupied, she entered the small sitting room of the Cartwright cottage, and found Mr. Bennett, their next-door neighbor from Pecatonica, waiting for her.

"Why, Mr. Bennett, I'm so surprised," she exclaimed. "When did you come over?"

"Today. I've come to take you home, dear child. Your father is very sick."

Sara was alarmed, and immediately began to ply him with anxious questions. Mr. Bennett tried to reassure her.

"Oh, now, Sara, don't be so troubled. It will be all right, I am sure. You'll probably be back in a few days. But your father is anxious to see you, and your mother thinks it would be a good thing for you to come home for the Sabbath. You get a good rest tonight, and we'll leave early in the morning."

In the morning Sara ran over to tell Mr. and Mrs. Vincent, but found that they already knew. As Mr. Bennett drove up to the door with the carriage, Mrs. Vincent walked to the gate with Sara, putting her arm around her and drawing her close.

"God be with you, dear child, in whatever is to come."

"Why!" exclaimed Sara. "Do you think anything is to come?"

"Of course"—Mrs. Vincent's tone was solemn but reassuring—"something is always to come, and we never know just what is before us. But whatever comes, you will be a woman, I know."

Full of foreboding, Sara remained silent during the long hours of the trip in the carriage, fearing to question Mr. Bennett, fearing to hear any further news. The 30 miles to Pecatonica took all day to drive, and it was evening before they reached home.

Sara leaped from the carriage the minute it stopped before the gate, and bounded into the house, stopping briefly to give a hearty smack to her mother, then rushing for the stairway to her father's room.

"No, no!" her mother called after her. "Not there, but in here, this way," and conducted her into the parlor, where Mr. Irish's bed had been made up. It was the airiest, pleasantest room in the house.

The windows were wide open, and the fragrance of apple blossoms floated in from the orchard, mingled with the scent of flowers. At this time of year the newly unfolded leaves of the trees and shrubs had a fresh delicate green and laciness that seemed to transform all the surroundings into a fairyland of beauty. The well-tended flower garden all around the house was in the height of beauty, a bright border of color.

Mr. Irish had always been in the most perfect accord with nature, and as he lay upon his bed of weakness, his strength gradually wearing away, he seemed still to be in that steady quiet current, with nothing to bring perplexity or care, with nothing to be desired, save that the omnipotent God operating through nature should have His way. Heartache and apprehension were out of place in that room. The serenity and faith of the sick man were strong enough to overlie the fears and distress of the family the moment they came into his presence. The only reasonable and natural condition of mind was that of a quiet, restful, and unquestioning trust in Him who doeth all things well.

It was not necessary to tell Sara that her father's days were few. She could see it in every line of his face, in the unnatural color, and in the strange light that burned in his eyes, now preternaturally large and bright. She took her station at her father's bedside, and from that time was seldom absent except for a few hours' rest at night.

One hot sultry evening as she was sitting by the bed while he slept, she could not refrain from brooding on what her life would be like when he was gone. He awoke and noticed the dejected look upon her face. Reaching out his hand for hers, he said, "Why do I see a shadow on your face, my child?"

Sara could not answer. Her heart was too full for words, and she struggled to restrain her tears.

"Can you not," he said, "turn your face to the light instead of standing in your own shadow?"

Sara was just opening her lips to answer when suddenly there came a loud roar, and a shock like a sudden concussion in the atmosphere. She glanced through the window and saw a strange light over the garden. The green of the grass and the foliage had taken on electric shades. Mr. Irish also noticed it, and said quietly, "Step to the door, and see what it is."

Looking from the door to the west, Sara saw a bewildering spectacle. Great smoke-colored clouds were being rolled together like a whirlpool in an inverted sea. The sun had just gone down, and the afterglow of the sunset was composed of many swiftly changing, metallic colors. There was a glow of burnished copper; the blue was tinged with a coppery green as across the face of this metallic surface rolled these tossing masses of vapor. The air was sultry and heavy, and seemed perfectly still.

As Sara stood silently watching, wondering whence came the shock of a moment ago, she saw a long white cloud slowly unroll from the whirling mass and drop gently to the earth. Instantly there arose as if to meet it an inverted cone of debris, in the midst of which were timbers and branches of trees, which were lifted as it seemed into a cloud, and then scattered in a shower toward the earth.

The tornado seemed to be coming directly toward the village. But while Sara watched in fascination, it changed its course, and passed over the river, bringing a cone of water from its bosom, which it carried into the woods beyond, releasing it in a brilliant shower against the last rays of the sunset. The wind began to blow in fierce sharp gusts, cutting the growing corn and the flower stalks in the garden close to the ground, as if by a knife. Its violence mocked the stability of everything in its path.

Sara closed the door and went back to her father's side. Although they were in the outer edge of the storm circle, they were perfectly safe, and could watch its progress through the woods and out over the prairie. Trees were torn up by the roots and flung into the air. Everything that came into the path went before it like chaff. It was an experience and a vision never to be forgotten by those who beheld it.

A strange light came over Mr. Irish's face. His daughter recognized in it the token of some great thought.

He took her hand and said: "I understand. It is called a tornado, and looked at from the standpoint of human life, it means destruction to everything that comes in its path. But it is simply another manifestation of the power of our God upon whom we have the right to depend. The power in the storm is the same power that lifted our crucified Lord from the sealed tomb and caught Him up bodily to heaven. It is the same power that Paul speaks of in the book of Ephesians as being 'to us-ward.' He refers especially to the manifestation of power by which Jesus was lifted out of the grave and made to live again."

"But Father," said Sara, "it seems to me that the storm is a fearful, irresistible, destructive force. It takes everything in its path. I cannot understand how you can compare it to the power of God."

"It depends upon our relation to the storm and our own position. Scientists tell us that in the very center of the storm there is a place so quiet that it will not ruffle a feather. If we have the peace of God in our hearts, we can abide under the shadow of the Almighty, and the power of God that is manifested in so many ways—in the sunset, in the flowers, in the storm, and in the hearts of men—will be 'to us-ward' and not against us."

And Mr. Irish, whose life had always been spent in the quiet center of the storm, was laid to rest, away from the ruin and swirl and roar of the tempest.

Of his passing Sara wrote in her diary:

"The next day, just at sunset, he left us. I will not attempt to portray the scene. I think that death never came to a home which had been more thoroughly prepared by all the teachings of the gospel, and yet I doubt if it has ever been more bitter to lonely women than it was to my mother and me."

Chapter Eight

JULIA'S COUSIN

I wish you could get acquainted with my cousin James, from York State," said Julia one warm summer afternoon as they sat on the veranda shelling peas. "He's different from anyone you've ever met."

"Every person is different from every other person," said Sara philosophically, her dark eyes twinkling, "but how is James peculiar?"

It was Julia who had first worn a path through the alfalfa field that separated the two farms. Friendly and cheerful, she had determined to "bring Sara out of her shell." And now that the close confinement to her father's bedside was past, Sara responded eagerly to the friendship offered by this girl of her own age.

"I didn't say he was peculiar," Julia said laughing, "but he *is* different. His ways are different. His language is different. His thinking is different. It's not that he is a city-bred person visiting his country cousins," she chuckled, "for although he is well educated, he actually comes from a farm. His folks have lived on a homestead in York State for generations. So they are hard-working people and have no notions of fancy ways."

"So far I don't see what is different about him," insisted Sara.

"I guess it's his thinking that is the most different. Well, take religion for instance. You know, we sort of take everything for granted—family worship, prayer meeting, and church. But his people aren't religious at all, and he just takes nothing for granted. Sometimes I think he questions everything. I know by remarks he makes and questions he asks that he thinks deeply though. Sometimes it seems that he sees things more clearly than I do. But I privately think he is an infidel, just an out-and-out infidel!"

"An infidel!" Sara was shocked. "How could that be?"

"I just wish you could talk to him, Sara. You are so good at explaining things. I know you could set him right."

"I've never seen a man yet that wanted to be set right. But I'm sure I'd enjoy talking with him. Why don't you bring him over?"

"It's not so simple as that," Julia said, not noticing that the bag of pea pods was full and spilling over. "I guess I might as well tell you. He has an aversion to women writers, and I guess I said too much about your poetry, because he said, 'Oh, a schoolgirl who scribbles!' with an expression of distaste, if I must be honest."

Sara's eyes flashed. "I suppose he thinks that women should not even go to school! I'd like to meet that cousin of yours!"

The affairs of the nation were reaching a critical point in that summer of 1859, and the agitation over the slavery question was the topic that was in everyone's mouth. The townspeople still gathered in the Irish parsonage to read aloud the New York *Tribune* and the *Congressional Globe*.

The speeches of Sumner and others were flooding the country, and sometimes this little company of patriots would become so excited as to forget their meals. It was a heterogeneous group, a cross section of groups all over the country. There was old Grandpa Taylor, blind and eccentric, feeling his way along the fences with his cane. There was Eddie Cobbler, sharp-tongued and sarcastic, who had a gift for seeing the other side, who livened the discussions with his surprising opinions and views, and sometimes—facts. Most of the listeners were humble, uneducated people, yet possessed of strong convictions. Sara and Julia, along with a number of other young people, made the occasion sparkle with wit and laughter.

One hot evening in July some of the group lingered on the veranda after most of the visitors had left the informal gathering. The veranda was long and wide, and the honeysuckle spreading out on the trellis at one end gave out a delicious fragrance to blend with the earthy and woodsy odors that descending night draws forth at the close of the day for the refreshment of those who are willing to step out from enclosing walls. The dark sky had that peculiar depth that seems to follow a hot day and makes the stars appear as though suspended against a curtainless backdrop.

Eddie Cobbler and James Henry were participating in a lively discussion of William Lloyd Garrison and his newspaper, the *Liberator.* Julia was piqued because on this particular evening when she had persuaded her cousin to join the group, Sara was not there. A call to help care for a sick child had come from one of the neighbors earlier in the day, and she had not returned. While listening to the conversation, Julia was alert for Sara's step along the walk.

"It is the duty of all citizens to support their government," Eddie was saying. "Since slavery is recognized by the Constitution of the United States, the abolitionists have absolutely no legal way to proceed. They should submit to the majority."

"If there comes a time in the history of any people," James Henry's voice was vibrant with feeling, "when it is apparent that certain fundamental principles upon which that government is founded are being violated, no matter what has been written into its Constitution, then I believe that provision should be made to hold to the original principles. William Lloyd Garrison says 'that the compact which exists between the North and the South is a covenant with death and an agreement with hell.'"

"That's pretty strong language. You mean you would denounce the Constitution and join the extreme group of radicals who are bent on destroying the nation?"

"Nothing will destroy the nation more quickly and thoroughly than the canker caused by holding a portion of its people in bondage."

While they were speaking, Sara had come up the walk to the gate, and Julia quietly slipped down the steps and went to meet her.

"I have a caller for you," she whispered. They stood under the elm for a few minutes listening to the discussion, and at the first pause Julia interposed and made the presentations.

Mr. Henry had risen from his position on the steps, and Sarepta held out her hand. They were then seated, and the subject of the evening continued. But only as the moon rose, a little later on in the evening, could they see each other's face. The face that Sara saw was a strong, handsome masculine face framed by heavy black hair and full beard and mustache, as was the custom of the time. The black eyes under the shaggy brows were frankly curious and interested. *A very charming, womanly girl, even if she is interested in politics,* James was thinking. *A very sensible, intelligent man, even if he is an infidel,* Sara was thinking.

From that time Mr. Henry became an almost daily visitor, joining the group at the parsonage, and adding his voice and opinions to the discussions. He fell into the habit of going after the mail and bringing it to the house in the early part of the evening. The reading of the news and the *Congressional Globe* was now divided between Sara and James, because Mr. Henry had a fine voice and was an exceptionally effective reader.

In this way the weeks passed until September, when Sara returned to the seminary and resumed her former studies and associations. She threw herself into her work with all the enthusiasm of her nature, ignoring the warnings of increasing symptoms that she had contracted the same dread malady that had taken her father's life. In the winter she had a serious attack of hemorrhage of the lungs, and in the spring was so weak she had to relinquish her part in the commencement exercises.

But there was another problem that was of greater concern to Sara than precarious health, providing a constant stimulus to her highest indignation, and that was the subject of higher education for women. As the school year drew on toward commencement, the topic of greatest interest was the future of the young men of the class, who were all preparing for Northwestern University. As they talked glowingly and happily of their plans and prospects, Sara's heart burned within her that there was not a school of college grade anywhere in the land that would admit women.

She waxed very indignant on the subject one day as she was talking to her old friend Stanley Maxson, who was still an ardent admirer of Miss Irish.

"No one seems to question that there is anything else for us girls to do but go back to our homes now and engage in whatever womanly occupation we might be able to find, while you boys go climbing the hill of culture." Her black eyes snapped wrathfully.

"Why, Sara, what a waste of time and money for a girl to go to college. What use would it be to you?" he said, half teasing and half in earnest.

"A lot of use. I want to be independent of circumstances and people. My mother may have to depend on me in her old age. The only thing my education has prepared me to do is to teach in the elementary grades, and you know the pay is hardly anything for such work."

"What about your literary career?" If Sarepta had been any less genuine, she would have detected the slight irony in Stanley's voice.

But the tone and the look were wasted on her, and she answered seriously, "Poetry is my hobby, but I am convinced that I could never make a living by writing. At best it would be uncertain."

Sara's feeling of indignation grew and grew during the last weeks of school. After the closing exercises of the last day, she and Ellen walked back to their room together, after the goodbyes had been said to the young men in the class.

"You know," said Sara, "I think it is positively unjust. Here we are, just as good students as they are, ranking as high as any of the boys, and just as proficient in any of the branches that we have studied together. But they get to go on, and we don't."

"It doesn't bother me," said Ellen. "I plan to get married, and I won't worry a minute whether I had the doubtful privilege of racking my brains over calculus and Greek."

"Well, Ellen, I am going to record a vow with you; if I ever live to grow up, and have a daughter of my own, she shall be educated in that university."

Ellen looked at her with amused eyes. "Your daughter will be a girl, and she won't be allowed to enter."

"But," Sara insisted, "this thing is unfair. It is an outrage. Because of the simple fact that you and I are girls is no reason that we have no right to the same opportunities as the young men. And you mark what I say—my daughter shall go to that university. No other will answer. She must come up to make good the lack of my own opportunities."

James Henry had come up from Pecatonica to drive Sara home. During the months she had been away James had made himself almost indispensable to Mrs. Irish, helping in many and various unobtrusive ways about the farm and home. The impersonal correspondence he had exchanged with Sara had deepened the respect she had for him, but had in no way led her to think of him in any sense but as a kindly neighbor and friend.

And now, sitting beside him on the seat of the buggy, she found his presence comforting and reassuring. It was such a day to lift the heart in gladness and fill the soul with the joy of living. The sun shone upon the wide and beautiful prairie whose rich, shining green stretched out in rolling dips to the horizon like a mighty ocean. Nothing was more breathtaking than to top a verdant grassy swell and feel the soft breeze curling past, to pause there and breathe deeply of the sweet-smelling air. Sara remembered the many trips with her father, and all the freshness of a thousand springtimes seemed packed into one and condensed into the fragrance of the prairies on this day.

She was discovering that James understood the language of nature and was able to translate it to her, pointing out patches of spiderwort and mountain pink, and naming the small frail blossoms star dusting the rolling green swells.

"I wonder what that spread of purple is on that sunny slope," Sara said with a wave of her hand.

"Wild larkspur, I believe, and those bushes along that meandering watercourse are currants. Just see all the bobolinks enjoying them!"

"What a wonderful Creator we have! Truly as the Scriptures say, His ways are past finding out!" Sara spoke with spontaneous enthusiasm, forgetting momentarily what Julia had said about James's attitude on religious matters. It was easy to forget. He seemed so understanding, so broad and deep. She fell silent at this revelation.

Even when she had poured out her indignation about the lack of higher education for women, he had sympathized, had seen her viewpoint, and had refrained from congratulating himself that he wasn't a woman. But suddenly they came back to her, the conversations with Julia, and her revelations as to her cousin's peculiar views. She glanced up at him doubtfully, feeling an invisible barrier.

But James was looking straight ahead, a serious, meditative expression on his dark face. They were both silent a long time until Sara could stand it no longer.

"What are you thinking about so seriously?" she asked.

"I was just thinking how true it is, as you quote, 'His ways past finding out!' I don't think any verse you could have quoted could express my sentiments more correctly. 'His ways past finding out.'"

"You do believe in God, then?"

"Why certainly. There are many things the churches teach, and that many people believe, that I cannot accept. But most certainly I believe in God—as the Father of mankind and the Creator of the universe."

Sara was satisfied not to probe any deeper for possible disagreements. She was convinced that James Henry was a man of integrity, one who abominated hypocrisy and hollow religious forms. She could respect such a man.

Chapter Nine

AN OLD-FASHIONED GAME

M r. Bennett dropped a heavy pine log onto the mound of crumbling embers in the fireplace, and settled back into his rocker to watch the shower of sparks bursting forth and the red-blue flames creeping out from the sides with a pleasant crackle. The reddish light from the fire was reflected in the burnished oak sideboard that stood against the opposite wall and in the flushed young faces of the group surrounding the large round table in the dining room.

"I'm tired of all this talk about war, war, war," said Alice. "I'd like to forget about the whole thing."

"There will be war, however," said James gravely, "but the war will result in the abolition of slavery."

"Everyone be quiet!" commanded Julia. "I want to show you how to play this new game. I guarantee it will be very amusing."

That morning Julia, her eyes shining with enthusiasm and her cheeks red with cold and wet with snow, had popped into the Irishes' kitchen.

"Tomorrow afternoon," she said, "there is to be a big mass meeting and public forum in Rockford to discuss the problem of coercion versus secession, and all the young people from Pecatonica are supposed to go and join the chorus that will lead out in singing

72

patriotic songs. I'm getting some of our friends organized to go with us, and we'll make a sleigh ride of it, leaving early in the morning. Why don't you come over and spend the night with me, Sara, so you'll be ready to go in the morning?"

The deep snow lay like a blanket around the Bennett farmhouse, and the cold penetrated cracks and doorways in a futile effort to assault the cheer and good spirits within. The group had spent the first part of the evening practicing for the singing, and then at Alfred Hart's suggestion had played some romping games, and now, panting from exercise, had settled down around the polished oak table.

Julia passed out slips of paper to each one and explained, "Write a line of verse on the paper, then fold and pass it to your neighbor showing only the last word, which sets the pattern for the rhyme. The fun comes when we read the medley aloud and see what nonsense we've composed."

Writing verse was just in line with Sara's talents and interest, and while she was busily thinking up hers, James Henry slipped a folded paper into her hand that had the words "For yourself" printed on the outside. Wonderingly, Sara opened the paper and read the most momentous question of her lifetime, cleverly expressed in a stanza of verse.

Sara seemed to be one of those rare women who can receive attention from men without perceiving intention. She had gone along enjoying a happy friendship without any thought in her mind of how it might end, or analyzing either her feelings or his in the matter. This had happened to her several times before, and had brought misunderstanding and reproaches. Her friendship with Stanley Maxson at Rock River Seminary had been full of misunderstandings because she was unable to understand his viewpoint or to realize that he thought he had a special claim upon her.

But she was a woman now, and here was a plain question to answer. She knew that Mr. Henry was too sincere and candid a person to trifle with. She reproached herself that she hadn't been discerning enough to have foreseen this. As she looked back and remembered little incidents she wondered at her own blindness.

She felt that an answer was called for immediately, but she was not ready with it. Her mind was in turmoil, which she tried to cover up by pretending to be absorbed in the game. Finally she wrote "Not tonight" on a piece of paper and passed it to Mr. Henry, knowing that she was just pleading for time, and that he would know it too.

She could not look at him again, and after a few minutes of effort to conceal her agitation she stepped from the room, going into Mrs. Bennett's own room, which was off the kitchen. Anything to get away and be alone and think. She had hardly shut the door when there was a light rap, and Julia, not waiting for permission, slipped in.

"You look as if you had a bad toothache or something," she said, scanning Sara's face suspiciously. "What on earth is the matter?"

"James has asked me to marry him!" said Sara as if in a daze.

"Well, what is so awful about that? Is that something to look so sad about? Surely you must have seen this coming through all these months!"

"But Julia, believe me, I didn't. I didn't have any idea."

"Sara, you funny little girl! Here I was thinking you were probably much wiser than you seemed. But now I see that you were much more innocent than I thought."

They talked the matter over girl fashion, and then Sara requested to be taken to the room where she was to sleep that night. Her cheeks were flushed as she looked in the mirror.

"I just can't meet James again tonight."

As soon as she had prepared to retire, she knelt beside the bed, as was her custom, and laid her case before her heavenly Father, and asked His direction.

She analyzed her own feelings, and admitted to herself a warmer affection for Mr. Henry than for any of her other friends. He was not her ideal in personal appearance, but in intellectual qualities, and inner nature as he had shown it to her from time to time, he came very near. As she sought for guidance in this most serious problem of her life, the conflict was not over the matter of whether she loved him or not, but whether she would please God by uniting with one who made no profession of Christianity. She remembered her conversations with him about God, and in her heart she pleaded that she knew him to be a man of fine principles and one who believed in God, even though he did not accept all the teachings of the church.

When Julia came to bed Sara feigned sleep to avoid any further conversation. But she spent a wakeful night, tossing and turning and revolving all the aspects of the question. Tired and distressed, she felt half resentful that he had opened a question that was to change all further relationships. Her mind alternated between visualizing herself as a beloved wife and mother and the torment of her doubts and fears. The problematic relations of marriage and its mysteries filled her with something akin to terror.

In the morning, as soon as she heard a stir in the house, she rose with her unanswered question still an intolerable burden. She crept softly down the stairs to the kitchen, drawn by the warm wood fire that roared in the stove. At the door she met Mr. Henry carrying a cup of unground coffee in his hand, which he was taking up to the garret to grind for breakfast. She had not anticipated such an encounter, but she met his eyes fairly, and inquired, "Would you like some help?" Her voice was steady but her heart quaked.

He looked down at her with tenderness, and from his face and eyes there seemed to spring a peculiar light and strength, the beauty of manliness that she had never seen in any other human face. Instantly she knew the answer of her heart.

"Certainly; all the help I can get," he said, and they went together to the old garret over the kitchen, where she stood and held the cup, which he emptied into the hopper and then ground the coffee into it. When there was no more coffee to grind and no more excuse for remaining, Sara told him of her perplexities, and said that she had decided to defer the whole matter to her mother.

"I must record," Sara wrote in her diary later, "that his conduct on this occasion was such that we went downstairs leaving coffee behind us scattered all over the floor."

"But please, you must remember," said Sara as they went downstairs, "that the matter is not settled, and will depend on my mother.

75

I have no idea how she will receive the idea."

James was determined to lose no time in finding out, so while the others ate breakfast he dashed across the five acres of snow that lay between the two farms. Sara was too excited to eat, and could not be drawn into the chitchat of the others at the table. She went through the motions of helping Julia dry dishes, but most of the time she was standing by the pantry window watching for a black figure returning across the snow. Finally, when he neared the house enough for her to see the expression on his face, she knew her fate had been determined.

Of the rest of the day she wrote in her diary:

"It would be useless to attempt to describe the day—the long ride, sitting in the bottom of the great sleigh on the straw, with the merry company piled in about us; the rhythmic play of the horses' feet upon the beaten road; the beauty of the winter landscape under the brilliant sun and sky; the harmony of all things with the newly awakened music of nature that was surging through my soul. The mass meeting was a magnificent affair; the spirit of patriotism high; there was no lack of enthusiasm. The great questions which were before the country were discussed and settled by the orators of the day in a most satisfactory manner, and it was with swelling hearts and unbounded joy that we took our homeward ride."

Chapter Ten

A PRAIRIE
SCHOONER
HONEYMOON

*I*t was decided that the wedding should not take place until the autumn, in the hope that Sarepta's lung trouble, which had been increasing, would improve. In the meantime there was much discussion, pro and con, of the prospective match by all the townspeople, who had known Sarepta since she was a small girl.

"She ain't no more fitten for weddin' than a child—don't know the fust thing about keepin' house," said one.

"Such a pity she didn't marry that aristocratic Stanley Maxson; he was just the ideal person for her. He'll go far, probably get to be Senator or something," was the opinion of her schoolmates from the Rock River Seminary.

On the other hand, James's aunt, Mrs. Bennett, and others of his friends thought that James, a vigorous young man, was making a great sacrifice to tie himself to a woman "who would always be an invalid, and could not do one practical thing." James Henry had accepted a position in the public schools at Pecatonica—a good respectable job—but it was not likely he would ever be rich or able to afford servants in the home.

Mrs. Irish herself had a few misgivings. The morning he had come across the snow to ask her consent she had said, "What do you want of a girl with one foot in the grave?"

And he had answered, "I want the right to care for her and make her well."

There were also whispered murmurs about Sara's "being unequally yoked together with unbelievers" and "tying up with an infidel."

One Sunday morning there was quite a stir and turning of heads by the staid members of the Methodist church when they saw James Henry accompanying Sarepta down the aisle of the church. After the regular preaching service he stayed with her and attended the meeting of her class. It was an informal occasion, and personal testimonies were offered by the different members. When nearly all had spoken, the leader stepped to Mr. Henry and asked him whether he would like to say a word too.

James rose. The room became very quiet, so each could catch his words.

"Since an announcement has been made in which our friends are greatly interested, I feel that it is no more than right that I should make a statement regarding my religious views. Above all things I wish to know the truth, and be led by it. However, I do not profess to know the truth, but I can sincerely state that I am a seeker of it.

"I know that the members of this group believe in prayer. I also have faith in prayer. I believe God is a real being, the Father of the race, and that He is willing to listen to His children when they speak to Him. I think of prayer as talking to God the Father. I would be grateful for anyone here to speak to Him in my behalf, if you are better acquainted with Him than I. I admit I do not know Him very well myself."

The candor of his appearance and words and the sweetness of his spirit made a deep impression on the hearers. After the meeting one of the older women whispered encouragingly in Sara's ear, "He certainly is a Christian, whether he knows it or not."

Sara was not afraid. She knew him for a man of deep and honest convictions and high principles, the soul of integrity. She was very much in love, and looked forward happily to the approaching marriage.

"You look out that window so much," teased her mother as Sara was standing by the kitchen window one bright morning in early March. "I suppose you are expecting to see James coming across the field at this time of day. You know he is at the school."

"As a matter of fact, he is coming across the field, and Julia is with him. They are walking rapidly and talking as if they had some news to tell."

Mrs. Irish joined her daughter at the window. "I wonder what it can be. Maybe war has really broken out."

"Oh, no, this is good news. I can tell. Possibly something about the inauguration."

The cousins, James and Julia, burst in the door together.

Julia got in the first word. "I had to come along and see what you think of this, I . . ."

James's eyes were sparkling with enthusiasm, and the words fairly tumbled out.

"Sara! Listen to this. Now don't say anything until you hear it all. For some weeks I have been talking with a Mr. Prescott who is representing a large land and business interest in the Spirit Lake region of northwestern Iowa. He has a large property on the east shore of West Okoboji that he wishes to make the site of a college—"

"Wait," said Mrs. Irish. "Isn't that West Okoboji district the place that was devastated by a terrible Indian massacre about two years ago?"

"Yes," admitted James honestly, "but of course that was two years ago. Mr. Prescott has asked me—us, Sara—to go out and take care of the erection of the buildings and the opening of the school. He wants me to be the president. It's a tremendous challenge, and a wonderful opportunity. It's just the kind of place you will love—in the heart of a forest, on the shores of a beautiful lake."

Sara was already fired with enthusiasm. But Mrs. Irish kept her feet on the earth with a few practical considerations.

"Sara's in no physical condition for a trip like that. She'd probably die on the road. I don't think you realize . . ."

James turned to her patiently and kindly. "Now, Mother Irish, I wouldn't want to be foolhardy or presumptuous, so I have already had a consultation with Dr. Jones about Sara, and he said that since the trip will be overland by slow transit, and she will be outdoors a great deal, that it will do her good and will be just the thing for building up her strength."

"And I'll help look after her too," put in Julia, who had been having difficulty in letting her cousin do the talking.

Both Sara and her mother exclaimed at once, "Are you going too?"

"Yes, isn't that wonderful? I think so. There are many things I can do to help in a place like that. There are a number of the others in our group who might like to go too, I think—Emory, and Alice, and Alfred Hart."

"Does everyone know about this except us?" asked Sara, amused. "By the way, when will we go? When does the expedition begin?"

James hesitated as if conscious that this really might have to be handled carefully. "There have been a number of uncertainties about the project, and I didn't want to get you stirred up until I knew for sure. Mr. Prescott has been planning to push off in three days, but if we can join them, they will wait until the seventh; that will be three days after the inauguration of Mr. Lincoln."

The women were absolutely nonplussed, not in reference to the president's inauguration, but because they had only five days to prepare for the trip and the wedding.

"Five days!" they both exclaimed. "Why, we haven't even begun to think about the wedding!"

The friends, neighbors, and townspeople joined in an orgy of sewing and baking to help the young couple and their friends as they prepared for this adventure into the wilderness. The girls designed their own traveling dresses to suit the nature of the trip, using durable material, and shorter skirts than the fashion of the time; in fact, they came only to the tops of their boots. They bought boys' riding boots with red morocco tops and caps with visors to protect their eyes from the prairie sun.

Into the heavy trunks Sara packed her silver spoons, bits of china, her new linens, and handwoven quilts. Her mother insisted on a place for the bean pot, trivet, and iron skillets. The English cloth that had been Grandma Irish's back in Albion was tucked in and carefully protected by layers of towels and soft woolen clothes. There were brass candlesticks to set beside the bed, and tallow candles to hollow out of the wilderness a glowing shrine of cheering light. Julia flew back and forth, chatting happily, helping and giving advice to everyone. The house was full of visitors bringing gifts and articles for use on the trip.

Each day was busier and busier as the time of departure neared. To set apart a single quiet hour, a solemn, sacred pause amid the hubbub of packing and loading and moving of trunks, for the exchanging of the marriage vows was an astonishing feat in itself. Through it all Sara remained calm and tranquil as if the possessor of some secret source of peace and joy that already was giving her new life and strength.

And so, on March 7, 1861, three days after Abraham Lincoln was inaugurated as president of the United States, Sarepta Myrenda Irish became Mrs. James Henry.

There was a special atmosphere of gaiety and festivity about this excursion, because the group who were making the adventure were all young people—intimate friends who were eager for the gypsy life of the wilderness trail—who were anticipating the hunting and fishing and camping and the new scenes before them.

The young men made light work of the loading of the prairie schooners. Trunk after trunk and box after box they hauled out and stowed away in the capacious beds of the huge wagons. Tents, sacks of grain, feed for the animals, barrels of water, bedding, and provisions of all kinds were loaded in and arranged in reference to their need on the long trip westward.

The cavalcade consisted of two prairie schooners, their new white canvas taut over hoops and bows and tightly roped on the sides, and two carriages, plus a number of saddle horses. The prairie schooners were awe inspiring in their ponderous clumsiness. The six-foot wheels of seasoned hickory turned on axles the size of trees and screeched protestingly as they turned under the weight of the tons of baggage. But such wheels were made to withstand the wear and tear of the sand and mud of the trackless wilderness ahead. Extra spokes and fellies, already shaped, were in readiness if repairs should be needed on the way. Five spans of matched red oxen for each schooner stood in their traces patiently waiting for the signal to go.

At last everything was in readiness, the whips were uncurled along the backs of the animals, and they were off amid a chorus of goodbyes and last-minute admonitions and a flutter of handkerchiefs.

The girls rode in one of the carriages; James and Emory and Al rode the saddle horses, galloping ahead at times, or falling to the rear as they chose. The boys were all excellent riders. Mr. Prescott was manager and pilot and drove in the fore wagon.

The speed was limited to the leisurely crawl of the ox teams. Sometimes the boys rode the horses beside the carriage and talked to the girls inside. James frequently felt the need of a glimpse of his bride, smiling out at him from the windows of the coach.

"Are you comfortable in there?" he shouted.

"Yes, but I'd like to be riding a horse," she answered.

"So would I," said Julia.

"When we get to Lake West Okoboji I'll get you a pony, dearest, and you shall ride."

Occasionally the girls discussed the location of their destination with reference to its isolation and the danger of Indian attack.

"Sometimes I wonder whether we aren't being a bit foolhardy," said Julia, "in going to a place that was so recently wiped out by the Indians."

The cavalcade was prepared to be quite largely a self-sustaining unit, lumbering on into the wilderness independent of towns, stores, and sometimes even roads, and provided with most of the necessities for the trip. There were widely spaced trading posts where supplies could be purchased—at a price.

In the late afternoon the search for a suitable campsite began. There was always the hope that they might find trees, water, and level ground for the night; but frequently a less desirable location—a boulder-strewn ravine or a treeless, unprotected spot—had to be accepted to avoid the necessity of making camp in the dark. The moment the oxen slowed to a halt at the selected site was the signal for passengers to emerge from carriages and wagons, riders to dismount from horses, and all set about their individual duties. The outspanning of the oxen, the setting up of tents, the making of beds, the building of fires, and the cooking of food all took time, and reduced the hours of travel. But the exciting sense of adventure kept their spirits high.

Even at best, from 10 to 12 miles a day was the most they could expect to cover. At the end of the first week they had crossed the Mississippi River and were beginning the long trek through Iowa. The weather had turned cold, and the bright skies that had favored them in Illinois had become gray and threatening. About 3:00 in the afternoon the light drizzle turned into steady, beating rain.

The oxen plodded on undisturbed; the canvas-covered schooners shed the rain; the horses and riders were shining and glistening with rain. Water dripped from the hats onto the shoulders of the riders.

James and Emory rode back to the carriage where the girls were riding and reported that Mr. Prescott said he thought there was a small tavern and inn not far ahead where they might be able to find a lodging for over Sunday, since it would be quite unpleasant to try to make camp in the downpour.

Just when it seemed that sky and road and horizon were blending in the wet, gray veil, and that the trackless wilderness was closing in on them, they passed a few crude shacks at the fringe of a small settlement, and soon stopped in front of a rambling building, badly in need of paint, with a shaky veranda along the front.

"Looks as if this is where we spend the night," said Julia with a gesture of disgust.

" 'The White Horse,' " read Sara on the sign, as they descended from the carriage steps.

A roaring fire in the fireplace greeted them as they entered the door. Otherwise the atmosphere was of threadbare shabbiness, pervaded by an odor of long-cooked cabbage, boardinghouse meals, and liquor.

The rooms were tiny and quite bare of all but the necessities for a night's rest.

Beside the little table with the single flickering tallow candle James opened the large Bible. Looking across at his young wife with tenderness, he smiled and said, "Do you know that this is the first evening we have been alone since our marriage? It seems strange, doesn't it?

"I do not profess to believe this Bible as you do, but ever since I began to think of having a home of my own, I have wished that my house should be a house of prayer, and that the Bible should be the guide of my life so far as I am able to understand it. I propose that we read it every day and pray together, that we have what you have always been accustomed to—a family altar."

Six weeks after leaving Pecatonica the caravan reached its destination beside the wooded shores of beautiful Lake West Okoboji. Mrs. Prescott and her seven children gave the newcomers a hearty welcome and found places for all in the large two-story house that was to serve as headquarters until the new buildings for the college were constructed.

The news they heard from the East was not reassuring. It had been a long time since they had heard what was happening in the nation, and they were eager to hear all the news since Lincoln's inauguration three days before their departure.

Mrs. Prescott summarized the events of six weeks for them. "Mr. Lincoln has had no easy time," she said. "In the first place, he has found that the members of his Cabinet are not altogether loyal, especially Seward and Chase. And Seward has even gone so far as to suggest to President Lincoln that, a month having passed since the inauguration without his formulation of a policy, either domestic or foreign, it would be a good idea for Lincoln to abdicate and let him take over the responsibilities of the government. Can you imagine that?"

"But President Lincoln didn't, did he?" they asked aghast.

"Oh, no. He even kept Seward in the Cabinet. The most important item of news is that Lincoln, in spite of the disapproval of his Cabinet, has sent relief expeditions to the garrisons at Fort Sumter and Fort Pickens. But this has led the Davis government to order the bombardment of Sumter. We haven't heard anything since, but you can see that we are right on the verge of war."

Mr. Prescott, Mr. Henry, and the others of the expedition spent considerable time each day discussing the plans for the projects to be carried out, but the imminence of war and the effect it would have on all their lives were a heavy damper on their spirits and caused grave doubts as to the realization of their plans for the school.

While they were waiting for developments and information from the center of the nation, they lived their life as merrily as possible. This spot, which later became a charming resort with magnificent accommodations for tourists, was nonetheless enjoyable in its primitive state; and the happy group of young people made the most of its woods for hunting, its waters for swimming and boating, and its trails for horseback riding.

True to James's prediction, Sara's health had improved with the outdoor life, and it may be guessed that happiness had also played its part. This was the happiest, most carefree period of her life, and she entered with enthusiasm into all the activities the group could invent. Most of all, she enjoyed the companionship of her husband, and the times when they mounted their ponies and rode off alone together.

James had bought her a horse, or rather an Indian pony, Black Hawk, which had never been mounted. She had always been a lover of horses, and had been trained to drive and ride in her journeys with her father, so she was perfectly at home with a horse harnessed or saddled. She insisted on breaking Black Hawk herself.

First she tamed him by feeding him sugar and dainties. He learned to put his nose to her pocket for something to eat, and would follow her like a kitten wherever she went. After she had secured his love, she fastened the saddle upon him. He remonstrated, but when he found she was doing it herself, he submitted. She led him around and made him wear the saddle and follow her for some time. Then she took her riding skirt and tied it to the pommel of the saddle. Black Hawk did not like this at all. He protested vigorously, but his love still kept him loyal, and with the skirt swinging under him and striking his heels, he would follow her about, careening and kicking but yet keeping on his feet. When both James and Sara were quite satisfied that he was accustomed to the saddle and skirt, she put on the latter, and mounted the former, and began her first effort to ride. The poor beast was very much perplexed. He could not understand what it meant to hear her voice talking to him so far above his head; but he listened while she talked, and James held the bit, fearing that something might happen. Finally she persuaded James to go away and leave her alone with the animal, who knew her better than anyone. At last he did, and Sara gave Black Hawk a little pat, and urged him forward.

He made a leap, then stood stock still while Sara maintained her position. Before they had finished their first lesson, Black Hawk went over the woodpile and up onto the back porch of the house, overturning a pail of water, and upsetting a churn in his effort to obtain freedom. He did not understand how to get rid of the accessories to which his old friend seemed to insist upon clinging!

"What makes you so pale, Jim?" teased Al Hart as the watchers relaxed and looked at each other when they saw she was getting the pony under control.

From that time Sara had no difficulty in riding Black Hawk wherever she wished. But no one else could mount him. James had a large chestnut horse for his own use, and he and Sara frequently went off for rides, ostensibly for game, but really that they might enjoy the beautiful air and each other's society uninterrupted. He taught her use of the fowling piece, and she soon acquired so true an aim that she could feather the cattails at a respectable distance. But she refused to aim at anything alive.

"I cannot bear to see the wing of the bird droop in its flight, or the little timid creatures about us murdered wantonly by those endowed with God-given powers. I cannot believe that the commandment, 'Thou shalt not kill' simply means 'Thou shalt not kill thy fellow man,' but am convinced it is also intended to protect animal life from unnecessary destruction."

Though James had never looked at it from this viewpoint, he

good-humoredly accepted the suggestion, and aimed his gun at a toughened prairie plant. "Hereafter we will get our sport out of feathered cattails and decapitated sunflowers," he said, "instead of from the blood of rabbits and blackbirds."

During these happy days Sarepta poured out her feelings in verse in a rollicking poem called "Joy."

THERE IS JOY FOR THEE, O EARTH!

"Joy! Joy! Joy!
There is joy for thee, O Earth!
The golden Morn
Of beauty born,
With its amber dews
And changing hues
With its tender skies,
Whose image lies
In the sparkling sea,
That exultantly
Lifts up its voice,
And cries, 'Rejoice!'
With its song that floats
From a million throats,
With its bursting blooms and
Rare perfumes—
All the glorious things
That the morning brings
On her quivering wings
Are a joy to thee, O Earth!

"Joy! Joy! Joy!
Each sound is full of joy.
From the faintest sigh of the swelling leaves,
And the twitter of birds beneath the eaves,
And the laugh of the rill down the mountain side,

To the booming roar of the tossing tide;
From the tenderest trill to the deepest tone,
There's a gushing fullness of joy alone—
Of joy that is thine, O Earth!

"Joy! Joy! Joy!
There is joy for thee, O Heart!
The life that fills
Thy veins, and thrills,
With quickening heat,
Each pulse's beat;
The power that dwells
Deep, deep below,
Like hidden wells
That silent flow,
But that upward spring
Like a mighty thing,
When a rushing thought
Into deed is wrought;
The aims that rise
Beyond the skies;
The love that lies
Like a peaceful sea,
Whose waters lave,
With songful wave,
Immensity;
Each glorious thing
That Life doth bring
On her glancing wing,
Is a joy to thee, O Heart!

"Joy! Joy! Joy!
O, life is full of joy!
And 'mid the sounds that swell on high
From the lips of Earth, triumphantly,

A Prairie Schooner Honeymoon

There bends for aye a low refrain,
A softer sound, a sweeter strain;
'Tis the voice of Life, and its thrilling tone
Sings the gushing song of joy alone—
    Of joy that is thine, O Heart!"

                          —MRS. S.M.I. HENRY

Chapter Eleven

ON THE INDIAN FRONTIER

One day in early June the Prescotts discovered that a newly purchased cow had broken loose, and was supposed to have returned to her old home, a town 50 miles distant. James and Sara volunteered to make the trip to find her. It would take three days, one to go and two to return. They would have to spend the second night on the prairie alone.

They started early in the morning with a horse and top buggy, a small shelter tent, and a well-packed lunch basket. They were well on their way when the sun came up, tinting the wide-stretching earth with a rosy glow. The prairie was covered with pink June roses as far as the eye could see. It was a sight never to be forgotten—hundreds and hundreds of acres of wild roses sparkling in the dew! They had their luncheon on the prairie, selected a campsite for the night of the return trip, and arrived at the town, which was in a river valley between the hills. The surmise about the cow's returning to her calf was correct, and the next morning they started home with the cow tied to the back of the buggy.

They made camp early, selecting a breezy knoll where the mosquitoes would not bother them. The tent was soon pitched, and the travelers were settled for the night. James slept at once, but Sara was wakeful, intensely enjoying the novelty of the situation. The

edge of the tent was drawn up, and she could look out at the brilliant, moonlit loneliness about them. The vast wilderness was so intensely still that the very silence seemed audible. The breathing of
the cow and the occasional stamping of the horse were the only signs
of life.

As Sara lay listening and thinking, she suddenly heard what
seemed to be the horse's footsteps, accompanied by peculiar sounds.
Peering intently into the moonlight, she saw that the horse was
walking away, dragging the rope and tether pin, which flew up once
in a while, and made the bumping sound that she had heard.

"James," she called, urgently shaking him. "Our horse is loose
and is getting away."

Mr. Henry sprang up immediately and started in pursuit, calling
soothingly, and stretching out his hand persuasively. But as soon as
the horse knew that he was discovered he quickened his pace.
Whether he found the mosquitoes troublesome or whatever was his
objection to spending the night in camp, he certainly did not intend
to be easily captured. James followed as close as he could, and tried
to grasp the pin; but the horse kept it just beyond his reach.

Sara came out of the tent and climbed into the carriage seat,
where she watched the receding pair as they went north along the
road farther and farther into the distance, finally fading entirely from
view. She could still hear her husband's voice calling to the horse
coaxingly and the steady stepping of the animal's hoofs. But at last
even these sounds died away, and the stillness became more and
more intense and the loneliness appalling.

Within her entire range of vision in that moonlit landscape there
was not another object so high as the carriage in which she sat. She
began to think of the Indian raids over the same territory scarcely
two years before, which had wiped out the settlements of this frontier, and to remember the rumors of hostile Indians that had been
coming in the past few weeks.

All through the long hours of the night she sat in the carriage seat,
her eyes glued to the horizon, hoping to see the return of her husband on the horse. Morning had begun to dawn when she finally saw

a tiny moving object upon the horizon. She tried hard to discern whether it was a friend or foe, but only when she heard the merry whistle that was her husband's signal to her did she know of a certainty that it was he returning. The horse had led him a long and weary chase, not being captured until within a few miles of home.

Not far from the boardinghouse were several log cabins that had been occupied by the massacred settlers, whose graves were in the dooryards. One of these cabins in the woods on the shore of the lake was the favorite resort of the young couple. They would take their dinner in a basket, with books and writing materials, and steal away to spend the day there.

One morning James had a bright idea. "I am going to propose to Mrs. Prescott that we take our bed and furniture down to the cabin and vacate our room."

The big house was very crowded, and now that hot weather had come, the thought of a cozy, quiet cabin all to themselves was very appealing. Mrs. Prescott laughingly assented to this request; and a wagonload of necessary things, including their trunks, was removed to the cabin, which they fitted up to suit their fancy. James made boxes, which Sara filled with moss and woodland plants, and they fastened them to the inside of the walls and to the outside of the house. Over the windows the young husband trained vines, and made a bower of beauty in the midst of nature's loveliness.

One evening just after they retired they heard a loud knock on the door, and James opened up a crack to see who it could be at that late hour. Emory and some of the other young men stood on the step.

"We've come to take you back to the house," they said. "With so many reports of Indians in the vicinity, it isn't safe for you to remain here. We don't intend to let you stay, and then some morning find you dead. Of all the harebrained ideas, anyway, coming down here!"

Neither James nor Sara was timid, and neither of them was worried about Indians.

"Well, boys," said James calmly, "thanks for the warning. We'll think it over and make up our minds tomorrow what to do."

"Oh, no, you won't," said Emory. "You're coming right back

now. Or if you want to stay down here, Jim, and be massacred, all right; but we have come down to take Sara up to the house, and we are strong enough to do it. We do not propose to have her carried off by the Indians."

There was nothing else for James to do but to give in.

"Very well, we will go with you," he said, and so they gathered up a few of their belongings and walked back with the boys.

When they reached the house they found that the chamber over the wing had been fitted up for their use. This chamber was long and narrow, having windows to the east and west, opposite each other. The bed stood between these windows. The east window looked toward the barn and the woods; the west, through a grove in front of the house toward the lake.

The conversation of the boys as they had walked back lingered in Sara's mind and prevented sleep after they had gone to bed for the second time that night. Her imagination was greatly aroused, and she tossed and turned and looked out the window at the moonlit yard with its lights and shadows. Along about midnight she distinctly saw moving figures, but her better sense suggested that her overwrought imagination might be playing tricks on her. Finally she became fully satisfied that they were Indians, and she saw them go to the barn, evidently to see whether they could break in and get at the horses.

She put her hand over to her husband and said, "James, James, wake up, but don't lift your head."

He awoke and began to get up, but she said again, "Don't move. Lie down. We are right between two windows. There are Indians out by the barn, and if anyone moves in this room, they can see him. There is an old fellow there keeping watch; he is looking this way. Don't lift your head, or you may be shot!"

James was anxious to ascertain for himself whether his wife was correct or only dreaming, but Sara persisted until finally he obeyed, and slipped down by the side of the bed to the floor, and crawled out to give the alarm.

Immediately the house was aroused—very much aroused when it was found that one corner of the kitchen was afire on the outside.

93

As soon as the Indians discovered that there were so many men in the house and the alarm had been given, they slunk off to the woods. But Emory and Al Hart could not resist making a few wisecracks about people who were so brave as to be foolhardy.

The increasing urgency of national affairs and the knowledge that participation in them was inevitable were considerations that could not forever be put aside. They overshadowed all the good times of the outpost. The idea of being able to proceed with the original plans was now generally conceded to be untenable. When the news came through that President Lincoln had made a call for troops, the spirit of patriotism ran high, and all the young men rode over to Fort Dodge to enlist. This first call for "three-month men" was issued under the antiquated militia law, which limited the term of national service to 90 days, but the president was not so short-sighted as to believe that the war would be over then. It was followed on May 3 with a call for 42,000 volunteers to serve for three years.

James Henry found himself a fraction of an inch below the very rigid military standard of height, and in a few days he and some of the others returned to the outpost. They brought with them papers filled with the news of the war, and also indications that there was present danger of another Indian uprising.

It was thought wise for the men who remained to organize into a company of home guards for the protection of the boardinghouse and the small settlement. The boys were uniformed with red shirts, and one was stationed as scout at each approach from the prairie over which the Indian bands might come. But after several weeks of vigilance with no sign of Indians, they relaxed their anxiety and began to pursue their ordinary life and outdoor recreation. The scout whose beat was on the northwest came in one morning with the statement that Indians had been seen on the trail frequently used by Sara for horseback rides. The party decided to send out the entire company of home guards to reconnoiter the surrounding area.

The kitchen of the boardinghouse presented quite a warlike appearance that morning as the boys cleaned their gun barrels and polished them for service. The girls were busily engaged in running a quantity of bullets to supply the deficiency of ready ammunition. Fortunately they had been able to find lead and molds that would accommodate the bore of some of the weapons, and had melted it down upon the kitchen stove. As usual James was getting a great deal of amusement out of it; in fact, all of them treated the whole thing in the light of a lark, thoughtless of the seriousness of their position in a spot that had been the scene of a terrible massacre.

All was ready at last, and the girls stood on the porch and watched the company march away in their red uniforms, passing the barn and following the road that led through the woods toward the mill and off to the prairie.

They had no sooner disappeared than the disquieting truth dawned on Sara and Julia that every man had gone and left the girls alone with the children. Mr. and Mrs. Prescott had gone East a few weeks before, and had left Julia as housekeeper, with one servant. There they were, the three girls with the seven Prescott children, alone, with half a dozen approaches unguarded, over which any number of Indians might come and attack, or carry them off by the hair of the head. The colossal stupidity of the whole thing was almost funny.

Sara and Julia went off by themselves and had a council of war. They did not want to frighten the children or the servant girl, but planned to take all measures for their safety.

Without attracting any attention they managed very quietly to fasten every window and door. Lizzie was given some housecleaning tasks to keep her busy. Down in the cellar, which was reached by a trapdoor, was a large bin of potatoes that needed sprouting. The children were told that they were to have a picnic, and it was to be in the cellar. Julia and Sara packed a basket with lunch and lowered it into the cellar with the children. The older children were assigned the work of sprouting potatoes, with a prize for the one who sprouted the greatest number.

"Don't try to come up until we call for you," Julia ordered. "We're going to be doing some cleaning up here, and will have some things on the floor above the trapdoor, and you might knock them off. Now be quiet, we don't want a lot of noise down there. If you get tired, you'll just have to think of some games to play."

They looked around to see what weapons they could find, but were limited to an ax, a hatchet, and one old gun. These Julia kept beside her while she kept watch from below. Sara took some lunch and mounted the cupola to watch. The cupola was a little square room on top of the house, with windows on its four sides—an admirable watchtower, built for this very purpose.

The hours crawled by. Sara strained her eyes, and allowed her imagination to work until it seemed as if every stump might be a crouching Indian. Finally, in the middle of the afternoon, she did see a faraway moving figure coming toward the house from the direction in which the boys had marched away. Yes, there were two, and they were coming steadily and purposefully forward. Her heart began to beat loudly.

She was just ready to go down and give the alarm when her common sense told her that two Indians would not be coming alone, or on foot, or at this time of day. The glad certainty that it was her husband and Emory finally broke through her fright, and she ran downstairs to open the door to let them in, meeting them on the piazza.

"What fools we were!" said James. "After we got out on the prairie we suddenly realized what we had done. 'We've gone off and left the women and children alone, absolutely unprotected,' we said, and so Emory and I immediately turned around and came back."

The detachment of home guards was gone for three days. On the evening of the third day they returned covered with glory. They had met the enemy and fought a battle almost on the spot where Sara had spent the night in the carriage waiting for James to return with the horse. Charlie presented Sara with what he considered a distinguished mark of his regard.

"See what I brought you," he said, pulling out of his belt the scalp of one of the Indians that had been killed in battle, and holding it out to Sara. Shocked and horrified, Sara shrank back from the long black hair with its grisly bloody skin still attached.

"And you, a Christian, have done that? And you wonder that

96

heathen Indians murder White settlers?" She spoke in sharp rebuke, forgetting for the moment the necessity that had taken the men out on the prairie to meet the enemy. In later years she regretted the incident, realizing that she had spoken too impetuously. "I have been sorry for this, because I think I lost an opportunity from lack of genuine spiritual power," she wrote.

By the end of the summer it had become evident that there would be no possibility of establishing a school or of completing any of the plans the group had made. Very few remained of the original company after the volunteers had gone to Fort Dodge and had been mustered in and sent to the front. The danger was too great for the small company in their exposed position.

In October Mr. Henry purchased a Democrat wagon, and fitted it with a canvas cover to protect them from the elements. The trunks were stored in the back, and with one horse Sara and James began the return journey to Illinois. It was a cold, cheerless trip. During the day there hung before them the smoke of burning grass, and by night long ranks of red flames gleamed on the horizon. Fires had blackened the prairie before them. Under them, in place of bloom and green grass, were the blackened stumps of the burned plains.

The sadness and desolation of the landscape were in harmony with the presence of war in the land. Already the fear and sorrow of it were everywhere present. There was scarcely a neighborhood out of which some strong men had not gone to make up the first 75,000 men. All the people they met, from the man who was busy in the field to the sad-eyed women standing in the doors of their sod cabins, were thinking of one thing: the armies that were marching against each other, and the hope for an easy victory.

James and Sara arrived in Pecatonica about the last of November. In the latter part of February their first children, twin boys, were born, and buried after 6 weeks of life. Sara was very ill after this, and her friends despaired of her life. The physicians gave her up to die of consumption.

From the first of her illness she begged them constantly to take her outdoors into the sunshine, but in those times such a thing would have been considered madness. However, when all hope was abandoned, and they felt that it was only a question of days, they decided to yield to her whim, and she was carried out on the porch in a reclining chair. Every day she insisted upon lying in the sun, persisting in the belief that if she could be outdoors, she would get well. James was soon won over to her way of thinking and under his nursing and nature's treatments she improved rapidly, so that by the first of May 1862 she was able to return with her husband to his father's home in East Homer, New York.

Chapter Twelve

END OF AN IDYL

Springtime at the Henry homestead in East Homer was especially welcome and significant to Sara in the year 1865. Springtime in any year was a peculiarly delightful experience at the old homestead. The sugar was running in the tall maple trees on the hill above the house; the clear, fresh water from the spring filled the conduit down the slope and splashed into the pool outside the kitchen door. A lacy filigree of green began to appear on the bare branches of the trees, penetrating the wooded hillsides that surrounded the cleared acres of the farm. Dogwood and redbud added their touch of magic, appearing here and there on the landscape in the careless disarray of the most perfect art.

No place in the world was more quiet and apparently undisturbed by the dreadful war that was being fought to a finish in the South. But even in this secluded part of the country there was hardly a home where there were not anxious hearts as the guns were heard in Homer firing a volley in celebration of the fall of Richmond. As she listened to the village guns Sara gave birth to her son Alfred, and wondered where his father was, somewhere in the heart of the conflict, and whether she would ever see him again.

Soon after the Revolutionary War, James's grandfather, John H. Henry, and his wife, Martha, had staked out the 160 acres of this homestead and established their home. Here they had reared their family; and here Abram, their son, and his wife, Polly, had lived and raised their 10 children. When John, the second son, had gone off to war they had written urging James, their oldest son, to return and manage the affairs of the farm.

Two years he had spent quietly at home, busy with the planting and hoeing and reaping of crops, but daily becoming more impatient as the war continued, and he was not helping with the fight to save the Union. Eagerly they had waited as the news came in of the battles lost and won: Bull Run and Gettysburg; Chickamauga and Vicksburg; Atlanta and Shenandoah. In October of 1864 once more he volunteered, and this time passed the examination for service, which had ceased to be so rigid as to height and weight. The need for every able-bodied, willing man was very pressing at this crucial period of the war.

After his acceptance James organized a company of a hundred young men among his friends and acquaintances, was elected captain by them, and the last of November they marched away. They joined Company E of the 185th Regiment of New York Infantry volunteers, which was detailed to assist General Grant in the siege of Richmond.

One of their first experiences was to stand knee-deep in Virginia mud for 36 hours, the only food being half rations of hardtack and salt pork. The ordeal was too much for even Mr. Henry's hearty constitution, and he became sick. Although from that time on he was in every march and in every battle in which his company served until the end of the war, about the first thing the doctor did on his rounds was to send him to the hospital. But James's intrepid spirit did not allow him to remain after he was able to stand on his feet, and then he would manage to get away on some pretext or other to the front and into service.

The news that dribbled back to the homestead in East Homer was not reassuring. Sara had received a letter from the surgeon of the hospital at City Point asking her to use her personal influence to persuade James to remain in the hospital. But from messages coming through from James she knew that he had returned to his company and was fighting with them. For two weeks before the birth of her son she had had no word except that Company E had lost half its number in crippled and wounded.

Every day Father Henry would go down to the post office and return with the same reply, "Nothing today." Sara's hopes grew fainter and fainter until she did not look for anything and could not bring herself to ask. With an expression of heartbreak on his grizzled, bearded face, Father Henry would go to the door of the room where she was convalescing from childbirth, look in at Sara, and turn away, unable to say a word.

The whole family was in despair. But one day, after about three weeks of this suspense, Father Henry came in with a different expression, and handed Sara what looked like a brown newspaper wrapper out of which the paper had slipped.

"Mr. Rose gave me this. He said that the paper had slipped out and was lost, but he recognized James's handwriting on the outside, and thought you would care for it, so he saved it for you."

Sara took the paper and looked all over the outside. There was no mark except the address. She laid it down, thinking about it, and wondering whether this were all that she would ever again receive from her husband. Then as she took it up again and held it before her face, it happened to break open a little in her hand. Eagerly she held it up against the light.

"Look!" she exclaimed, "there is writing inside!" The family gathered round, while Sara, as carefully as possible, unfolded the crumbling pieces of paper, and removed a tiny letter written with the end of a burnt match.

"He is alive and well," she told them excitedly, "and will write more as soon as he can get letters through the lines."

It was August, however, before he was finally well enough to leave the hospital, discharged as incurable, the shattered wreck of the strong man who had left home less than a year before.

He was received back into the bosom of his family with inexpressible joy, and tenderly given the best of food and care. After two years he was able to resume his old work of teaching, taking the school in the village of East Homer.

They lived now on the little farm he had purchased soon after bringing Sara and his little daughter Mary to East Homer. A second son, Arthur, was born in 1867, and when, a few years later, another beautiful blue-eyed boy came to them, their delight knew no bounds. "With this trio of boys," James said, "and our Seraph," as he called his dimpled, curly-haired daughter, "we shall grow into an old couple gracefully, if I am permitted to remain, and if not, you will never be alone."

James Henry adored his children and devoted his time and strength to making them happy. He was their companion and playfellow, enjoying their romping and their games. Because of his bright and merry disposition and his ability to conceal his own feelings, he was able to hide from his family that he was seriously ill. If at any time his illness became too severe to be endured, he would absent himself, going alone to the woods or barn so that his pain would not cause anxiety to his family.

During the long evenings he would lie stretched out on the lounge, with his shoulders lifted on pillows and the stand with the lamp at his head, reading aloud to Sara as she sat with her sewing.

In the inscrutable providence of God he was not permitted to remain, and in May 1871 passed away after a sudden attack of what was called in those days inflammation of the bowels, but known today as appendicitis.

Sara returned from following the flower-decked casket to the green slope on the hill and shut herself in her bedroom to wrestle with her grief alone. She sat hour after hour with tearless eyes, staring fixedly ahead, motionless. Desolate and stunned, she felt that the end of all things had come.

Outside, the children were playing noisily with the healthy forgetfulness of little animals. Their careless chatter grated harshly on Sara's open wounds. Several times she half rose, intending to check them in their play. They should be made to understand, to remember, to suffer. How could they laugh and play while she was crushed, heartbroken? But a numbing inertia possessed her, and she allowed the impulse to pass, her mind returning to her relentless absorption in her sorrow.

How long she would have continued thus it is impossible to say, but after several hours had passed she became conscious that Arthur was calling to her, knocking persistently on the door.

"Mama, Mama! Open the door please! I want you."

Woodenly, as in a dream, Sarepta rose and went to the door. Her heart melted at the sight of his sweet, wistful, little-boy face.

"Mama, what are you doing in here by yourself? Why is it all dark?"

Sara could not answer, but stood regarding him pityingly. The other children came up, eyeing her suspiciously. The smiles faded from their rosy faces, flushed with their happy play, and they began to look tearful.

"Mama, don't stay in that dark old room anymore," said Alfred crossly.

"Mama, why are you so sad?" asked Mary. "Didn't you say that Jesus came and took Papa away?"

"Yes, dear, but . . ."

"And that now he will never hurt anymore and will be always happy?"

"Yes, but . . ."

"Aren't you glad that he'll never be sick anymore, and that he is up in heaven with Jesus?" It was an echo of their Methodist training.

But I miss him, and I want him here with me. Sara didn't say the words. Instead, she said, "You are right, darling. I tell you, let's all go for a walk up on the hill and see whether we can find some anemones and trilliums."

The children's faces changed at once, and the happy smiles returned. And from that hour Sara left the gloom of the darkened room and turned her face to the sunshine.

There were also practical considerations that forced themselves upon the young mother's mind. Heretofore her husband had borne the largest share of the responsibilities, having fulfilled his promise to Mrs. Irish of years ago when he asked for the privilege of taking care of Sara and making her well. She knew nothing of the practical demands of life. Up to the time of her husband's death she had never

103

bought herself a dress, or a child a garment.

No wonder that her husband's family and the neighbors thought she ought to give her children away and go back to her mother! But the young mother, with her pale face and the great reproachful eyes into which the anguish of widowhood had struck deep, looked with unspeakable distress at those who would take her children, and gathered her little ones into her arms with silent resolution.

As far as she knew she had not a penny in the world, and her only possessions were her few household goods and her children. She didn't know how she would manage, but she was confident that God would guide and provide. She hadn't the strength for hard labor, but she could write and she could teach.

While pondering these things her hand dropped into her pocket, and she pulled out a forgotten check for $10, payment for a poem written during her husband's illness. It was a good omen! With courage and faith she began the task of providing for her children. She got busy with her pen and from poems and magazine articles brought in sufficient money to help her through the summer.

Evidently it was intended that her cup of sorrows should overflow, for three months after James Henry's death the youngest babe, a delicate but beautiful little creature, was laid to rest beside his father on the hill.

In the fall Sarepta took over the school her husband had been teaching, taking her children with her to the schoolhouse. For the same job her husband had performed she received only a third of the pay—$20—the difference being that she was a woman! But it kept her children from hunger and herself from having to depend entirely on others.

The struggles and trials of the new life brought out latent qualities in her character that otherwise might have remained hidden, and there grew a new feeling of strength and self-reliance. She was eventually to realize that the terrible blow that had fallen so quickly, as well as everything that had gone before in her life, was in the nature of a preparation for that which was to follow.

Part Two

THE CRUSADE

*T*he Lord giveth the word: the women that published the tidings are a great host" (Ps. 68:11, ARV).

"For death is come up into our windows, and is entered into our palaces, to cut off the children from without, and the young men from the streets" (Jer. 9:12).

Chapter Thirteen

THE WHIRLWIND
OF THE LORD

*W*hile blood was flowing on the battlefields of the South, and homes were being torn and shattered as the nation struggled to settle the question of slavery, another enemy, another devastator of the home, another form of slavery, was gaining strength in both the North and the South. While the minds of the people and the legislators were turned toward the problem of national union, the liquor dealers had busied themselves to bring about the repeal of all the prohibition laws save in the state of Maine.

For more than 50 years different groups had attempted to bring some sort of controls over the widely expanding business. The first temperance society was founded in 1808; in 1826 there was a national movement resulting from the efforts of the preacher-orator Lyman Beecher; in 1836 there was formed an American Temperance Union, and in 1846 a Total Abstinence Society, whose membership reached the 7-million mark, backed by such outstanding personalities as John B. Gough.

Some idea of the seriousness of the menace that alcoholism was to the nation at the close of the War Between the States may be formed from Abraham Lincoln's statement: "The next snare we have got to straighten out is the liquor question." Just how he would have attacked this national problem, and what difference it would have made to the country, is a matter of speculation, for the leadership of the nation was soon in other hands, and the liquor traffic "practiced and prospered."

Owing in part to the influx of immigrants after the Civil War there was a great increase in the consumption of liquor. The government tax sanctioning it gave to the business a protective legal standing. For the next 10 years and more the people were generally preoccupied in trying to regain their lost fortunes, and consequently they protected the business that promised to help fill the treasuries and lessen taxes.

This was an era when women were beginning to take off their kitchen aprons and step out of their homes with determination to participate in wider interests than recipes and patterns. The colleges had been slow to open their doors to women, but Wesleyan Female College in Macon, Georgia, had led the way, and others were slowly following. However, higher education for women as a general thing was hardly dreamed of. Very few women took part in public affairs, and the choice of a career for women was limited chiefly to the historic role of schoolteacher. Women had not yet discovered the power that later came to them through organization and concerted action. But they were beginning.

For 25 years a small group of women, led by such personages as Susan B. Anthony, Carrie Chapman Catt, and Elizabeth Stanton, had been pushing the cause of woman suffrage, and in 1867 had brought their cause before the federal government for recognition. Although the right of women to vote in political matters was still nearly half a century in the future, the reaction of the women of the country to the conditions in their towns and cities brought about by the coalition of politicians and saloonkeepers was remarkable. It illustrates the fact that when sufficiently aroused and aware of the need, women in any country will arise, and throw off the restraints of custom and convention to attack the enemies of their hearths and homes.

Simultaneously in all parts of the country, without being aware of concerted action, little groups of women banded together to plan, to act, and to crusade against the saloon. Frances Willard later described it as the "whirlwind of the Lord, which in fifty days swept the liquor traffic out of two hundred and fifty towns and villages."

"It was like the fires we used to kindle on the western prairies," she said, "a match and a wisp of dry grass were all that were needed, and behold a magnificent spectacle of a prairie of fire sweeping across the landscape, swift as a thousand untrained steeds, and no more to be captured than a hurricane."

Somewhat akin to the stones crying out was this occasion when the women rose up as one person in Puritan wrath. Women who had never appeared in any capacity but that of gracious homemakers stepped out and faced the liquor dealers in their places of business, and confronted the politicians with insistent demands for reform.

One of those who least expected to be drawn into this struggle was Sarepta M. I. Henry, who since the death of her husband had been absorbed in a private struggle of her own—to keep her children and provide for them in spite of all her well-wishing friends who thought it would be impossible, and advised dividing them up in other homes.

In September 1873 Mrs. Henry and her three children returned to Pecatonica from New York on the request of her mother, who wanted some company in the home for her youngest daughter. She felt that it was a calamity for this beautiful girl in her teens to grow up in a home with two old people, mother and grandmother, both long past the age for bringing up children. So Sarepta had gladly joined the household, bringing youth and activity with her family of three little ones.

Almost immediately after her return, the pastor of the Methodist church had visited her and asked whether she would be willing to travel and read her poem, "The Two Cups," in the interest of relieving the debt on the church. This poem was based on the biblical history of the Rechabites and Daniel, closing with Belshazzar's feast. It required three quarters of an hour to read, and was considered very fine for an evening's entertainment. By special request she had given it twice before the Good Templars of Cortland and Homer.

She agreed, and had gone on tour, with all arrangements made and expenses paid, and the proceeds to go toward the payment of the church debt. One of the places she visited in this way was the growing town of Rockford, Illinois, where she had been entertained in the home of her old friends, the Alfred Harts. While there she had visited the superintendent of the public schools, Professor Barbour, who urged her to come to Rockford to teach in the grammar department of South Rockford. It was an opportunity to be independent and make a home for her children. Her family and friends thought it would be impossible for her to teach and take care of her children, but after a few experiments in parceling out her family, she was confident that it was necessary for her happiness and theirs to be together. Against all the well-meaning advice, therefore, after a few months she brought her children from Pecatonica to be with her in Rockford.

It was a tiny little home of three small rooms, with no carpet, or curtains on the windows, but with happiness and joy within. In addition to teaching in the public schools, Mrs. Henry was working on a series of books for the Methodist Book Concern, whose editors had asked her to prepare some helpful literature for boys in the teen age. She called the series After the Truth, the four books being entitled *Finding the Truth, Teaching the Truth, Using the Truth,* and *After the Truth.*

One critic in reviewing them after publication said, "This gifted writer here felicitously blends facts of history, science, and art into a charming bit of fiction, so that one reads for delight, and rejoices for the gain he has made, and is all the while brought into contact with gospel truth and Biblical exposition in a most ingenious way."

Busy and happy in her work, Sarepta Henry was quite unconscious of the life outside her intimate circle of activities. She was a dreamer and an idealist, and above all else a lover of her children and her home.

Rockford was a city of 15 to 16,000 inhabitants, with 21 saloons operating under a system of license that had grown up under the fostering care of the leaders in some of the city's 16 churches. Probably no one in Rockford was less aware of the inroads of the liquor traffic than Mrs. Henry, who probably passed a dozen saloons every day on her way to teach, without knowing they were there. She knew absolutely nothing about the ways of the world, had never been in a saloon, or had friends who used liquor, or been in the company of people who drank.

Life might have gone on in the same even tenor for an indefinite time if it had not been for a small incident that lay at the foundation of her whole public life. She described it in her autobiography as follows:

"One day I sent my youngest son upon an errand to the house of a friend. Soon after he started I had occasion to go down to the Public Library, which was on State Street. As I came to the intersection of Court and State Streets I saw Arthur coming out of a tall brick building on the corner next to Court Street Church. I had noticed this building as one that finished the church neatly, but had never thought about what might be in it. When I saw my child coming out of it, however, my curiosity and interest were at once aroused. As soon as he saw me, he came running toward me, and I said,

" 'Why, Arthur, I thought I sent you to Aunt Georgia's. What are you doing here?'

" 'Oh yes, Mama, you did; and I am going right away. But that boy . . .' and I noticed a boy standing on the steps holding the door partly open with his hand, 'that boy—he is a very nice boy, Mama; he has talked with me over the fence lots of times. That is his papa's store, and he told me that if I would come in a minute he would treat me.'

" 'Treat you!' I said, 'what does that mean?'

" 'Oh,' he said, 'give me some candy.'

" 'Well,' I said, 'did he give you some?'

" 'Yes,' and he put his hand into his little blouse pocket and drew out a handful of dirty-looking candy, all colors of the rainbow. He held his hand open, and I began to pick out the colored dirty lumps, and to throw them on the ground. He, childlike, while still loyally holding his hand open, said:

" 'Don't throw it all away!'

" 'It is not fit to eat,' I said. 'Throw it down, and when we get home Mama will make you some nice creams.'

"But all the while I was looking at the building and wondering about it. I saw no signs of a confectionery establishment. Instead, there were bottles in the window, which I had never before seen or thought about. I had learned a great deal theoretically of the evils that were in the world and had become afraid of them for my children. Instinctively I felt that I must know everything that came into their lives. I felt that this thing across the way which dared to open its doors to my boy, and call him thither, must be investigated. So, after a moment I took Arthur's hand, and said:

" 'Come with me. We will go and see what is inside that building.'

He drew back on my hand a little and said:

" 'Oh, Mama, I don't think I would go in there if I were you. It is not a nice place. I don't think there is anything in it for ladies. It doesn't smell nice.'

" 'Well,' I said, 'since my little boy has been in there, I think I will go and see what it is like.' And so, holding his hand, I started.

"As soon as I turned toward the building the boy standing on the steps swung the door and ran inside. When I opened the door and entered I was confronted by a green Venetian screen, and by the vilest of odors. A tremor passed through my whole frame, so that I was tempted to run before I went any farther; but I was determined to see what this all meant; so I went on around the screen.

"The scene that met my eyes can never be forgotten. It was an American saloon in full blast. It is photographed on my memory— there was the long counter with the bartender in his white dress. He was just placing two glasses on the bar, one of foaming beer, as I have since learned, and the other of some colored liquor. Before the bar were two men and one boy, the boy probably not more than sixteen. There were a dozen or more half or wholly intoxicated men lounging about. One, who I learned afterward was the proprietor, was tilted back in his chair against the wall. All who were not asleep were smoking or drinking, and the air was heavy with the vilest of odors, and blue with tobacco fumes.

"As soon as I entered the room, everything stopped, unless it might be the clock. My presence had the effect upon the company of an apparition. But after a moment of embarrassed silence, the proprietor dropped his chair heavily on its feet, arose, and started to approach me. I felt that I could not have him approach a step nearer. He evidently thought I was some drunkard's mother or wife, although I had not at that time experience enough to understand this. In my alarm, holding my child by the hand I turned and fled and ran, dragging him with me until he brought me to my sense by saying, 'Mama, you hurt!'"

When soon after this Mrs. Henry read in the papers about the action that women in other parts of the country were taking against the liquor traffic in their towns, she was stirred as nothing in her life had ever stirred her. She could understand now why women were concerned about making their communities safe for their growing children, and she could almost understand how they could go into the saloons and pray, and how they could kneel on the sidewalks in the slush and make agonized appeals to the saloonkeepers.

Gradually the interest she felt in this war of the home against drink became a matter of personal responsibility to help, and grew into a burden too great to evade. Daily she felt a conflict within her, between her natural instinct for seclusion and retirement, and her growing recognition of the need for something to be done in her community. She pleaded with herself that really there was nothing she could do, because she had to earn a living for herself and her children, and this whole effort against the saloons seemed so very public.

Mrs. Henry began to look around among the women of the church for those who ought to begin the movement in Rockford. She invited a number of the leading women to her home, and tried to impress upon them the thought that Rockford needed crusade work as much as any other city. They all agreed, but were equally unanimous in refusing to take the lead in the matter, saying that if someone else would start they would help. She then went to her pastor and suggested that he do something about it, but he replied, "This is woman's work wholly. It is not for us men. When the women of the city are ready to do anything about it, they will find a friend and helper in me; but it is not for me to begin it."

Try as she would, Mrs. Henry could not escape the burden that seemed to have been placed on her. Daily it grew heavier, and she was conscious of the influence of the Spirit of God impelling her to take the leadership that everyone else so easily brushed aside. Mrs. Backus, a woman of wonderful Christian experience, faith, courage, and good judgment, in whom she had a great deal of confidence, charged her impressively in these words, "Mrs. Henry, you feel very strongly about this. It seems to be laid upon you in such a way that I believe God wants you to do this thing. Have you never thought that it was your duty to make a start in this new work for our city?"

"How can I make a start?" she asked. "What can I do? I am alone with my little children, with no money except what I can earn by my pen. I have no influence; no one knows me but a little circle of church people. What can I do?"

"That depends on whether God wants you to do anything or not," she said. "Have you never thought that you have something to do?"

This burning question kept boring into her soul until she was in a state of continual unrest that interfered with her work. Day after day she sat at her writing, trying to keep her pen going, but she would find the ink drying on it, and her thoughts afar off with the crusade women, trying to visualize the future of her children and the state of the nation if this terrible evil should not be driven from the land.

At last there came a day in which she could neither work nor sit still in her study, a night when she could hardly pray with her children when she put them to bed, and in which she could not think of sleep. She walked to and fro until she was too tired to take another step, and then threw herself upon the floor, wrestling with the question of whether she would or would not accept a challenge so foreign to her inclination, one that might change her whole future. At last it seemed to be just a simple basic question of "Will you obey?" or "Will you not?" She realized then that it was a matter of her soul's salvation. If she did not obey, she would lose her standing with God, something she could never do.

Immediately the thought came to her to write notices to all the prayer meetings for the next Wednesday evening, calling all the Christian women of the city together to consider what could be done in reference to the saloon.

"Is that all? Was it for a little thing like that I have been holding my soul's salvation in the balance, and struggling over it for days?"

She rose quickly from the floor, sat down at her desk, and wrote notices to the pastors of the 16 churches in Rockford, and planned how to have them delivered in time for the Wednesday evening prayer meetings. She also wrote to Father McKinley, the church father of the Court Street church, asking for the use of the church parlors for their meeting. Then she wrote a notice to appear in the daily paper.

After she had prepared some notes for the meeting, relief came to her mind and soul, and she was ready for rest. Dawn was beginning to break, but she went to her room and lay down on the bed, fully clothed, and slept.

Out of this very intimate personal struggle the campaign against the saloon in Rockford took a form that was to influence the whole nation. On the twenty-seventh of March, as a result of the forward step taken by Mrs. S.M.I. Henry, this group of women organized what they called the Woman's Temperance Union, with Mrs. Gilbert Woodruff, the wife of the mayor, as president, and Mrs. Henry as secretary and treasurer. All of those who had a part in the first organization of the Woman's Temperance Union were those who had been brought up in the shut-in sphere to which women had been relegated from time immemorial by the social customs of the world.

They realized from the beginning that their first step should be an intelligent investigation of the laws of the city and state relating to the sale and control of liquor, to find out the legal status of the saloon under the law, and what measures might be taken to protect the rights and privileges of the wives and mothers of the victims of this traffic. In other parts of the country the women were making open crusades through the streets and into the saloons. They questioned the advisability of this means. A description of the crusade as it was conducted in some parts is found in the writings of Frances Willard, who, although she admired the courage of the women who participated, had not joined with them until this occasion when she decided she would go with them as a sort of pragmatic experiment.

She wrote of it thus:

"We paused in front of Sheffner's saloon, on Market Street. The ladies ranged themselves along the curbstone, for they had been forbidden in anywise to incommode the passers-by, being dealt with more strictly than a drunken man or a heap of dry-goods boxes would be. At a signal from our grey-haired leader, a sweet-voiced woman began to sing, 'Jesus, the Water of Life will give,' all voices blending in the song. I think this was the most novel spectacle that I recall. There stood the women of undoubted religious devotion and the highest character, most of them crowned with the glory of grey hairs. Along the stony pavement of the stoniest of cities rumbled the heavy wagons, many of them carriers of beer; between us and the saloon in front of which we were drawn up in line, passed the motley throng, almost every man lifting his hat, and even the little newsboys doing the same. It was American manhood's tribute to Christianity and to womanhood and it was significant and full of pathos. The leader had already asked the saloon-keeper if we might enter, and he had declined, else prayer meeting would have occurred inside his door. A sorrowful old lady, whose only son had gone to ruin through that very death trap, knelt on the cold moist pavement and offered a broken-hearted prayer, while all our heads were bowed.

"At a signal we moved on, and the next saloon-keeper permitted us to enter. I had no more idea of the inward appearance of a saloon than if there had been no such place on earth. I knew nothing of its high, heavily corniced bar, its barrel furnished with a faucet, its shelves glittering with decanters and cut glass, its floors thickly strewn with sawdust, and here and there a table with chairs, nor of its abundant fumes, sickening to healthful nostrils.

"The tall stately lady who led us placed her Bible on the bar and read a psalm, whether hortatory or imprecatory, I do not remember, but the spirit of these crusaders was so gentle that I think it must

116

have been the former. Then we sang 'Rock of Ages.'. . .

"It was strange, perhaps, but I felt not the least reluctance as I knelt on the sawdust floor, with a group of earnest hearts around me, and behind them, filling every corner and extending out into the street a crowd of unwashed, unkempt, hard-looking drinking men."[1]

There were many different ideas among the women as to how the campaign in Rockford should be conducted, but it was generally agreed not to make any move in ignorance that would discredit their efforts. Although there were widespread rumors that they planned a line of march up and down State Street, visiting the saloons, praying and singing, they decided instead to meet every day for study of the municipal law and discussion of the best methods of procedure.

They were surprised and astonished at their findings. Mrs. Henry, as secretary of the organization, stood before the churchful of women and read the statutes aloud, section by section. In the course of her reading she came to this phrase, "As many saloons may be licensed as the public good requires." She stopped, thinking she did not see it right, or that it must be a misprint, and then finding it read as she had first noticed, she said:

"Here is the strangest thing I ever heard of, but I will read it, and see if you can understand it. 'As many saloons may be licensed as the public good requires.' It cannot be that this is the way they intended to have it, for how can the licensing of any saloon serve the public good? If you ladies can understand this, I can't."

A buzz of discussion filled the room. It seems that in that assemblage of the leading women of the town there was not one worldly-wise enough to explain the phrase. They unanimously agreed that they could not understand it, and appointed Mrs. Sawyer, the wife of one of the leading attorneys, to ask her husband the meaning and bring a report the next day.

"Yes, it is true," she reported. "The saloon has a legal status. Most of the men in town are for it, whether they drink or not. My

---

[1] Quoted in Anna A. Gordon, *The Beautiful Life of Frances Willard*, pp. 98, 99.

husband is one of the best men that ever lived, but he instructs us to leave it alone. He says it is a necessary evil, and that society and the government cannot get along without it. The forces behind it are too well protected, too long established, too deeply rooted, for us to do anything about it."

This news brought deep dismay and discouragement into the ranks of this earnest but unsophisticated group of women. It was necessary that they face, early in the campaign, something of the power and strength of the foe they were challenging, and of the long, hard fight they had ahead of them.

Chapter Fourteen

MASS MEETING
TONIGHT!

*M*ass meeting tonight! Mass meeting tonight!" the newsboys shrilled. "Hear the latest in the women's war on the saloon! WCTU will tell plans in big rally in Congregational church!"

The time had come, the women felt, to make the public acquainted with their purposes and plans, and they announced their intention of holding a public meeting. The press, some friendly, some hostile, gave plenty of publicity to this controversial project.

But while the carriages were pulling up to the church, and well-dressed women and their escorts were crowding the vestry, and filing into the pews, the speaker of the evening was prostrate on her bed at home. For the first time in her life Sarepta Henry was the victim of absolute terror.

That morning, when she had attempted to get up, she found that she was unable to raise her head. Ever since she had realized that the duty of presenting the message of the evening had devolved upon her, she had become increasingly appalled at the idea of standing before the great audience of men and women, and trying to speak. How had she ever allowed herself to get into such a position? She knew she could never do it. She had been wakeful most of the night, and now she was deathly sick, so that she sank back upon the pillow.

She called Mary and Alfred and told them they would have to do the best they could about getting their breakfast, that she was unable to rise. The children, alarmed, told the woman who lived in the other part of the house. She came in and was so concerned over Mrs. Henry's appearance that she insisted upon calling the physician.

When he arrived Mrs. Henry explained the situation. He said: "You are suffering from nervous shock, and you must not think of getting up today. As for going out tonight, or making any attempt to meet your engagement, that is out of the question. It would be dangerous to do it."

Chagrined and embarrassed, she sent word by Alfred to the women at the afternoon meeting telling them how she felt, and admitting frankly that it was fright and nothing else. "Make up the program from some of the ministers who will be there," she suggested. "I want every minister who does anything in that meeting to pray especially for me. I want the one who presides to tell the audience the reason why I am not there—it is because I am afraid. Perhaps that will break the spell." She promised that if they would appoint another meeting, and would pray for her she would be there.

Consequently, another meeting was appointed for the following Thursday, which would be held in the State Street Baptist Church, for the Congregational church had not been large enough to hold all the people who had come to this first public gathering.

Although Mrs. Henry had had no formal training as a public speaker, she was not without a number of valuable qualifications and some experience. Her voice, referred to in the press write-ups as possessing the "tone of a silver bell," had an unusual sweetness and carrying quality, and was trained through the hours she had spent reading aloud in her girlhood and young wifehood. Her stage presence and facial expression were pleasant, and her dark eyes large and penetrating. Most valuable of all was the knowledge of the Scriptures gained at her father's bedside, and the transforming power of that knowledge, which gave purpose to the life she demonstrated in her public service.

During the happy years she had enjoyed with her husband on

their little farm at East Homer, both before and after his war experience, she held little cottage meetings in her home for the neighbors and friends who were too far away to attend church. Here she had stood before them and spoken as easily and naturally as a mother talking to her own family.

It would seem that these experiences might have fortified her against stage fright. Her first appearance before the women whom she had called together to organize against the saloon had not occasioned her any distress in this line, and she had been so on fire with the purpose of their gathering that she had entirely forgotten herself, or the fact that she was speaking in public.

The struggle now was not the same she had fought out the evening before she made the decision to enter this work. She had accepted the challenge and set herself to the task. But this was something physical, something she did not seem to pray herself out of, something she could not cope with.

The next day after the meeting was supposed to have been held, she found herself perfectly well, without the slightest trace of the illness of the day before. She did a good day's work at her writing, and went to the daily 3:00 meeting as usual. Entirely convinced now that this was something she should and would overcome, she went ahead with her plans to speak at the Thursday evening meeting.

All went well until Thursday morning, when again she found she was prostrated with extreme nausea. Again the woman came in and saw the condition she was in and ordered the doctor. He came, as before, and said that it would be dangerous, under the circumstances, for her to get up. She must abandon the effort to meet this engagement, he said, for she certainly did not have the strength for it.

"But I must do it," she said. "This is a call from God. You are a Christian man, are you not?"

"I hope I am," he replied.

"Then I think you will understand me," she said. "I must overcome this. I must be at that meeting tonight."

"Under those circumstances," he said, "you are taken out of my hands. As a physician I would say that you must not go, but this whole thing is something that I do not pretend to understand. God is in it. He has been with the Ohio women; He has evidently been with our women here, and I must keep my hands off. But yet," he hesitated, "my judgment is that it is very unwise for you to attempt it."

"I will stay in bed all day," Sarepta said. "I will not go out this afternoon."

By afternoon she showed no improvement, and sent a note to the women that she was in the same condition to which her terror had brought her on Monday, but that they must pray for her and she would overcome it. Some of them came over to see her, and upon observing the condition of their prospective speaker, were quite dubious over the outcome of the proposed event, and inclined to think that maybe the doctor was right. But Mrs. Henry insisted that this time she would not give up.

"Mother, a closed carriage has come for you." Her children came running in to where she was still unable to rise from the bed. The women came in, dressed her, helped her out to the carriage, and supported her while they were riding to the appointment.

As they approached the church they found themselves among a dense mass of people, horses, and carriages. Mrs. Henry looked out the carriage window and saw that there were about three or four times as many people outside the church as could get in to the meeting. This sight had the tonic effect of restoring her strength. She forgot herself and her weakness. Her mind cleared, and with a prayer to God for help in putting across the message to this great crowd, she left the carriage and with the others made her way slowly through the people and into the church.

Recalling the meeting afterward, she said that once on the platform in the concentrated focus of a thousand people, she felt no embarrassment or weariness. Those who heard her reported that she spoke eloquently, as if inspired, with an absolute unconsciousness of self.

And so was launched a campaign that was to grow and expand throughout the country, effecting vast changes in the social conditions of cities and towns, influencing the lives of countless thousands of people. From this time on, Mrs. Henry found herself as either the leader or speaker of a meeting two or three evenings a week, and eventually her entire time was consumed by the demands upon her.

The first thing the women attempted, after having become conversant with the legal status of the saloon, its privileges, and the protection that the law afforded it, was to arouse public sentiment concerning the dangers of those who were frequenters of these drinking places.

Their first personal work, therefore, was for the victims of drink. They districted the city and went out, every woman among them who could possibly take part, in a house-to-house visiting, by which they attempted to secure names for the temperance pledge.

Women of wealth, who had never thought of putting their hands to their own housework, would lay off their elegant dress, and in something suitable to the occasion go down into the homes of the poor, wash the faces of the children, dress them in the clothing they had helped to make, show the discouraged wife of some bad husband how to make the home comfortable and attractive in the hope that he might be won to stay in it; show her how to prepare food and place it on the table neatly, and in every way possible to embody her best ideals in the limited material with which she had to work. These women of culture and refinement were trying to follow in the footsteps of Christ.

Chapter Fifteen

A CHALLENGE
TO INVENTORS

O n a drizzly afternoon in April 1874 Jonathon
B. Sawyer, gray-haired attorney at the bar in
Rockford, Illinois, leaned back in his swivel chair, elevated his feet to
the new rolltop desk, filled his pipe with tobacco, and then unfolded
his copy of the Chicago *Evening Post*. Puffing contentedly, he glanced
briefly at the headlines: "Woman Suffrage Defeated in Ohio
Constitutional Convention," "Effort to Reduce President's Salary,"
"Honors to Dr. Livingstone's Remains in London."

Turning to the editorial page, he read Oliver Willard's commen-
tary on the new Civil Service Commission appointed by President
Grant. Willard denounced the opposition of the politicians to this
hard-won forward step, calculated to trim down the number of office seekers clamoring their demands on the president. Sawyer's eyes
glanced briefly over a number of items on the opposite page, finally
halting at some figures in the temperance column. Since Greeley in
the New York *Tribune* had established a special column for temperance news, many other newspapers had followed suit, reporting the
developments in the war of the women against whisky, and keeping
their readers informed concerning the "progress of the war" or "this
praying infection," according to the editorial viewpoint.

Sawyer was not so much interested in Willard's soft-soaping defense of what he thought was a ridiculous crusade, but one of the statements struck him with the surprise of a cold draft of wind. "In March there has been a falling off of internal revenue in Ohio and Indiana to the extent of $350,000." Reading further that 3,000 saloons had been closed, and that Congress was now receptive to a bill asking for official investigation of the liquor traffic, he frowned, reread the column, not omitting anything this time.

Sawyer, of course, was familiar with the women's crusade. He knew of its phenomenal growth since the previous December, when a group of women in one of the churches in Hillsboro, Ohio, had organized themselves into a band, and had marched out of the church in a column of twos, singing "Give the Wind Thy Fears," right down to John's saloon. Since then the movement had spread rapidly from street to street, from town to town, and from state to state, until finally attention was given to it by the press, and discussion of it was in every mouth.

Sawyer's attitude had been one of detached tolerance, even when the women of Rockford had united to contribute their share in the nationwide effort. His wife was an enthusiastic member of the group. Naturally, he hadn't expected anything else. She was a respectable, religious woman; she was the wife of one of the leading citizens; her friends were the most important people in town. They were all in it; she couldn't do otherwise. He hadn't tried to oppose her. He was even a member of the council that had received the delegation of women bringing their petition that no more licenses should be granted, and that the saloons should be closed.

It had been a notable occasion, an outstanding example of manly chivalry and tolerance. The council chamber had been packed. People thronged through the halls and looked out from neighboring office windows. A dense crowd waited on the sidewalk, and others kept coming up the stairway into the hall. All the gentlemen rose as a messenger escorted the women bearing the petition into the presence of the council. Every honor and courtesy possible was shown to them. Many of them were wives of the councilmen.

Sawyer remembered that the speeches made by the women in

presenting the petition had been very forceful and eloquent. One was by a clear-eyed young matron, Mrs. Henry, one of the teachers in the public school. Mayor Woodruff, whose wife was president of the group, presided. He received the petitions, said a few appropriate words in the most correct manner, and appointed committees to give the matter its careful study and attention.

Of course, nothing ever came of it. The touching and eloquent speeches were rehearsed in the papers, and frank admiration was expressed for the beautiful courage of the organization. But everyone knew that this was an impractical way of dealing with the tricky questions of revenue, of supply and demand. Women couldn't be expected to understand such things. The petition had been treated with great respect and laid on the table.

Jonathon Sawyer considered the item in the *Post*. Maybe this thing could go too far. "A falling off of $350,000 in internal revenue in Ohio and Indiana alone." If that were to continue, there might be repercussions in the political and economic structure of the whole country. Opening a drawer, he withdrew a clipping from an envelope. It was from the New York *Tribune* that had been sent to him in March by a friend in the East.

"The day when the liquor dealers laughed at the women's movement has passed. Whatever the secret of its success, and however ridiculous it has appeared, it now seems very formidable to all who depend for income on the manufacture or sale of whiskey and beer. Hundreds of liquor stores have been temporarily and permanently closed.

"It cannot be without political effect. It is not uncommon to hear the remark that 'this thing will break up the Republican party if it goes on much longer.' In the municipal elections this spring, a temperance question will be the main issue in nearly every town where the women's movement has been tried or talked about."

At some time during the day nearly everyone in Rockford passed by the window of the lawyer's office, which was on the ground floor of a frame building on the north side of State Street. To the left about a block away Sawyer could see the unimposing but substantial Methodist church, rubbing shoulders with the sturdy two-story brick building that was Mike's saloon. Between the hours of two and four crowds of women were upon the street going to and from the meetings they held daily. In fact, business had been more or less upset by all this agitation.

The lawyer had no difficulty in spotting Mrs. Henry as she came down the street with a group of other women. Her leadership of the Rockford women and her frequent public addresses during the previous six months had made her a familiar figure.

Mr. Sawyer stepped to the door of his office, bowed courteously, and accosted her, "Mrs. Henry, I would like to have a talk with you for a few minutes. Will you please come in?"

"Certainly, Mr. Sawyer." The half-surprised glimmer in her penetrating deep eyes dissolved almost immediately into the cordial, eager expression that was habitual to them.

The man stood uncertainly for a few moments after seating her, as if in doubt how to begin. Then he said, "I have been wanting to speak to you for some time about this unusual state of affairs that exists in the city. This intense agitation is upsetting all our social conditions and disturbing the peace. Some of us men have been talking about this matter, and we think it is time it was stopped. We cannot tolerate it any longer!" He paused, then repeated emphatically, "It must stop!"

"Well, that is just what we women think," she replied seriously. "We think it ought to stop, but how can it so long as things are the way they are, and with the dangers which threaten our children from these open saloons? What can you expect? If you men will devise some way by which the saloons can be closed up, the agitation can stop very soon."

"That is just what I want to talk to you about. You simply don't understand. If you did, you would not insist so strenuously upon this question of throwing up the licenses. We must license the saloon! That is the only way to keep it under control at all. If we do not license it, it will run just the same, and we shall have free whisky that anybody can sell anywhere. We shall have no end of trouble with illicit dealers." He then gave a summary of the factors involved in suddenly changing the order of the economic structure by dropping out the revenues from the liquor wholesalers and retailers, and by pushing to the wall businessmen of long standing.

"You see," he concluded, "it is not as simple as you think. It is impossible to close the saloon. Now, I have gone into this matter and explained it to you so you can tell the other women. You can put it before them in your next meeting, so they will understand it, and when they do they will certainly desist, and we shall have quiet again in our city."

"I wish we might stop," Mrs. Henry spoke in calm, low tones; "we all do. In fact, we're pretty tired of this thing, and would much prefer to go back to our homes and stay there. We will do it quickly if you men will do just one thing."

"You mean close the saloons?" he asked angrily.

"No," she shook her head sadly. "No, I don't. Not this time. We have found out that you won't do that. I for one have no more heart to ask you."

"Well, then, what do you want?" His angry expression began to soften. "We will do anything in reason."

"Just this: invent some way to run the saloon business by machinery. You can get machinery to do anything else, it seems. Get an automaton and put it behind the saloon bar; organize a long procession of automata to file along the streets and in at the saloon doors—we women will give them the pavement and walk in the gutters—have them throw down the nickels and dimes, while the automaton behind the bar slings the glasses so that this little exchange of coin and whisky that is so necessary to the life of the nation may go on and hurt nobody." Gradually her words accumulated more force until Sawyer listened as he would to the raving of an insane woman. He turned away contemptuously, as if to bring the interview to a close.

"No, you must listen to me," Mrs. Henry insisted. "You called me in and threw down the challenge—now I must speak. Do you expect the mothers to sit quietly at home, teaching their boys the principles of purity and truth, while the saloon on every corner is waiting to catch them and grind them up for the sake of revenue? Do you expect them to stay behind closed doors and sing and pray and close their eyes to what awaits them outside the home? We've done too much of that in the past. No, sir, I tell you, the mothers of this country are awake at last, and I assure you they will never go back into the old quiet life so long as a saloon and a law protecting it exist in this nation."

Mrs. Henry delivered this speech with the vehemence of an orator, pouring out the words as only an indignant woman can, and rising to her feet as if to give more room in her small body for the growing spirit within. Her eyes lashed at him in righteous indignation.

Impatiently waiting an opportunity to conclude the painful scene, his face flushed with anger, Mr. Sawyer attempted to restrain his sarcasm.

"Mrs. Henry, understand this. We men who are interested in the public welfare, and understand public conditions and have had the responsibility of regulating these affairs—if we have done the best we could in reference to this saloon business, and if we feel that we are following the most satisfactory plan, just what can you women do about it? You might as well give up right now."

Mrs. Henry closed her lips on the rebuttal she was prepared to make as the full significance of his words struck her. Maybe he was right! These men were more experienced, better educated, more powerful than the women. Maybe they had honestly tried and that the present municipal laws were the best method of handling this situation so potent for evil.

Completely silenced, she sank back into the chair. Sawyer glanced at her in a sort of patronizing pity mingled with masculine pride, and turning to his desk, picked up some of his papers and ostensibly attempted to resume his work. Privately he was hoping the dear woman would not break into tears, but would be sensible now and go home.

Conscious of a crisis in her own relation to the future of the work that had begun so earnestly and prayerfully, Mrs. Henry sat brooding over the question, her mind reaching out desperately for an answer. Suddenly it came. It was so simple and natural she was amazed. With renewed energy she rose to her feet once more.

"I will answer your question, Mr. Sawyer. There *is* something we can do about it. And we'll do it too. The majority of the temperance women are mothers. A great many are teachers. We will begin a program of education, training, and development. We will take the children in the cradles, in the schools, and in the slums, before the saloon has a chance to instill its depraving habits, and show them the effects of alcohol on the body, brain, and soul. We will show them how whisky can wreck the home, put a man out of business, cause murder and death. It will take time. But give us 35 years, and we will present to this nation a majority on the right side of this question who will snow under the liquor traffic with a pure man's ballot."

Convinced of the possibility, certain of the future, she could now smile at him without rancor. For a moment Sawyer had nothing to answer, but no woman had ever had the last word with him.

"An excellent idea!" he said, "I would advise you to do it. It will keep you out of mischief."

"I will," she retorted. "I will go out and begin now."

She departed and went immediately to the office of the man who had the renting of Brown's Hall.

"Will you let me have the audience room for next Saturday afternoon?" she asked. "I want it for a children's meeting."

"Certainly," he said.

This was the first step toward the organization of what has since developed into the Loyal Temperance Legion of the Woman's Christian Temperance Union. Mrs. Henry organized an army of children into three full companies of 100 each, between the ages of 8 and 16, which she called the Cold Water Army. An old drill master from the army was engaged to teach the boys military tactics.

Wooden guns were contributed to their equipment by a manufacturer who had three boys in the "army." On the barrels of the guns was printed "Our guns are ballots. Our bullets are ideas." They were uniformed in white summer waists and caps. Company A wore red belts and red bands on their caps; Company B wore white belts and white bands; Company C, blue.

In addition to open-air drills conducted every day, lessons for both boys and girls were presented every week. The girls were organized into bands too and given a place in the exercises. Since at that time there was no material of any kind available to use for instruction in temperance, Mrs. Henry spent much of her leisure time preparing lessons, using the Bible as a textbook.

After weeks of training, the Cold Water Army paraded for its first public ceremony to swear in the troops on the square of the courthouse green of Rockford. Thousands of people came from all over the country to witness the administration of the Triple Pledge:

"I do solemnly promise that I will forever abstain from the use of all alcoholic beverages, including wine, beer and cider, and from all profane and impure expressions, and from tobacco in all its forms, God being my helper."

Chapter Sixteen

WHOSE
BUSINESS
IS IT?

T he "Whirlwind of the Lord," which zigzagged across the country and tossed into the air the rubble of social and political evils, gradually spent its fury, but left in its wake a tremendous work to be done in cleaning up the debris. It left, moreover, the women depressed and bewildered at the contempt and opposition they had aroused in the saloonkeepers and distillers, and the indifference of the lawmakers and politicians. The overwhelming evils of the world upon which they had just opened their eyes filled the women with dismay and discouragement. The need for leadership and concerted action was great. In August 1874 at the Chautauqua Assembly, a handful of women organized the National Woman's Christian Temperance Union, with Mrs. Jennie F. Willing, as president, and Mrs. Emily Miller, as secretary. Plans were made for a national convention in November.

Just at this time Miss Frances Willard had resigned her position as dean of the women's branch of Northwestern University at Evanston, for the sake of a principle of government that she could not conscientiously yield. Deeply interested in the work that had been begun by the temperance women, she accepted the presidency of the Chicago union in October, and at the Cleveland convention in November was elected corresponding secretary of the National organization. Immediately upon her return from the convention she wrote to Mrs. Henry requesting her to come to Chicago for a month at least, to assist in organizing the work upon the practical gospel lines that had been tried out in Rockford.

This was the beginning of a close friendship between the two women. Miss Willard affectionately called Mrs. Henry "Smi," being the first to cope with the problem of the unusually long name, Sarepta Myrenda Irish Henry. Miss Willard had strong qualities of leadership and a background that prepared her to take the helm and steer the new organization through rough political waters. She had, however, little idea of the difficulty of the job the women had committed themselves to perform.

"When we began the delicate, difficult, and dangerous operation of dissecting out the alcohol nerve from the body politic," she said, "we did not realize the intricacy of the undertaking, nor the distances that must be traveled by the scalpel of investigation."

She recognized the unusual talent and power that Mrs. Henry possessed in the field of evangelism and helped open up a wider field of usefulness for this phase of the work, that the union might receive the fullest possible benefit from her abilities.

Mrs. Henry described her work as having two objectives—formation and reformation. *Formation* was the term she used to comprehend the idea of education of the youth, a work of prevention, and of organization in a positive way. They agreed that the work for youth seemed by far to have the most promise for the future. Miss Willard had said, upon the occasion of her reviewing the troops of the Cold Water Army in Rockford: "I tell you, Smi, this is the right place to begin. Nothing is so discouraging as a hopeless man, and nobody that I know about comes as near being that man as a drunkard. We must grow a crop of hopefuls—that means men chock full of hope, and this is the way to commence."

The work of organizing the children began at once in nearly every state in the Union, and went forward with the energy of a forlorn hope, for the more they tried to evangelize the masses, the more they saw the desperate need of preventing the formation of such a vicious, sensuous appetite as that for strong drink. Miss Willard aptly phrased it: "The stronghold of the rum power lies in the fact that it has upon its side two deeply rooted appetites, namely: in the dealer, the appetite for gain, and in the drinker, the appetite for stimulants."

In the interest of the Cold Water Army, Mrs. Henry traveled widely, as the organization of the youth became a recognized department of the WCTU. Miss Julia Coleman, of New York, was appointed to prepare a textbook on alcohol to accompany the new Bible temperance lessons of Mrs. Henry. Anna Gordon and Mrs. Rice came forward with enthusiastic interest in this type of work, and helped to select and combine the best from all former organizations into the Loyal Temperance Legion, until they became satisfied that they had the most complete system for training the young idea that could be developed.

As the others took hold of the training of the youth, Mrs. Henry's public work turned more and more to the reaching out for, and the assisting of, the habitual drinker. To her there was no more glorious challenge than to present the gospel in some skid-row meetinghouse, and follow it up with personal work, agonizing and praying with the men as they struggled to break the shackles of evil habit; and weeping when they failed, or were once again drawn into the snares of the enemy. Somehow these men and women felt the sincerity of her interest in them as individuals and opened their hearts to her as to no other person. Out of this wealth of human experience she wrote the volume *The Pledge and the Cross*, an account of people reached and won during the beginnings of the work in Rockford.

In many ways this work was comparable to the program advanced by the Alcoholics Anonymous today. It was a personal work with individuals; it made use of the reformed man in the saving of others; it recognized the social and psychological factors back of the habit; its success depended on the victim's recognizing his helplessness and need of dependence on a higher power. Their work differed, however, from the Alcoholics Anonymous in its public phases. That was a different age, an age when people were not ashamed of their emotions, when feeling played a large part in evangelism. It was an age of great evangelists who swept great audiences along to conversion with the surge of their oratory. Dwight L. Moody was at the height of his eminence in Chicago. Spurgeon was drawing great crowds to his tabernacle in Essex, England. It was a time of great religious awakening, as foretold in Bible prophecy.

The work that was done by the women of Rockford, as by other groups in other places during those early days of the temperance movement, was aggressive, militant, persevering. No one needed to gather them together every so often for a pep talk on home missionary work. Seeing the prostrate figures lying in the gutters beside the curbs, in the filth and litter of the streets, was enough.

There seemed to be a greater awareness of the evils of drunkenness at that time than is evident today. Now there is a smug complacency by too many people who feel that this present generation has learned better how to handle its liquor. You don't see drunkards lying in the gutters anymore, do you, or staggering home along the sidewalks? Of course not; the reason is that today people rarely walk home from the taverns and drinking parlors. They get in their cars and drive home. Instead of being on the streets, they are in their cars, and you will meet them on the road! It is so much more respectable.

One of the remarkable things that comes to light in the study of that period is the welcome that was given by the alcoholics themselves to the work these women were doing. The women opened up rooms in the middle of town, where they conducted meetings, and were patently scouting for pledge signers. The men came in seeking for the help so offered. Some notorious characters who operated disreputable places shook in their boots, expecting callers; but if the women failed to visit them, they seemed to feel slighted!

These women gave of their time freely and willingly to gather in and save these wrecks of the liquor business. Once the victim had signified any willingness to overcome the habit, they did all they could to help. They knew the struggle and agony ahead in the battle with thirst. They used everything they had to help: psychology, prayers, encouragement, money, and medicine. They went out to the homes and helped the families with food and fuel. They followed up cases until they were sure the pledge signers were on solid ground. They distributed bouquets to new signers, visited them frequently, and assisted them in finding new employment.

Great impetus was given the work by the reformed men themselves. Having been rescued from slavery and reinstated in the ranks of free men, they banded together to help their friends and relatives. Reform clubs sprang up everywhere, and the movement snowballed across the country with great rapidity. They were glad to swing their influence and assets, whether of name or position or money, into the service of the cause. There was nothing anonymous about their testimony! And their witness was convincing.

One of the secrets of Mrs. Henry's success was the charm of her very feminine personality. In the early days of her public work her slim figure, black hair, soulful eyes, and deeply spiritual expression seemed the embodiment of the ideal of young womanhood to the unfortunate men and women who sought her aid. As the years passed, her figure rounded into more matronly lines, and her hair became tinged with gray, giving an overall impression of that of a good mother with a "Can I help you?" look beaming from her eyes. She drew people to her by the irrepressible concern for their happiness and well-being.

Although in answer to the call of God she was to go far and wide in public work, she never thought of herself as a preacher, doing a man's work. She had a firm conviction that the home is woman's sphere, and she was in definite disagreement with those who wanted to see women equal with men in politics or in the ministry. To some this attitude might seem inconsistent in view of the heavy public program she carried on, and some of these were ready to point this out to her. How did she come to preach the gospel and at the same time teach that the place of woman was in the home? they asked. Her answer to this was:

"For the same reason that God had to do some things. He had to profane the princes of the sanctuary, give Jacob the curse, and Israel to reproach, because our first father sinned, and our teachers transgressed against the Lord; because nothing was any more as it had been in the beginning. Because an emergency like that of a railroad smash-up was upon us as a race, and everyone who could get hold of a light must carry it out into the darkness, and take a hand in the work of rescue, regardless of age, sex or condition."[1]

There were those who thought it was unwomanly to campaign against the saloon, to go into the places of vice and crime, to associate with reformed men, to become a target for the hostile press. Some of the women said, "Stay at home and make home pleasant, and all will be well." Of them she said:

"Didn't they stay at home until the tide of sin set in so far as to bear them off their feet? What was the use to stay home any more, and make home pleasant and cheery, and spread the evening meal, and light the evening lamp, when the husband and son, for whom all this was done, were down in the saloon? The day came when a woman's housework took her out into the drinking holes of the city, and sent her even to the platform."[2]

Some women argued that there was no necessity for them to get involved in the dispute as long as they could keep the invader out of their own homes. This was akin to an isolationist attitude.

"Why should we be concerned about this matter?" they said. "It is really nothing to us, for our home is in no sense exposed to the influence of this evil. We will let it alone, and it must let us alone."

Mrs. Henry's reply was characteristic:

"To any such let me say that you cannot enclose your homes so securely, you cannot build your walls so high, or plant your foundations so deep, or sweep the circumference of your power so wide that, with existing institutions as they are in our land at this day, this evil of drink will not find a way over, and under, and through to your hearthstone until it has made itself felt in every fiber of your being, except you actively, positively and in God's name bend all your powers to its overthrow. . . .

---

[1] Mrs. S.M.I. Henry, *A Woman's Ministry*, p. 38.
[2] Henry, *The Pledge and the Cross*, p. 11.

"It has branded the brow of the boy in his crib who was supposed to be so securely sheltered that no evil could so much as breathe upon him; it has lain in wait to catch the lad just from Sunday-school with the sacred songs and golden texts fresh upon his lips, and has corrupted his soul before he could reach his mother's side; it has stolen in under the porch of the temple of God, and has hung its hook and chain upon the very horns of the altar, as it has waited for the son set apart and dedicated to the holy office, and has dragged him from the sacred place, tramping his vestments in the mire, leaving behind him an offense like that of carrion upon a king's table; and it has proved that there is no man or woman who can look up and say, 'All this is nothing to me or mine.'

"I know a woman who made us feel her scorn as we went out and in before her in the ways of this work—a woman who, sitting in her elegant home, with her two sons about her, dared to speak lightly and contemptuously of 'reformed men'; who said it was an 'unlady-like thing' to be interfering in the saloon business so much, going into these places with tracts and such things; that the saloon was no place for a woman. The time came to that mother when her sons staggered into her presence or were borne as they bear the dead; when she trailed the silk of her skirts through saloon filth at late hours of the night, searching for her boys in the haunts of vice; the time came when she would have given all she had in the world could her sons have been honestly called 'reformed men'; and now, if those sons ever bring any comfort to her heart or home, or ever enter the home of the pure above, they must begin by being 'reformed men.'

"And there are thousands of women of whom all this is true today. They sit where we all sat awhile ago, unconscious or unbelieving concerning the great danger which threatened us all; and to such we send out the cry: 'Awake, for death is near; it is looking in at your window, it is creeping into your palaces, it is cutting down your children from without, and your young men from your streets!'

"Awake, and with us strike for God and Home and Native Land!"[3]

---

[3] *Ibid.*, p. 191.

Chapter Seventeen

JACK'S HARD LUMP

No better picture of the work that was done by the women of Rockford in those early days can be found than is given in Mrs. Henry's simple stories behind the names on their "pledge roll." Two of these from the book *The Pledge and the Cross* are chosen to reveal something of the devotion of the women, and the struggle on the part of the men to overcome the narcotic influence of alcohol, "Jack's Hard Lump," and "Christmas Eve With the O'Connells."

Jack's Hard Lump

The first New Year's after we had opened the Temperance Rooms our ladies decided to serve refreshments and receive their friends in the rooms instead of their houses, giving a general invitation to all gentlemen interested in our work to manifest the fact by calling on us.

Many women closed their elegant homes and joined the company in our halls. A substantial collation, with coffee and tea in abundance, was served, and a continuous procession of gentlemen in broadcloth and kids, and in the plainer dress of workingmen, farmers, and professional men thronged our rooms and were received at the door by our president, and from thence escorted to my table, where were the register and pledge roll, and then taken in charge by the committee on refreshments.

A little while after noon there came in together a company of young men, bringing in a strong odor of the saloon. They were "under the influence" to a considerable degree, and altogether unkempt in appearance.

Some of the well-dressed gentlemen looked annoyed, as though this were an intrusion, but our ladies were glad these men came in, and took special pains to make them feel welcome. Mrs. Woodruff, our president, gave them her hand as cordially as though theirs had been covered with gloves of delicate hue. None who sat at our tables was more carefully served, and by none the well-prepared food more highly appreciated than by some of these men. They were hungry and had obviously been drawn to the rooms by the free lunch available to all.

One of these men, whom I will call Sam Stevens, somehow kept thinking of his wife and three little children in the miserable place he called home. He knew well enough that while he sat drinking his coffee and eating the food provided they were shivering and hungry on this New Year's Day.

The reason for this he knew was the bottle tucked away in his ragged coat, bought with the money that should have gone for fuel and bread.

He looked about and saw the reform boys merrily assisting in the work of entertaining or serving, or mingling among the guests—men with whom he had often drunk who had gone just as ragged as he, but were now well clothed and appeared as well as any gentleman in the room. He thought, *This temperance is a pretty good thing. I think I'd better join and see what it will do for me.*

When he had finished eating, he came over to my table and said, "Now I want the pledge, ma'am."

I handed him the roll, got out the pocket cards, and wrote my name in the proper places, while I kept thinking, *How he will need help, poor fellow. Lord, help him!*

He was an intelligent-looking man, and wrote a fair hand even while drunk. There was an air of shrewdness and quickness about him that interested me greatly. He took the pledge with an evident appreciation of its import that was an assurance of his purpose to do the best he could in the new effort, and soon joined the procession moving outward.

I made it a point to call upon this man's family early in the week, as my experience with others had made me determined to allow but little time before looking up these cases. I found them in a condition of wretched want, aggravated by the fact that Mr. Stevens had been taken sick with strong symptoms of delirium tremens. Everything was crowded into one little room scarcely large enough for any one of the many purposes it served, and the tokens of suffering were everywhere. Three little children in the thinnest of garments, the bare skin blue with hunger and cold, scarcely covered by their rags, were huddled upon the bed where the sick man lay, while the wife sat in the attitude of one who had nothing to do and less to hope for.

Relief was furnished by our women at once in the form of food, fuel, and clothing; a physician was summoned for the sick man, and every attention shown that the comfort of the family required.

I visited them daily, and sitting beside the sickbed read portions of the Bible, and talked with Stevens about the sinner's Friend. He was constantly distressed about the condition of his family and the fact that he had so neglected them, and I often told him that now he must put his case in the Lord's hands, do the best he could and trust the results with Him, and better days would come.

When I talked thus his expression was that of the most intense interest. One day as he was getting better, he spoke of the pledge card I had given him.

"I have kept thinking of your name on it," he said. "I could see it as I lay here with my eyes shut, and I knew it was the name of a friend."

"I have a better name than that to give you," I replied, "the name of the Lord Jesus. You may trust in His name."

He interrupted me quickly, exclaiming, "Now, Mrs. Henry, what can you mean by that? You've said it before. I often thought to ask you, but didn't like to make so bold. But I didn't know there was any good in that name, only to use in swearin'."

At first I thought I could not have heard him correctly, or that he was trifling with me. I had never dreamed of really encountering ignorance like this, especially in our city of nearly a score of churches; but as I looked into the solemn eyes of the sick man as he gazed into mine with his head partly lifted by his hand, I knew that he was in earnest, and I began to question him, and in his replies gathered a brief outline of his life.

He was Scotch by birth, his home being in Liverpool, until, when about 10 years of age, he ran away from home and shipped before the mast on a merchant ship, and had followed the sea all his life until three or four years prior to this time. He had become so addicted to drink that he was unfit for duty, and he was put ashore at New York, while his vessel sailed away leaving him a stranded wreck of his former self.

He had a wife and two children in Liverpool. She had many excellent qualities, among which was a strong and loyal attachment to her husband, worthless as he seemed. She followed him to America with the youngest child, not being able to pay the passage of the other, whom she left with her mother.

They made their way west as far as Chicago, where he found employment for a time at the stockyards; but soon he drifted on, sailorlike, and found himself in our city.

How they lived he never knew. His patient wife always managed somehow to keep the little family together, while he drifted here and there spending all his earnings for drink. He knew no associations but those the saloon afforded; never had a thought of any other way of life. Not a sound of gospel truth had ever fallen upon his ear until he was led to the Temperance Rooms, and later to these earnest talks by his bedside.

As I gathered these facts how my heart was stirred! I thought, *How is it possible with an active Christianity in our midst that a family should have lived right in the center of it all for three years and not know the sinner's only hope? How many other such are there among us?*

At length I asked, "How then did you come to think of being

sober—better—or signing the pledge?"

"Do you mind the tract you gave me in Joe's saloon a few weeks ago?" he asked.

"I don't think I do, really," I said. "I have given a great many tracts to men in saloons, and I can't just remember the occasion."

"Well," he replied with a keen interest almost amounting to enthusiasm, "it was a famous tract. It was called 'Jack's Hard Lump.' Jack was a sailor like myself, and I thought you knowed and gave it to me a-purpose."

"I did give it 'a-purpose,'" I replied, "and I remember the tract very well, but did not know you at the time."

"Well, it just hit my case, anyhow. You see, Jack, and it might ha' said Sam just as well, had been a poor drunken sailor just like me, all knocked up, and could never save nothin'. He went on a long voyage and kept sober, gave the grog the go-by, and when he came into port he had a good sum of money in a little bag in his jacket. He was going up the street, past the Sign of the Lion, when the keeper of the inn called him to come in. Jack said, "No, I thank you."

"'Why not' said the innkeeper. 'Come and get a drop. I'll treat ye myself.'

"'No,' said Jack putting his hand on his side over his wallet, 'I've got a hard lump on my side, and I can't drink; thank ye all the same.'

"'A hard lump!' said the innkeeper. 'Of course you'll be havin' all kinds of hard lumps if you stop drinking a little ale for your health. You'll be havin' one on the other side 'fore long.'

"'Yes,' said Jack, 'that's just what I expect.' And pulling out his wallet, he held it toward the innkeeper and cried out:

"'This is the hard lump, and you never said a truer: if I don't drink I'll be havin' one on t'other side before long. Good day, sir.' And the laugh was turned on the keeper of the 'Lion,' you see.

"Well, that set me to thinkin', and I brought it home and read it to Mary Jane here, and she said she wished I'd try it, and I thought I would, but somehow I kept putting it off. I hated to part company with my bottle, we'd jogged along together so long, and I kept putting off the beginning. But that night before the New Year I found the devil walking by the side of me.

"It's true," he said with emphasis, as he noticed my surprise, "just as true as you sit there, and I saw him just as plain as I see you, right at my elbow. He came in and went out with me, and walked along the street and over the bridge, and I could not drop him nowhere. I tell you it was pokerish.

"I was afraid to go to bed that night, and in the morning I was sick enough. I felt better after I had an eye-opener and got my bottle filled, and then the fellows said, 'We'll go up to the Temperance Rooms, and see whether they'll give us anything to eat.' So we went up. It was pretty nice to be treated like somebody as we was, and so I signed the pledge. I had my bottle of whisky in my pocket, and when I came down and got half way over the bridge, comin' home, I took her out and dropped her into the river; and the next minute I'd ha' given anything to have her back again. But I came home, and I've been plagued with the devil ever since, I tell you. But he's kinder lettin' up on me now, and when you've sat here and talked about that Jesus bein' a Lord and able to help me, I've wished I knowed Him, and that I hadn't used His name so rough."

As Mr. Stevens ceased his narration I began at the beginning and told him the story of Jesus and salvation, just as I would tell it to a child. He listened with open-eyed wonder, drank in the truth as a parched field drinks in the rain, accepted it as fast as he could hear it, and began to believe in Jesus as his own personal friend.

He was some time in recovering from his sickness so as to be able to do much work, but when he was able he began to manifest unusual ability to adapt himself to any work, being not only a Jack-of-all-trades, but able to do readily and well almost anything from mending and making over of clothes for his children to laying a brick wall, running a derrick, or doing landscape gardening. While he was still unable to do hard work he sat at home busy with his needle, fixing over garments that were provided for his little boys, who had gone almost naked. He soon had them comfortably dressed for taking out with him, and used to bring them to the rooms and the gospel meetings.

The deep, still gladness that grew upon the face of Mrs. Stevens was touching to see, and the patience with which she toiled and endured hardship, counting it all joy since her husband was sober. When asked what she needed, she would reply, "Nothin' more, ma'am; I have all I want now. My man is drunk no more."

And by this spirit she seemed lifted above poverty and want such as seemed for a time almost beyond need of relief from resources. Mr. Stevens joined the club and became an earnest and efficient member. He grew into an intelligent understanding of his relation to Christ and the gospel, and with his wife, who was converted, united with the church, and although many efforts were made to drag him back to the old life by those who made gain off his quick wit, he went steadily forward in an even, upright course.

Many were the battles he had to fight with the strong appetite for drink that was woven into every fiber of his being; but by the grace of God he went from victory to victory, until his strength became a matter of assurance to him as well as his many friends.

He had obtained the situation of gardener for one of the members of our union, and was rapidly squaring his account with the world, as well as making his family comfortable. He was a man of wonderful energy, and carried enthusiasm into all his work; and he had a desire to do to the utmost ability for the cause by whose influence he had been rescued and lifted up to manhood.

One day, more than a year after his reformation, Mr. Stevens came to me with a plan of work in saloons that he had dreamed out and had made up his mind to undertake, first intending to lay the matter before me and ask my counsel. I told him it would not do.

"You must keep out of saloons," I said, "or you will be likely to fall; and all work that will take you into danger had better be left undone."

"But," he insisted, "this is God's work, and He will keep me. And besides, the appetite for drink is all taken out of me. I don't want it, and you need not be afraid on that score."

"You will find that the appetite for drink is there, sir," I replied, "and while I know God will keep you while you are in the way of His commandments, yet if you go off onto the ground of the enemy you will put yourself outside His grace; and you take your salvation into your own hands."

"But I feel it my duty to go," he replied.

"Then your feelings mislead you."

"Then how shall I know my duty?"

"By the exercise of judgment, together with the Word and Spirit of God."

"I am trying to do that."

"Then add to that the best judgment of those who can look all around this question, and who cared for your soul long before you did."

He seemed for a time almost persuaded because of my pleading to give up the scheme; but not convinced that danger was in the way he had marked out, at last he said with considerable reluctance, "Mrs. Henry, I must do it. I am sorry to go contrary to your advice, but I must this time; and I promise if I find there is danger I will get right out; but I must try it."

I saw that it was useless to try to change his purpose, so I said, "Well, if you will go, promise that you will report to me as early as eight o'clock this evening."

"Certainly I will promise that," he said, and soon after took his leave. With a heart too heavy for even prayer, I waited. I knew that the chances were very great that he would report drunk.

The day passed slowly, and as it drew toward evening my anxiety became such that I could do no more work, and every faculty seemingly was strained to the utmost. I went home, and prayed and waited.

One portion of my house was occupied by a young man and his mother. The old lady was in her own room, my children in theirs, and John had gone down the street, so I was alone in the sitting room when I heard an unsteady step on the walk. It came on toward the house, then up on the porch to my door. I did not wait for a signal, but sprang and opened the door, and saw, just what I feared, Mr. Stevens staggering toward the entrance; and although the great fear of this very thing had been with me for hours, I was not prepared for it when it came, and was unwilling to believe the evidence of my eyes. As he came toward me I exclaimed, "Sam, don't stagger so; don't try to make me believe you are drunk."

"But I am drunk, Mrs. Henry," he said, coming into the room; and the thick guttural of his tone, and his whole appearance as he stood in the light, left no ground for hope. I gave him a chair, and wished John would come home. John's mother came to the door, and looked in, but was too terrified to remain.

Mr. Stevens took from his pocket a flask partly filled with whisky, and handing it to me, bade me take care of it; and he kept talking incoherently of the events of the day until he had, as he supposed "made his report," and then he rose and said, "I must go back now" and came toward the door near which I had seated myself.

"Wait for John," I said, "he will be in soon."

"No, I must go back now."

"Go back where?" I asked, while a cold terror at the thought crept over me.

"Where?" he repeated.

"Yes, where?"

"Well, I guess I won't tell," he replied, hesitatingly.

I felt that if he left the house alone and got out into the street again, with the saloons all along the street, and some of the police only too glad to lock up a member of the Reform Club, all would be lost, as far as he was concerned. So as he was approaching the door, and I feared he would go out, I turned the key in the lock and put it in my pocket.

He stopped and stepped back a little, and sternly demanded:

"What did you do that for?"

"So you would not go out," I replied.

"You had better unlock that door and let me out," he said, taking a rapid step toward me. I was somewhat frightened, but I did not dare to let him think I was afraid.

"No, sir, I shall not," I replied, standing with my back against the door. "I have spent too many prayers and too much effort; our union has helped your family up out of want and you out of the ditch; we have all done too much to make it possible for me to let

147

you out now. There is too much at stake. Wait till John comes, and he may go home with you and stay all night."

He stood looking at me as I talked, and for some time after, without a word. Then as I saw that he was making calculations how to get the key, I began putting on my waterproof and rubbers, which chanced to be nearby. As he saw this he asked, "What are you going to do now?"

"I know you are stronger than I," I replied, "and may get this key away from me, and may get out. But if you do, wherever you go I go."

"No you wouldn't," he said in surprise. "You don't know where I would go."

"You would go directly to a saloon and get more drink. I shall go with you, for I know there is not a saloonkeeper in this city who would sell you a drink with me standing by."

He looked for a moment like a tiger at bay; and yet as I stood there and looked him in the eye, he saw there something in my plan, and that there was not much hope of getting away from me, even if he got out the door. Soon he dropped his hands and stood in a listless attitude, and I began to sing, almost without thought, "I Need Thee Every Hour," and I felt it as I had never done before.

I sang the hymn over and over, while he shifted his position occasionally from one side to the other, sometimes looking up with an air of determination for an instant, then settling back again, until he dropped himself into a light rocker that stood nearby. I sang on softly, that same hymn. The town clock struck the hours twice while I stood against the door singing the same song until his head began to droop to one side, and at last with a heavy lurch forward, he fell to the floor with the chair upon him. He was asleep.

I hastened to call the old lady, who came tremblingly in and assisted me to straighten him out and put a cushion under his head, which I did and thanked God.

John came soon after this, and took his station as a watcher, while with his mother for company, I went to see Mrs. Stevens and inform her where and how her husband was. It was very late by this time, and we found her walking her floor in an agony of fear. I told her the whole story and assured her that her husband would be taken care of until he was himself again, and left her with her little ones to spend a night of such prayer as comes only from the heart of such a wife.

That was a night of such watching as can never be forgotten by any of us, and early in the morning Mrs. Stevens came over leaving her little ones asleep. Her husband still slept on the floor. We prepared coffee, and when it was ready awakened him. His mental faculties were very much disturbed, and he sat for a long time on the floor, looking from one to another as if seeking a solution of what was evidently a mystery to him. We assisted him to recall the events of the day and evening before and then urged him to take some coffee.

"No! No!" he exclaimed in disgust as I handed a cup toward him, "I can't take a drop of coffee."

He began to walk the floor, trembling in every limb, and evidently suffering. Suddenly he stopped before me in his nervous walk.

"It's no use, Mrs. Henry. I must have a drink to steady me."

His wife sobbed, and I uttered an exclamation of anguish as I thought, *Is he really lost? Has it come to this—can we not save him?*

"Don't say that, Mr. Stevens," I implored.

He stopped again in his walk, and looked down at me with real sympathy in his face.

"It would be too bad," he said. "I mind me now of all you have done to save me; of how you have watched me and advised me, and prayed for me, and come between us and want; of how you locked the door last night, or God only knows where I should be now. You were a brave woman. I had it in me to have killed you; I could have done it."

"Yes, I know it. Oh, don't drink anymore," I pleaded, as all the terribleness of that struggle for his soul came back. He laid his hand upon my shoulder and continued in a low, candid tone, modulated like that of a reasoner:

"I'll tell you what, Mrs. Henry, you see you don't know quite as well what to do for me just now as I do. You generally know, but—but now you see, here is this awful hankering. Sick! Ah! It's deathly. Just see how my hand shakes. I haven't any power of my will now, but if you will just give me a thimbleful of the bottle I gave you last night, I'll promise you I'll go home and stay there till I can walk past a saloon, and never, never go in one again as long as I live. But I know I can't go past one this morning with this devil crying for drink inside of me. Give me just enough to stop his mouth till I can get home."

"That's truly what we'll have to do, Mrs. Henry," said the poor wife, whose pale face told the story of an aching heart.

I stood irresolute. To do this seemed the most terrible of anything in the world to me; and yet I knew if he would make me a solemn promise to go right home with his wife, he would keep it. But if he got out into the street without his resolution fixed, he would go into one of the many saloons he must pass, and God only knew how it would end. At last I asked, "How little will do to help you home?"

"Give me a tablespoonful, and I will promise all you ask." His plight was pitiful and I was irresolute.

"You will go right home with your wife, and stay there until to-morrow—until I get over to the house?"

"Yes."

"And will keep away from the saloons forever?"

"I will, so help me God! But please get me the whisky—a good drink."

I had started for the closet where I had hastily put the bottle the night before, but at the last words I stopped and turned and looked at him, while my heart sank. He saw my thought, and hastily said, "No, no; I won't ask it. Just a tablespoonful. It is hard—hard—but I will be true."

I went out and closed the door; and feeling like a criminal, with a hand that shook violently, I poured out an honest spoonful of the stuff, put it into a glass with as much water, and returned with it to the room, taking the precaution to empty the bottle before I left it.

Mr. Stevens was standing as I left him, evidently trying to hold himself. I went slowly toward him with the glass. He eagerly took it from my hand, lifted it out at arm's length toward the light, and looked through its shallow measure. As he held it, a soft and manly expression came to his face, and he said, "Mrs. Henry, you shall never repent this. You shall see I will keep my promise. You are brave; you are true to us poor wrecks. God bless you and help me!"

He put the glass to his lips and sipped slowly, drop by drop at first, compelling himself to check his eagerness, until with something like a spasm he threw it down his throat; then turning upon me with the look of a madman, exclaimed with an oath half muttered:

"You watered it, you—" But checking himself as he saw me cover my face with my hands and drop on my knees beside a chair, he asked gently, putting his hand on my shoulder, "Didn't you know any better than that?"

"No, I did not," I said. "I honestly thought it would do just as well."

I had risen to my feet as I replied. He stood silent a moment; then reaching out his hand, he said:

"Yes, I see. You didn't know the difference. You are true; I will be. I promise it all over again. I will keep my word, if you did water the whisky; but don't you ever do that again. Come, wife, let us go home."

"The Lord go with you!" I sighed, while my strength seemed slipping away, for the strain upon heart and brain and nerves had been terrible for the 12 hours since he first came staggering in. Just as he was passing out of the door he turned back a moment and said:

"Mrs. Henry, a man like me never could forget this. I should not have believed there was anyone in the world who would have done all this to save me. Don't fret; I'll keep my promise."

And he did. He took the whole lesson home and profited by it. But he had to fight the long fight over again with the demon of appetite. By diligent attention to his work, by constant prayer and trust in God, and by care of his company he was able to overcome, and in his quiet sphere has become one of our best and noblest workers for the reformation of men.

In the course of his correspondence with his friends in

Liverpool, England, he told the whole story of his own reformation and conversion and the change in his home. He gave accounts of the Reform Club, and its members and work; and one day he received a letter asking for the club pledge and constitution, with instructions for organization and work.

He sent them at once, and in the course of a few weeks we were all made happy to hear of the formation of a club of about 40 men—his old friends and cronies—who had signed the same pledge he had taken.

UP AND ON

Out of the darkness into the light,
Hasten, my soul, with pinions white;
Out of dishonor, and sin, and shame,
Into the purity whence you came.
  Out of continual worry and strife;
      Out of contentions that never cease,
  Into the hope of a better life,
      Into the hope of perfect peace.

Thus I command thee, soul of mine!
O that the will to do were thine.
"The spirit is willing, the flesh is weak;"
The strength of Jehovah you must seek.
  Body and soul together rise.
      Body and soul together fly,
  Together run for the heavenly prize,
      Or together faint, and sink, and die.

Out of the darkness into the light,
Upward, my soul! exert thy might;
Nerve, and muscle, and heart, and brain,
Come to the rescue or all is vain.
  Out of the heavens, O God look down!
      Help, for I fain would come to thee;
  Help, that I win the victor's crown;
      Help, that my heart be true to me.

—MRS. S.M.I. HENRY

153

Chapter Eighteen

A $250 SIP
OF WHISKY

*A*s long as the women spent their time in at-tempting to rescue the cast-off products of the saloon, and set them on their feet again, they were praised and commended on all sides. But as soon as they began to make any effort to secure privileges from the law, all sorts of animosity and bitterness appeared. Since Mrs. Henry had called the first meeting in Rockford, and was everywhere recognized as a leader, she became a conspicuous target for the hostile press. Some of the papers published the threat that the city would be made too hot to hold her. But she refused to be frightened, and declared that she would cease to read the papers, would walk carefully before God and be guided by Him, and pay no attention to anybody else.

One of the conflicts with the city machine came out of the effort of the women to uphold the law that forbade the selling, delivering, or giving of liquor to habitual drunkards or minors. Those who had complaints against them from family or neighbors were put on the black list, and this was hung in every saloon, but generally disregarded by the bartenders against the pleas or demands of the thirsty patron. When, as it often happened, a wife or daughter was endangered by the drunkenness of the husband or son, the women of the WCTU stepped in to help. They had a company of volunteers who stood ready to answer any call where a case was to be tried in court, thinking that their presence might be helpful in securing justice. However, as they saw and listened to the evidence of the law, they were disheartened and desperate at the futility of their effort.

Several plans for securing evidence had been tried, but when the case came before the judge, usually the opposition could find a flaw somewhere that would throw it out of court.

One day there came to the temperance headquarters a woman who had a very sad story to tell of cruelty and suffering on account of the drunkenness of her husband.

"There's times as we're afraid to have him come home, he's thet bad," she said. "And many a time he's threatened to kill me and the little ones. But still he will have it! His name is on the black list, has been there for a long time."

This was not a new story. "How then is he able to obtain it?" Mrs. Henry asked.

"I hates to tell ye this," the woman said, "but Harry sends out little Tommy to the saloon to get it, and he brings it home to his father, and then he drinks until he's madly insane, and we are in terror for our lives."

"How old is Tommy?" asked Mrs. Henry.

"He's just 7, but very quick for his age."

An idea of how she might qualify as a witness began to form in Mrs. Henry's mind.

"This is indeed a pitiful story," she told the woman. "Will you come over to my house to see me, and bring Tommy with you? I'd like very much to get acquainted with him."

Consequently, by the close of the visit the next afternoon she and Tommy were on excellent terms, having discussed at length a number of interesting topics, such as Tommy's pet dog, Mrs. Henry's Indian pony, Black Hawk, the habits of guppies, and the colors and patterns of birds' eggs.

The following morning Mrs. Henry moved her desk so that she would command a view of the bridge over which the child would have to come on his way to the saloon. She had learned about what time he was usually sent, but as an extra precaution against her missing him, she wrote all day literally with one eye on the bridge and the other on the paper.

Finally she was rewarded by seeing him come sauntering across. She immediately put on her wraps and placed herself on watch at the head of the stairway, but out of sight. She let him pass, and then went down to the street, and slowly walked behind him, far enough so that he could not observe her.

The saloon to which he was in the habit of going was just opposite the restaurant. She stepped into the restaurant and waited. It was not very long until he came out and passed the door. His coat was now buttoned up tightly, not entirely concealing a slight bulge. Mrs. Henry was waiting and spoke to him.

"Why, hello, Tommy," she said in a friendly way.

Tommy looked surprised, and not altogether happy about the meeting.

"Hello," he answered without much enthusiasm.

She started walking along with him. He looked up at her with a friendly smile, but at the same time not hiding his unhappiness to have had this encounter at this time.

Mrs. Henry took hold of his hand, and said, "Tommy, show me what you have under your jacket, please." Tommy gave her one startled look, and then puckered up his face to cry. But at Mrs. Henry's gentle, reassuring manner he composed himself and managed to muster a wry smile.

"Don't be afraid. Nobody will hurt you. I will give it back, but I must see what you have." She put her hand on his breast and felt the bottle. Then she unbuttoned his jacket, and took it out.

Just at this point she looked across the street and saw the saloonkeeper standing at the door, watching them. Remembering her determination to qualify herself thoroughly as a witness, she uncorked the bottle, put it to her lips, and took a mouthful.

The saloonkeeper went into action at once. He sprang on his horse, which was tethered in front, and before Mrs. Henry had returned the bottle to the boy and sent him on his way, the man was galloping across the bridge. He knew she had evidence against him which meant fine and imprisonment unless he could get in ahead of her. Before she had time to move in the matter, he had complained of himself to the judge, and paid his fine. That one mouthful of whisky that Mrs. Henry took had cost him $250, and closed every saloon in the city to the little boy's father, so that he was compelled to be sober. He afterward became a Christian and a good citizen. He often told Mrs. Henry that her little stratagem must have been inspired by God.

The next evening, however, when Mrs. Henry and the children were preparing for bed, they heard a knock on the door. Wondering, Mrs. Henry opened the door, and found Alfred Hart, their good friend, and an influential citizen.

"Get dressed," he said in a commanding voice. "You can't stay here tonight."

"Why, what's the matter?" she asked in surprise. "Come on in."

"Well, if you're going to insist on making enemies of the most powerful people in this town," he said bluntly, "I'm going to insist on protecting you. Don't you know your life is in danger?"

"As long as I am doing God's work," she said, "my life is never in danger."

"Just the same," he said positively, "you aren't going to sleep here tonight. I've arranged for you to go to Mrs. Starr's tonight, and I'll take the children with me."

For three weeks after this Mrs. Henry was constantly guarded, unknown to herself, and never allowed to sleep in the same place, until the excitement caused by her effort to "qualify as a witness" subsided.

THE MANTLE

"Charity covereth a multitude of sins."

All day long at the loom of love,
A beautiful angel sat and wove.

The woof was of silver threads of light,
The warp was of gossamer, dainty white,
Beaded with dew from the tender skies,
That lay in the depths of the angel's eyes.

Back and forth the shuttle flew,
Weaving a web of texture new.
Nothing like it in heaven was known,
From the veil that hung before the throne,
To the mist-like robes, so strangely fair,
That the star-eyed infant angels wear.

. . . . .

Alone, in silence, the angel wrought
The secret of her holy thought;
Something was needed down there below,
In the sin-cursed world of death and woe,
To hide from the sight of earth and heaven
The strains of sin by Christ forgiven:

Something to hide the faults of men
From the venture's eye—whose greedy ken
Hunted them out, by night and day,
That human souls might be its prey.
To meet this want, the angel wove
That wonderful web in the loom of love.

And she fashioned a mantle, with sweeping train,
That nothing of earth could ever stain;
A mantle for Christian hands to take
And backward bear, for Christ's dear sake,
And cast, wherever a soul doth lie
In shame, a sport for the passer-by.

—MRS. S.M.I. HENRY

Chapter Nineteen

WOODRUFF'S
ADDITION

*A*lthough the work the women were trying to do suffered from the opposition of a great many influential men in the city, Mrs. Henry and her cause had a very substantial friend in one man, the mayor of the city and the husband of the president of the local temperance union. Mayor Woodruff had been interested in the work from the beginning, and had great confidence in the women and their methods.

He was a manufacturer on a large scale, employing a great many men. Many years ahead of other industrialists of the time, he was much interested in the welfare of his men and in making laboring conditions more attractive. One of his projects was a plan by which it would be possible for them to own their own homes. He had a large tract of land southeast of the city, and this was added to the city corporation under the name of Woodruff's Addition, and divided up into lots. He gave his employees the opportunity to purchase and build, and furnished the capital himself for the buildings, giving easy terms so that the men might eventually own their own homes.

He bought the church building of the Swedish Methodist people, when they were starting on a new building, and moved it to Woodruff's Addition for the accommodation of his working people. Then he sent a message by his wife to the next regular meeting of

159

the temperance union that he wished them to occupy this church with their own services. He agreed to pay whatever extra expense was considered necessary to put the building in order, as well as the expense of a conveyance to take Mrs. Henry back and forth to conduct the services.

Most women, mothers of three children, would have felt that their time was pretty well taken up without this new request. At this time Mrs. Henry was putting in regular hours at the temperance headquarters from 9:00 to 6:00 every day; she was holding special temperance meetings for the working men and women in the center of the industrial area of the city. A large hall had been made out of an old tack factory, which had been cleaned and renovated and provided with 800 chairs. Every day Mrs. Henry with six helpers went there to conduct a noon service. The people came in eating their lunches, and as soon as they had eaten they would join in the singing. At 12:25 the prayer service would begin, consisting of a reading of the Scriptures, and prayer, consuming about 15 minutes. The remainder of the time was given to whatever the meeting seemed to call for—testimonies, prayer, or roundtable, sometimes a regular revival service. The room in which the meeting was held was directly over the wheel that started the machinery for the great system of manufacturing. The wheel started exactly at 1:00, and at that moment, no matter what was going on, every man and woman must be at his or her post. It was so arranged that precisely five minutes before one the organist would start with some lively march or song, and the audience would disperse. Mrs. Henry made it a point never to forget the signal, so that these tired, anxious working people could settle themselves for a half hour of rest and enjoyment. Many people were converted in these meetings.

Despite the heavy load she was already carrying, Mrs. Henry felt that the opportunities for reaching another group of people in Woodruff's Addition were too great to be neglected. But it meant close planning of her time.

Sunday morning, after conducting a large Bible class in her own Sunday school, which met immediately after the preaching service, she took the carriage to Woodruff's Addition to take charge of the regular preaching service at a 1:45. It left her only 30 minutes to make the trip and eat her lunch, which she took with her and ate in the carriage on the way to the church. After the preaching service she opened the Sunday school, and then left it in other hands while she took the carriage back to the temperance headquarters to take the regular 3:00 meeting. At 6:00 she had a class meeting at the Court Street Methodist Church for a special group who had become interested in gospel meetings. The evening she spent in the regular Sunday night service at the Court Street church.

During the week there was one evening service held in Woodruff's Addition. These meetings were attended by a remarkable manifestation of the power of God. In her diary Mrs. Henry referred to this in these words: "This power was so manifest that even those who were believers were silenced by the things they could not understand, and which were so remarkably in harmony with the teachings of God's Word that they could not be accounted for in any way except upon the fact that God is real and the gospel is true and that the Spirit of God accompanies His Word. . . . Very often the only preparation that I could make was purely mental in the few minutes that were free for thought between services in making the journey from place to place, so that the results of these meetings could not have been due to human eloquence or learning."

Through the cold and blizzards of winter, the meetings were held without fail. There came a week of terrible storms, in which the snow was piled high and the weather bitterly cold. All day Friday the storm raged so severely that few people were on the street. Mrs. Henry had learned that very often she was needed more on a stormy day than on a fair one, so she kept her appointments as usual. She found only a few men at the temperance headquarters in the morning when she went down, and they had likely gathered to keep warm by the fire.

As the storm grew worse, the proprietor of the livery stable who always sent his carriage to take Mrs. Henry to Woodruff's Addition sent a boy to say that no carriage would go out that night. But

Sarepta Henry was her father's daughter, and weather had never prevented him from going out to carry on his work of seeking the lost. She turned to the messenger and said she would certainly go if they would send some kind of conveyance. But the carriage owner stoutly declared that they would not do it.

Then she appealed to the men in the reading room who had conveyances, and one of them finally consented to allow her to use his horse and sleigh, if one of the others would go and drive. But they all tried to dissuade her from making the attempt, assuring her she would freeze on the way.

"When we find that snow has completely blocked the road, then we will abandon the effort," she said as she resolutely prepared for the journey.

When the sleigh came, there were plenty of robes and wraps. It was a difficult trip, but when they came in sight of the church and saw it was lighted, Mrs. Henry was satisfied that they had done the right thing. As they entered the door, she heard the exclamation, "There, I told you so!"

The stove was red-hot, the lamps burning brightly, and five men were waiting.

"Some of these fellows," one of them explained, "said you would not come, the weather was so bad, but I told them you would never be discouraged by the weather. Now I'm glad we came, for it would have been too bad if you had come and found a cold, dark house."

They gathered about the stove and had their meeting, the one woman and six men. Mrs. Henry was the only one of the group who professed to have faith in God's Word, but before she closed the meeting all five men who had come from the neighborhood had been converted, and the one who had driven her over in the sleigh admitted that the foundation of his unbelief was shaken. About 20 years later she had a letter from him, saying that he at last surrendered to the gospel that he had begun to believe that evening, and that up to the time of that cold night he had never been in an atmosphere in which he was conscious of the Spirit of God.

The fruit of the work in Woodruff's Addition, at the close of the year, was a company of believers ready for church organization. This was the origin of the Ninth Street Methodist Church in Rockford, which soon became a self-supporting and flourishing body.

Chapter Twenty

ANNIE

*F*rom the minute Mrs. Henry had begun to speak, Annie had listened with intense fascination. *It's almost as if she were talking right to me,* she thought, *and she doesn't know me at all.* She almost forgot the strangeness of her presence in the large hall, her dislike of crowds, and her suspicion of strangers as her eyes clung to the inspired face, and her ears drank in the comforting words of the musical voice. She was glad she had come now, glad that Fanny had told her about the meetings. "I don't think I'll like a woman preacher," she had said, "and I don't want anyone to convert me." But for some reason she could not explain to herself, she had come. *She's not like a preacher really,* she thought now. *She's just like a mother.*

And as she listened, a great resolve had come into her heart, a resolve so daring she hardly believed it herself. *If I only could talk to her!* The idea grew into a wish that persisted so strongly that part of the time Annie hardly heard what the speaker was saying. *If I had had a mother, a mother like her, I know I would never be like I am.*

But Annie hadn't had any mother since she could remember, and her mother's sister had adopted her. Her uncle was a profligate and a pervert. And there had never been any woman she could talk to. Only men. Too many men.

A few days after the meeting she approached the rear door of the temperance headquarters in downtown Rockford with fear and trembling. *If there is a crowd in the waiting room,* she thought, *I won't stay. I'll go right home.*

She knocked timidly, and then almost fled before there was a chance for anyone to answer. Mrs. Henry opened the door and invited her in. *It's almost as if she were expecting me,* thought Annie, returning the cordial greeting, but looking anxiously around the room. The room was empty, but the doors to the reading room beyond were open. A number of loungers sitting in the chairs could be seen.

"May I talk to you a few minutes alone?" the girl asked in a low voice.

"Certainly," said Mrs. Henry, closing the door and placing a seat for Annie beside the desk. She busied herself for a few minutes with some papers on the desk and waited for the girl to speak.

"My name is Annie Lawton, and I . . ." she looked at her hands in her lap and swallowed a few times. She could not see to go on.

"How old are you, Annie?" Mrs. Henry asked encouragingly.

"Nineteen, ma'am." The lovely face framed with wavy brown hair gave little clue to the torment and distress within, save in the large blue eyes that were hard and sad. And now the expression on her face tightened, and she said quickly, "I'm sorry to have bothered you, Mrs. Henry, but I cannot tell you what I came for. I cannot say what I have to say. I thought I could, but I can't. I will come again." And before the other could say a word to stop her, she hastened to the door, and down the stairway and out of sight.

The next day at the same time a very similar incident occurred. Mrs. Henry heard a light tap and met Annie at the door. The girl came in, sat silent, and then declared she couldn't do it.

"Why can't you tell me what you came for?" Mrs. Henry asked kindly.

"Because if I did, you would not listen," the girl said sadly; "you wouldn't have anything to do with me."

"Oh, you are mistaken. I am sure there is nothing that you can say that will make me have anything but love for you."

But again Annie left abruptly, saying, "I think I will come again."

"Dear God," Mrs. Henry prayed after she had left, "this girl is desperately in need of help. Show me how to help her."

For the third time Annie stood in front of the door to the temperance headquarters. *I don't know why I keep coming back here,* she thought, *but I don't seem to be able to stay away.*

The door opened almost immediately after her light tap, and Mrs. Henry took her by both hands and drew her into the room.

"O Annie, I was so afraid you wouldn't come back, and I have wanted to see you again so much. Just wait here a minute while I get my things."

"Why, what are you going to do?" Annie asked in alarm.

"I am going to take you home with me."

"You don't mean that!"

"Yes, I do. I have everything ready. My work is done for the day, and you and I are going to my home together. I want you to have dinner with us."

"Mrs. Henry," the girl said positively, "I can't go home with you."

"But you must. This is not a good place to get acquainted. And there are so many things I want to know about you. At home we can relax and have a good visit."

Annie said, "If you knew what you are doing, you would not say that. If you knew who I am, you would not ask me home with you."

"My dear little girl, you could not be anything or do anything or say anything that would prevent me from taking you home with me tonight."

But Annie set her face and said, "I won't go."

Sarepta Henry had never been one to give up easily. She put her arms around the girl and said, like a mother to a daughter, "Oh, yes you will."

The unmistakable affection in the woman's manner brought tears to Annie's eyes, and she said, "I will go to your home, but I will not go with you. You walk on, and I will come behind you."

"Oh no, you are going right with me. Come."

When they reached the street, arm in arm, Annie suddenly drew herself away and would have fled, but when she saw how determined Mrs. Henry was, she finally acquiesced and walked with her to the house.

Mrs. Henry took Annie to her study and left her quietly alone with some books while she went to prepare the dinner with her little 14-year-old daughter's help. The mother explained to her children the visitor's presence in some casual way so that she would be accepted without surprise or comment. When all was in readiness, and Mary was serving up the dinner, Mrs. Henry went to call the guest. Annie came with her into the cheerful dining room, attractively set with the evening meal, but the sight of Mary, dimpled and smiling in her ruffled pinafore, so happy in this Christian home, so upset her that she returned to the study and asked not to come out to dinner. All Mrs. Henry's efforts to persuade her were unavailing.

I should never have come into this home, she thought to herself as she remained in seclusion in the study, her mind a turmoil of conflicting emotions. *Why did I come? Why did I ever think there is any hope for such as I? But Mrs. Henry didn't act as if she despised me. She probably has no idea. How kind she is! And that darling little daughter of hers! She has probably never known anything but love and goodness all her life!*

She ate little from the tray of tempting food that Mrs. Henry had brought her. Thankful at first for the seclusion and privacy she soon became restless and walked about the room, looking at pictures on the wall and the titles of the books, until Mrs. Henry returned after her dinner with the children.

"Do you know how to knit, Annie?" asked Mrs. Henry when she came in and seated herself with a half-finished stocking on her needles.

"No, but I'd like to learn."

"Next time you come we'll have to have some yarn and needles, and I'll teach you." Mrs. Henry led out in an impersonal feminine conversation which she hoped would put the girl at ease and temporarily divert her from the troubling theme that seemed so hard for her to discuss. She talked on about her early days on the prairies, her travels in all kinds of carriages, and the needy people she met from day to day.

When the evening became quite late and Annie made a move to

return home, her hostess objected, saying, "You cannot go home at this time of night, and I've been planning for you to spend the night with me." She took her up to her own room and showed her the bed, beside which was a comfortable lounge.

"This is my room," she said, "and I'd like very much to share it with you tonight. You are to sleep in the bed, and I'll sleep on the lounge."

This simple gesture of kindness opened the floodgates of Annie's tears, and she dropped to the floor beside the bed and wept until she could weep no longer. Mrs. Henry sat down on the floor beside her and put her head in her lap and stroked her back. After a long time Annie was calm again, and she poured forth her story without any coaxing.

"You've done just the right thing to come to me with this story, Annie," Mrs. Henry said when she had finished, "and I think it has been good for you to tell it and get it out of your system. Now I don't want you to think about it anymore. The thing now is for you to let me help you plan for the future. You must forget about this ugly past. You aren't to blame that your uncle mistreated you in this way. You are young and have many years to live a useful, happy life."

"Oh, no, Mrs. Henry, my life is just utterly ruined. I know it will be impossible for me to reform. I don't know why I have told you this, but when I heard you speak at the meeting, something inside me just seemed to make me come and tell you about myself. I wanted you for my friend, but I was sure if you knew my story, you would want nothing to do with me."

"But don't you feel now that I am your friend, Annie, and want to help you?"

"Yes." The blue eyes started to fill with tears again. "But there is nothing you can do to change the past."

"No, Annie, I cannot change the past, but there is One who can wipe away all the sins of the past, and all tears from our eyes, and who can clothe us with the robe of righteousness, if we'll only let Him. He is the truest Friend there is."

But Annie sat brooding. She was not yet ready to comprehend the truth and beauty of these words.

"I know you wouldn't have come to me at all, Annie," Mrs. Henry continued, "if you hadn't thought that I could help you. Telling me your problem has been the hardest part of the battle. Now we must lay some plans for the future. Where are you living now?"

"With my father. I left my uncle as soon as my aunt died. Father is an old soldier, and he doesn't have very much, and he depends a lot on me for support. There are three men in this city, men who stand high, men whom you know, Mrs. Henry, and of whom you would never believe it, who will make it just as hard as possible for me to reform."

"I'm sure I can find some other kind of work for you to do. I know of a number of women who need someone to do special fancy ironing for them. Can you iron? Oh, I'm sure there is a way out. But first of all you must find some good associates. We have some lovely young people coming to our meetings, and I want you to meet them and get acquainted." Annie looked at her in astonishment.

"Do you really mean that?"

"Why, surely. Your secret is safe with me. You're going to have to get busy quick now, and make up for all the happy times you have missed." She smiled warmly, and for the first time Annie felt a little ray of hope creep into her heart.

The next few months saw a remarkable change in this girl. Mrs. Henry kept her supplied with plenty of work, and drew her into the association of other young people, who accepted her, and other women from the union who knew her only for a sweet young girl who had a struggle with poverty. Annie attended the meetings and gave her life to Christ, developing the modesty and manners of a beautiful Christian woman.

But there came a day sometime later when Mrs. Henry responded to a knock on the door of her office, and was surprised to find Annie there, greatly agitated.

"I must have a private talk with you," she said. "May I come to your house to see you this evening?"

"You can come with me right now. I am taking you home to dinner."

When the meal was concluded and they were in the privacy of the study once more, Annie told her that a young man, one of the reformed men of well-established Christian character, had begun to pay her special attention, and had already intimated that he wished her to become his wife.

"You know I can't marry him. It would be impossible, and I don't know what to do. I have told him, but he will not listen. He wants to know the reason, and he asked me if I could not care enough for him, and I had to tell him that I did. I love him surely, but I cannot marry him."

"Why not? You are probably just as good as he is."

"I cannot marry him, for first I would be obliged to tell him the whole story, and that I can never tell."

"Of course, that would be necessary," agreed Mrs. Henry, "or it might make trouble later on. But I can see no reason that you should not marry. You are both leading true and useful lives, and God has forgiven the past. Why shouldn't man?" They prayed together that God would guide them in their plans, and if it were right, would interpose some way to bring it about.

Again, a few days later Mrs. Henry recognized Annie's timid tap at the door. When seated alone together, she said, "Mrs. Henry, I think I shall be obliged to tell Will the whole story. He will not be satisfied otherwise. But I cannot do it. Will you do it for me? If I send him to you with a note asking you to do it, then will you tell him for me?"

Sarepta was silent a moment as she pondered the dangers of accepting this responsibility.

"I want you to think this over very carefully, Annie. For me to tell him this story might arouse in you a feeling that would make it impossible for me ever to help you again. There is a great risk in telling him. I have no idea how he will receive it. He might be bitterly angry and turn against you; and feeling toward him as you do, you might react unfavorably. We must think it over and pray about it. If after longer consideration and prayer you still wish me to do it, I'll do the best I can."

In the months that passed after that, Annie's face as it was turned toward Mrs. Henry in the meetings seemed thinner and full of pathos. She realized that the girl was unhappy to the point of illness, and feared that the burden she was carrying was weighing on her health.

One Sunday afternoon when she was seated with her children in the study the doorbell rang. Alfred went to the door and returned saying that Will B. was in the parlor and wanted to see her. He was a fine-looking young man with a strong face, and she was drawn to him at once. Since Annie had told her about him she had observed him from time to time, always with interest and approval.

After a few moments of general conversation Will drew a letter from his pocket and handed it to Mrs. Henry. Guessing the request it contained, she asked Will to go into the study, and she followed soon after reading the letter. It was from Annie, as she had surmised, and it said, "The time has come when I cannot refuse to tell Will my story. Something must be done about it, and so I send him to you."

It was a hard assignment, and Mrs. Henry felt weak at the thought. She lifted her heart to God for strength, and remembering her promise to Annie, went into the study.

"Have you any idea of the contents of this letter?" she asked the young man when she had seated herself.

"Annie told me that she would send me to you to tell me something that she wanted me to know," he said. "I have no idea what it is, but she has informed me that you understand my wish concerning her; so I suppose it is something with reference to that. It makes no difference to me what it is. I want to marry Annie."

His manly attitude made the task easier, and Mrs. Henry told him about Annie's first coming to her, about the repeated visits, and the whole sad story.

Before she finished there were tears in the young man's eyes, and he dropped his head upon his hand.

"Mrs. Henry, Annie is just as good as I am, a good deal better; and this makes no difference, only that it makes me believe in her all the more. This has been very hard for you; and I thank you for it. And now I am going to see Annie." He left immediately with a determined look on his face, and Sarepta rejoiced that now, probably, everything would turn out all right.

But a few days later Will came back. He was very much upset. "Have you heard?" he asked, "Annie has disappeared!"

"No!" Mrs. Henry exclaimed, astonished. "Come in, and tell me. I thought everything was going to work out happily for you two."

"I did too. After I left you that day I went to Annie, and she promised to marry me, and we were very happy planning for the future and our home. And then I think she suddenly seemed to be afraid, and without letting me know she has left the city."

"This is terrible, Will. I am so sorry. We must find her!"

But for three years there was no clue, and after a while Will also left the city and Mrs. Henry lost track of him.

Chapter Twenty-one

RED RIBBON CLUBS

*F*or other foundation can no man lay than that is laid, which is Jesus Christ. Now if any man build upon this foundation gold, silver, precious stones, wood, hay, stubble; every man's work shall be made manifest." Mrs. Henry was beginning the Scripture reading that preceded her Thursday afternoon study in the Methodist church in De Kalb, Illinois, when she looked up and saw a strange group coming into the church. The meetings had gotten off to a good start on the previous Sunday. The women of the WCTU and all the church people of all denominations had cooperated in distributing invitations all over town, at every house, in every place of business, and at every saloon.

Everyone recognized the saloonkeeper as he and about 20 of his customers filed down the center aisle and found seats near the front of the hall. Their walk was unsteady and their faces flushed with intoxication, and they were greeted with a mixture of stares, smiles, and frowns.

But Mrs. Henry continued her reading of the third chapter of 1 Corinthians, "And the fire shall try every man's work of what sort it is. . . . Know ye not that ye are the temple of God, and that the Spirit of God dwelleth in you?" She then proceeded to her discussion of building, and the loss or gain that comes to the person according to the materials he uses. She never gave an address without making everyone hear the call of God to his soul and feel the yearning love of the Father for His children.

That evening at the gospel meeting the men all returned and were early in their places. The presence of the Holy Spirit was clearly manifest in the response of the crowds who came out. The church could not begin to hold them, and they clung to the message like hungry souls.

"It was almost impossible to dismiss a congregation," said Mrs. Henry. "In fact, sometimes after they had been regularly dismissed they would linger, some would request special prayer, or something would come up so that we could not close. I have known the meetings to be dismissed three or four times, and to continue until midnight in spite of everything reasonable that we could do."

On this particular evening the saloonkeeper and many of his friends went forward at the close of the service and signed the pledge.

The next morning some of the women went down to the saloon, not out of curiosity, but feeling that these men might need help in carrying out their expressed desire for reformation. They found them all there, surrounded by all the familiar appliances and equipment, standing around idly, scarcely knowing what to do, yet still determined to stand by their newly formed resolves. They were happy to see the women, and immediately turned over the premises into their hands.

The liquors were spilled, the billiard tables were taken out, and the place was thoroughly renovated; pictures were hung, reading tables were put in; periodicals, books, and newspapers were supplied. The saloonkeeper was installed at a living salary as keeper of the reading room, and began his new life and new work amid his old surroundings and old cronies.

The remodeled saloon made such a fine hall, in fact, that the women decided to hold their morning and afternoon meetings there from that time on, and thus come in contact with the very people they desired to help.

The news of Mrs. Henry's success spread from town to town, and she was in constant demand to spend two weeks, 10 days, or three weeks in a place. She brought a message of love and hope and peace and repentance. She showed the beauty of holiness, the relation of salvation to habits of living, and automatically the saloons closed down for lack of patronage. It was not unusual for two, three, or more saloons to go out of business at the close of a series of meetings. In the city of Paw Paw 53 men of the town formed a league for the protection of their community from the liquor interests, determined that no saloon should ever obtain a foothold among them again.

Their method of procedure required that one of them be at every train and watch every newcomer. If he appeared at all questionable in character and aims, he was shadowed until the league became satisfied as to what he intended to do. They had several encounters with saloon men who secured a place and opened a business, but they would be immediately visited by members of the league—all businessmen—who would tell them that they were not wanted in Paw Paw. If they refused to listen, the visits would be repeated with more and more frequency, until at last the intruder made up his mind that it was best to leave. The liquor interests concluded that it was a very bad place to establish a business, and during Mrs. Henry's lifetime no saloon was ever opened in that town again.

In these early years of her public work Mrs. Henry had no agent to make her engagements, but simply went from point to point as the calls came, spending from 10 to 14 days at a place, organizing all the churches and temperance groups for a regular, systematic, and prolonged siege, expecting them to carry on the work after she had gone. It was hard work, and the expenditure of physical and nerve energy was tremendous. Strange that a girl given up to die should be able to meet such heavy demands on her strength.

The hardest part was the separation from her children. For although Sarepta rejoiced to do the work of the Lord, and threw her whole soul into the work she felt called upon to do, yet her mother heart ached every time she had to go away from her children. They were growing up now, and could be left for a few days at a time. They had been trained in self-reliance and domestic efficiency.

In understanding Mrs. Henry one should think of her as two personalities—the public figure, calm, poised, powerful, and fearless; and the recluse in her home, vigorously scrubbing and cleaning. She could paint and paper a room, upholster a couch or chair, mend a broken latch. She had very decided opinions regarding the sphere of women, and differed sharply with Frances Willard, who campaigned strongly to compel ministers to let women into their ordained ranks. She didn't think of herself as a preacher, but took her place on the platform as a "voice for the home," crying out against all evils that would destroy the home and ruin the children.

Shortly after the work in Paw Paw, Mrs. Henry received a call to spend a year in the state of Michigan doing gospel work in the Red Ribbon Clubs, which had been organized by Henry A. Reynolds. The Rockford Union finally consented to give a year's absence to allow her to fulfill what seemed a larger field of usefulness. She was forced to break up housekeeping temporarily. Mary was sent to preparatory school in Evanston, and Alfred and Arthur to homes in the country.

Not long before she was to leave for her work in Michigan, she received a call from the Red Ribbon Club of Shabbona, Illinois, an organization of temperance men, to lead out in some special meetings that were being arranged to help some of the "weak members," as their leader expressed it. They didn't know that her approach to the matter was almost certain to be evangelical, and she didn't know that this group were infidels, almost to a man.

The only suitable place to hold the meetings was the Baptist church, which was also used by the Methodists. The Red Ribboners had some difficulty in getting the use of the church, because the attitude of the men in the club toward religion was well known. A reluctant consent was given, however, when it became known that Mrs. Henry was a gospel worker. One pompous gentleman of the flock was so angry that the pastor was going to allow the meetings in the church and so prejudiced against work of this sort by a woman that he took away the pulpit and Bible, to prevent their being desecrated, and stored them in his own home.

"I'll never come back to this church as long as that woman preacher is here!" he vowed.

Mrs. Henry was entertained in the home of one of the leading citizens, a merchant, who was much interested in the success of the lectures. Soon after her arrival, Mrs. Henry was called upon by the president of the Red Ribbon Club, and they began to lay plans for the work.

She outlined her usual plan of opening exercises and mentioned casually that she would expect him to take care of the singing, prayer, and Scripture reading. He soon interrupted her with, "But, Mrs. Henry, you are talking to me as if I were a Christian!"

"Are you not a Christian?" Her dark eyes turned to him in surprise.

"Far from it."

"What, then, are you?" she asked.

"If you should go out here on these streets," he answered, "and ask anyone what I am, they would tell you that I am an infidel. I do not know that I am quite an infidel, but I am very far from being a believer. This is true of our club almost to a man."

Mrs. Henry was so astonished she couldn't say anything for a moment.

"Why did you send for me?" she asked soberly.

"Because we knew of your work," he said, "and what it has done in other places, and we have some men among us whom we believe you can help. We want to hear you, and so we have sent for you."

"Well," she said, "in sending for me you have laid yourself liable to gospel dispensation! I shall be obliged to preach the truth as I understand it. The only thing that will help any man, whether he is considered weak or strong, is the gospel of Christ. If my work means anything at all, it means salvation through the Lord Jesus Christ. If it means anything to any man in this community, it means something to you personally. If you are willing to go on with the arrangements, and accept my work with this understanding, we will arrange for it. If not, I will take the evening train home."

"Oh, you can't do that," the man said quickly. "You cannot go home, of course. The meetings are advertised all through this country, and people will be here from all about. Of course we want you to speak. I am willing to do anything I can to assist you, but you won't call on me to offer prayer, will you?"

"No, not tonight," she promised. But she assured him that she would expect him to open the services with singing and to read the Scripture she should select, and find someone else to offer prayer.

This seemed to be a problem. "There will be mighty few people upon whom you can depend to pray," he said. "There will be the Methodist minister, if he happens to be there, or the Baptist minister, should he be there, which is doubtful, since he has opposed our using the church at all."

"Very well," she said, "if you think of anyone who might be a help and will introduce me, I will get along the best I can."

Soon after the president had left, the secretary of the club came to see Mrs. Henry, and practically the same conversation ensued. Both men, though professing their religious unbelief, seemed tremendously interested in the projected series of lectures.

The church was filled to overflowing. Although it was October, the weather was mild, and the windows were open so that those who could not be seated inside could participate in the service from the outside. Mrs. Henry had planned a temperance lecture, but felt impressed, after her visit with the two leaders of the Red Ribbon Club, to present the "straight gospel," because, as they reminded her, the evangelistic appeal had proved the most effective approach to the temperance question.

During the opening exercises on the second evening the president stepped forward to the desk beside Mrs. Henry, just as she was going to offer prayer, and said, "Just a moment, please, Mrs. Henry. I guess everyone in this congregation knows me, and how I have always stood on religious matters. I have never been a drinking man. I went into the Red Ribbon Club with the purpose of helping, and with my brother, Captain A., was instrumental in bringing Mrs. Henry here to give us three lectures." Then he went on and told of his visit with their speaker, and quoted her statement that her work meant salvation if it meant anything at all, and that it would mean

178

something to him personally. "I found out last evening," he continued, "that she was right. It does mean something to me personally, and my wife and I both wish to ask you to pray for us, that we may find all that there is for us in the gospel."

So great was the interest in this place that it was impossible to close the meetings after the three lectures. Instead, Mrs. Henry remained three weeks, holding two services every day. Each evening meeting was preceded by a prayer service and followed by an inquiry meeting. Since it was almost impossible to dismiss the congregation, often it was late at night before the last personal consultation was finished.

The community was stirred to its depths. At the close of the meetings Mrs. Henry conducted a special service for the 200 converts, most of whom had never before held church membership, 73 of whom were members of the Red Ribbon Club, and avowed infidels.

Chapter Twenty-two

CHRISTMAS EVE
WITH THE
O'CONNELLS
(From *The Pledge and the Cross*)

*I*t was Christmas Eve. About 5:00 in the afternoon a large, broad-shouldered, good-looking Irishman came into the rooms. He had a determined, businesslike look on his face, which at once attracted my attention. I made him welcome, and he took a chair beside the table, and picked up an illustrated paper. A few minutes later, as I glanced up from my writing, I saw he was sitting with his eyes fixed upon the page, which was upside down, while his whole expression betrayed the most perfect abstraction. He was in a brown study, and utterly oblivious to all his surroundings. I watched him. His face bore the traces of drink, and yet was stamped with so much that was manly and honest that it was a pleasure to look at it.

A candidate for the pledge, I thought, and went on with my work.

Considerable time elapsed. He said not a word, scarcely changed his position or looked up, although people were coming and going almost constantly, until a man came in and asked for the pledge.

Then my Irishman dropped his paper, turned quickly in his chair and sat bolt upright, and looked and listened with every faculty on the alert.

The new candidate was in a hurry, and having signed the roll and the pocket pledge, went immediately out.

The Irishman sat in the same attitude for some time after, often fixing his eyes upon me with an anxiety that almost made me break my resolution not to be the first to say anything about the pledge. He evidently did not know how to introduce the subject of the pledge until he had heard it called for by the man who had just gone, and now was embarrassed by the presence of others or by his own self-consciousness. I offered a silent prayer for him and went on with my work, leaving him to his thoughts.

In a little while all had passed out of the rooms but us two. Then, as I looked up, he quickly rose, and coming toward me, said, "I would be afther a takin' that plidge, ma'am."

"All right, sir!" I responded heartily. "I shall be very happy to give it to you."

"Only first," he said, "I have no money now."

I did not understand him, and as he hesitated, and stood awkwardly and with shame on his face, I waited for him to go on. After a moment he added, "To pay for it, ma'am."

"Oh! bless you," I exclaimed. "There's nothing to pay for. This is a free gospel—free as God's good grace."

"Is it thin? Thank God!" he said devoutly.

I opened the book and brought out the pocket pledges, and, as we sat with these between us, asked him some questions about himself. But he was very reticent; so at that time I learned nothing further than that he had spent and lost all by drink, except his wife, who was with him in a wretched hovel not far from us, just across the river. He seemed filled with a deep sense of the wrong he had done her, and with shame for it all, read the pledge, and repeated in a tone of real supplication the prayer at the end, "Lord, help me!"

After signing the pocket pledge and putting it away in his breast pocket, he sat with his hand over his face for a long time, and often sighed heavily. At length he looked up and said, "Would it be too much to ask? But I would like another of the card pledges to put in my wife's stocking this night, a bit of a prisint, ye know."

There was a pathos in the tone as well as words that went clear down into my heart, and I assured him that it would be a fine thing to do.

There was something about this case that took strong hold of me, and I would find myself recurring to it very often while busy with work that should have taken my entire attention. This was so much the case that a day or two after Mr. O'Connell signed the pledge I determined to visit the family. It was a wild day to be out, snowy and windy, but I could not rest or work for the thoughts of this man and his wife that kept crowding upon me. I prepared for the storm and went out to find them.

There was need. The door of the hovel—for it was nothing better—was opened by Mr. O'Connell, and as soon as I saw him I knew there was trouble.

He seemed amazed to see me, and for an instant hardly knew what to do. I stepped in, being assured that I was welcome, whether he bade me enter or not. He shut the door quickly behind me, for the storm rushed in, and then, turning, he took my hand and said with a deep-chested sob, "God be praised! He sent you, shure."

The room was a basement, dark, cold, and damp with mold. A stove was there, but only a spark of fire, and no fuel visible. A bed was in one corner, and upon the side of it sat a little girl of a woman with a week-old baby in her arms, and she was shivering with cold and red with crying.

"Have you no wood or coal?" I asked in surprise.

"No, only what is in the stove," said the woman. "But Pat here has been off all day yesterday and today to find a bit of work, and gets nothing; and that bit of bread is all there is to eat, and not a cent of money, as sure as God lives. Oh! dear, oh, dear, the bitter day." And she began crying again like a grieved child.

"And you with this wee baby!" I said, while my heart seemed melting in my throat. "You must get into bed and be covered warm; you will catch your death."

"It was so cold in bed," she replied, "I thought I might warm by this bit of fire. Baby is warm, the little dear!" she said, smiling up in my face as I bent down over the bundle she was holding so tightly.

And baby was warm, for Pat had taken off his coat to wrap her in, and was shivering in his thin shirt sleeves. He sat on the foot of the bed, with so much of honest shame on his face that anything like reproach for this terrible state of things would have choked in my throat.

"Well, God did send me, and now, cheer up, friends, there're better things ahead. I am going out now, but will be back soon." And I hastened out.

There was a wood and coal office within a block. I went and ordered fuel sent at once; and to credit the tradesmen of our city, I wish to record that such orders given in the name of our WCTU were always promptly met—did not have to wait their turn on the list. From the coal office I went to a grocery and ordered a long list of foods, and then hastening to the rooms, I enlisted one of the boys, and then sent him with a note to one of the wealthy members of our union, stating the case, and asking the remains of their dinner— meats and any cooked food—as soon as possible, with bed changes and anything for the baby that could be gotten together at a moment's notice, with more to follow at leisure. I made it clear that the situation was desperate.

It was not long before the dark room was warm and cheerful, and everything wore the aspect of a prophecy of better days.

Before leaving, I said, "Now we want to kneel down together and thank God for His goodness, and ask Him to help you lead a new life from this day."

"Yes, God help us indeed!" said Pat.

When we rose from our knees Pat said, "We are of a different religion, but I like that you pray for us; it has done me good."

"You are Catholics?" I asked.

"Yes, but not very good Catholics, I fear."

"Well," I replied, "you must go to your church now. Father _____ is a good temperance worker, and I know a good many of your church people will help you. But even if you are a Catholic, you can come over to the gospel meetings on Sundays."

"Yes, I will, ma'am," he replied, and he was faithful in keeping his promise.

Mr. O'Connell began to pick up small jobs of work, such as wood sawing, snow shoveling, and so forth, our people looking out for him and giving him anything that came to hand. He always did his work religiously, and could be depended upon. The wife and baby were clothed and the house looked after, and before many weeks they moved into better quarters, and things looked favorable for comfort and prosperity. Pat used to come to the rooms for a few moments almost daily, but usually was too busy to stay long. One day while we were talking, he said, "Mrs. Henry, I find I've got to have more help than I ever have had somehow, or the old life will be too strong for the likes o' me."

"I'd like to help you in any way I can," I said. "What can I do for you?"

"I want to know about your religion. If it won't put ye out too much, I'd like if ye would talk to me a bit."

And I did talk to him, explaining the way of justification by faith, and the true priesthood of our Lord Jesus Christ. And he, eager for truth as the "hart panteth after the water brooks," took it into his heart. As he listened he saw Jesus as He is, and accepted Him with an intelligent faith.

There was something very touching in the manner in which he would request prayers for his wife from this time. He would arise and say in the prayer meetings, "I have a dear friend; I ask prayer for _____ ; Mrs. Henry knows who it is." This was done again and again, until she was led into the acceptance of Christ for herself, and with her husband united with one of the Protestant churches.

He subsequently occupied a place of trust that brought him good support. His pleasant home was provided with all needful furnishings. There was an air of refinement about it that was an inspiration to contemplate.

The little girl of a woman, with the beautiful little Mary whom they called my baby, kept the home so dear a place to Pat that he was seldom outside its enclosure. Working and living for each other, they became as truly a happy little family as is not often found.

Chapter Twenty-three

NATIONAL
EVANGELIST

*R*ecognition of the power that attended Mrs. Henry's efforts in the field of evangelism was given when she was asked to fill the position of national evangelist for the WCTU, a newly created post. In this capacity she traveled far and wide over a long period of years.

Very early in her work she realized the need of trained workers, women who knew how to work for others; who had practical experience in handling people, in winning souls, in giving aid to mothers who had little idea of the proper care of their homes and children. At the temperance convocation held at Lake Bluff, Illinois, in 1877, the first effort was made to organize such a training school. Here they discussed principles and methods, as well as needs, and how to bring about the very best application of the one to the other.

The first institutes for mothers were held in the little hall erected by the WCTU in Chicago for their meetings. Although the beginning was small and experimental in nature, from this idea grew a greater work, culminating in the home and school for WCTU evangelists and missionaries, situated in what was known as "hell's half acre," a section of New York City.

The advantages to accrue from trained workers became at once so apparent that the training school was adopted and made a department of the national organization at the next convention, and Mrs. Henry was appointed superintendent. Since she already had her work as national evangelist she could not accept, but Mary Allen West, an experienced teacher, who had been for many years superintendent of public schools in Galesburg, Illinois, was induced to take the responsibility of organizing this important department.

But the work of the evangelistic institute remained Mrs. Henry's special province. Local unions would call for an institute of several days' duration, and sessions of two hours each would be held during the morning and afternoon, with a public lecture in the evening. The women were enrolled, and came to classes like pupils in school.

These institutes were always occasions of great spiritual growth and power. They were not confined to members of the union. Ministers, teachers, members of churches, and many others joined in studying methods and discussing problems connected with the drive for better, purer homes. But they did more than study and discuss. They went out into the homes of the needy people, caring for the sick, counseling the discouraged, cleaning up the premises, and bringing the gospel.

Ever since Sarepta Henry's eyes had first seen the inside of a saloon, her work had brought her into close contact with all kinds of crime and corruption and social evils. Each new phase brought surprise, shock, and horror, and built up again her desire to fight the destroyers of home and happiness. In the work with the institutes in the big cities the women faced a new problem.

In the 1870s there was still no legal protection for child laborers. Little children not yet in their teens worked 12 to 14 hours a day in conditions that were detrimental to mind and body. Standards of sanitation, ventilation, and remuneration were very low. Many of the same outrages against childhood that had caused Dickens to excoriate the industrialists in England were also present in the United States.

Young girls in their teens were a special prey to the greed of men. As the women visited here and there in the tenements of Chicago and other large cities, they listened to many a sorrowful tale from worried mothers.

The sweat shops where numerous teenage children were employed operated under such shady methods of coercion and extortion that many a girl became a victim of the moral slavery that went largely unchecked in the large cities of the land. It offered easier money than the dawn-to-dusk factory labor, and many a family lived unwittingly off the stained virtue and soiled chastity of its daughters.

The arousement to these horrible facts, as they were discovered piecemeal in the low and out-of-the-way holes of the big cities, brought terror and despair to many of the women. Mrs. Henry said: "I have tossed sleepless on my bed night after night, often finding my teeth set and my hands clinched with the nails pressed deeply into the palms, every nerve strained to the keenest tension in the intensity of thought as I was trying to work out this problem of rescue for those who had been caught in the snare that had been laid for the unwary which was always baited with *bread*, and which always led to a bondage from which death was a welcome release."

The women appointed committees of investigation to make a thorough canvass of the situation and give the world the facts. The conditions revealed were so appalling that they felt absolutely helpless before the political power. The greatest commercial forces in the world seemed to be in league with the demon of greed whose heel was upon the throat of the poor little girls in toil and suffering.

The women were moved to indignation and wrath at the mercenary employers and corporations who required a seven-day week of work, and who wrenched from the people their one day of rest and for hearing about God. The more they faced the need of these child laborers, the greater impetus was given the movement for women to share in the lawmaking power.

Although they were still denied the vote, the women could wield considerable influence on public opinion, by making themselves heard as loudly as possible, both collectively and individually, on this issue. It seemed to them then that the best solution to the problem lay in the making of a law to compel employers to close on Sunday, thus allowing the oppressed workers to have one day in the week for rest or worship.

Mrs. J. C. Bateham, one of the strong, earnest, self-sacrificing women of the organization, rose in a convention of the WCTU and asked for a department of Sabbath observance that would push with all the means at their disposal the enactment of such a law. The request was considered, warmly discussed pro and con, and finally accepted. Many of the women were instinctively opposed to it, having a premonition that there were possibilities involved in such a department that they could not foresee, and that might cause trouble.

Mrs. Henry was not present at the convention, but as she learned about it from published reports and from the conversation of those present, she gave it her hearty endorsement, for she was convinced that the foundation principle was right, namely, to bring the law to bear against the oppressor to let the oppressed go free. It was never intended to force Sunday observance, but only to make it possible for those who wished to observe the day. Later Mrs. Henry said, "If only we had known enough to leave the choice of a rest-day open to each individual!"

At that time, however, they were unaware of any minorities who might suffer by the enactment of such a law. Little did they realize the repercussions their agitation would engender both within their own organization and in the social problems of later reform movements.

PLENTY TO DO

There's plenty to do in this world of ours:
There are weeds to pluck from among its flowers;
There are fields to sow; there are fields to reap,
And vineyards to set on the mountain steep;
There are forests to plant, and forests to fell,
And homes to be builded on hill-side and dell.

There are fountains of sin and of sorrow to seal;
There are fountains to open, the nations to heal;
There are brave words to speak, and songs to be sung;
There are doors to be opened, and bells to be rung;
There's a conflict to wage with the armies of sin;
There's a fortress to hold, and a fortress to win;

There's plenty to do all over the land—
Work, crowding the brain, the heart, and the hand;
There are millions to feed in the world's busy hive;
There are railroads to build, and engines to drive;
There are pathways to mark over mountain and lea;
There are ships to be piloted over the sea.

There's plenty to do; there are children to teach;
An evangel of love and of mercy to preach;
The fallen to lift, the proud to abase,
To bring right and wrong to their own fitting place;
There's an ensign to plant on the heights by the sea;
There's work for the millions—for you and for me.

—MRS. S.M.I. HENRY

Chapter Twenty-four

ANNIE AGAIN

*M*iss Helen Hood was kept busy making all the engagements for Mrs. Henry and working out schedules of her speaking appointments. She was considered infallible with reference to railroad routes and arranging dates that would not conflict. But there was one time when she made a mistake.

Mrs. Henry had finished her work at a state convention on Friday afternoon, and went to the railroad station to buy her ticket for the next appointment, only to find that it would be very difficult and inconvenient to get through until Monday. Since the WCTU in a nearby town two miles away had already asked her to remain over Sunday and speak to them and she had declined because of this previous engagement, she now wired them and told them she could come.

She went on to the small town, found a room at the hotel, and began to prepare for her work.

As she stood before the audience at the Sunday afternoon meeting in the temperance hall, suddenly her eyes passing over the sea of faces spotted the pretty, familiar face of Annie. But it was white and drawn, and full of distress, and looked at least 10 years older than when she had seen her last.

When the meeting closed, and the people gathered around to speak to Mrs. Henry, Annie came and stood at the outskirts of the crowd. Continuing to shake hands, Mrs. Henry reached out and took her left hand, and tucked it under her arm, holding it tight until at last all were gone.

"Annie, how does this happen?" she asked.

"Mrs. Henry," Annie returned, "I want to ask you how it happens. What brought you here?"

"I am here, I had supposed until now, because a blunder was made by the one who arranges my engagements," she said, "and because I could not reach the point where I was to be on Sunday. But now I know there has been no blunder. I am here because you need me. What is the matter?"

"I can't tell you here," she said. "I want to see you though."

They went to the little hotel room, and Annie poured out a story of great discouragement, of a hard life and hard treatment. Her efforts to be true to what she believed to be right had seemed to bring her only hardness all the way. And at last she had been discovered by Will, who again had urged her to marry him.

"Mrs. Henry, I cannot marry him. You know how I feel about my past. And I had determined at last that I could not stand the pressure any longer, that the only way to escape was to die, and I was going to take my life. I had already made all the arrangements, had secured a bottle of poison, which I was going to take last evening and end it all, when I saw a notice in the paper that you were to be here to speak."

She threw herself on the floor, sobbing uncontrollably and laying her head on Mrs. Henry's knees. "I could not forget how you had been a mother to me, and the longing to see you once more took such a possession of me that I made up my mind I would live to see you, and then I would do it. But the minute I saw you today I knew I could not do it. And when you took my hand and drew me to you, I knew I could never do it. But what can I do? I can't marry Will."

When Annie's emotions were finally spent the older woman calmly read to her from the Word of God and prayed with her.

"Annie," she said, "don't you believe that God has forgiven your past?"

"Yes, I'm sure He has."

"If God has forgiven your past, don't you think it is very foolish, if not wrong, for you to keep bringing it up and letting it stand between you and your happiness? If you are unhappy, you can't do the work that God would have you do."

"You really think I should marry Will, then?"

"I certainly do, and I think God had a definite part in my coming here to help you to see this thing in the right way."

Three weeks later, while engaged in her next convention, Mrs. Henry received notification of the marriage of Will and Annie. They said they were going to a Western state to live, amid entirely new surroundings, but gave no address.

Mrs. Henry traveled widely in her work as national evangelist, and three years after this time was on a tour of the West. At one of the state conventions she was entertained by a beautiful and wealthy woman who was interested in all kinds of work for the poor. A widow with a large income, she had begun rescue work for unfortunate girls, into which she was pouring her whole heart and soul and a large share of her funds.

"Do you see that cottage over there?" she asked one day when they were driving out together. "One of my best helpers lives there." On another occasion they stopped at an attractive confectionery and bakery establishment. She went in for some pies, and when she came out, remarked, "This is the business of one of my lovely helpers, whom I have spoken to you about. She makes these pies and cakes herself, and is altogether a very nice person—a great treasure to me."

A few days later Mrs. Henry was on her way early to church when she saw a woman about two blocks away suddenly stop and look at her, and then begin running toward her. She soon recognized Annie, who ran and threw her arms about her neck, and said, "How does it come that you are here? Are you attending the convention? How did it happen that I have not found you before? The fact is," she laughed, "we have been so busy that I have not even been to the convention. I have not read the papers, and I did not know that you were to be here."

She told her about the success of her candy shop, and invited her to the cottage, where she and Will and a beautiful baby boy were happy in their love for each other and their work for God. And Mrs. Henry thanked God for the work He had given her to do.

Chapter Twenty-five

OLD MAG

Yes, Annie made things unnecessarily hard for herself by her extreme sense of guilt, which was altogether natural considering the prevailing attitude of harshness of the righteous toward the guilty in those days. The pendulum had not yet swung from the intolerance and severity dealt out to offenders of Annie's class to the nonchalance and indifference with which moral lapses are treated today. Society sat in judgment upon those who made the slightest deviation from the path of rectitude, and the more sanctimonious drew back from brushing garments with those who bore the slightest tarnish on their respectability. A young woman's good name could be smirched by even the acquaintance of some less-proper girlfriend, and there was always Dame Grundy to circulate stories and spread scandal. This social attitude was responsible for many an outcast who might have been held to a useful and happy life if there had been sympathy and understanding in times of stress and temptation. Sarepta Henry was far ahead of the Victorian age in which she lived. The girl who would not wear hoop skirts when all her companions wore theirs distended like balloons, or who would not participate in harmless flirtations at the boarding school, was not likely to be swayed by the changing tides of public opinion. Her progressive attitudes had not been molded by the sentimentalism of contemporary novels or by the artificial standards of a society that put an exaggerated emphasis on the appearance of morality. In contrast to the false modesty and prudery of the age, she believed in frankness and honesty in matters of sex; and true kindness and graciousness in social relations instead of blind adherence to the formality of manners. Two of her books, *Studies in Home and Child Life* and *Good Form and Christian Ethics*, show that her thinking on parental responsibility and the conduct of life was far ahead of her Victorian contemporaries.

Probably one of the reasons for her success in reaching so many of the apparent untouchables was her abandonment of the Victorian smugness and the friendly rapport that was quickly established between speaker and audience. She was convincing in her down-to-your-level manner because she was genuine. It is not enough to tell about the love of Christ. People want to have a living sample, and Mrs. Henry was a true exemplar of the gospel she preached.

She treated each individual as though he or she was a real person for whom not only Christ but she herself had a great deal of interest. Each person she encountered whose heart was opened to her was a potential full-length book. Many of these stories did appear in the books she was writing for young people, published by the Methodist Book Concern and the National Temperance Society. *The Voice of the Home, Mabel's Work, One More Chance, Beforehand, Afterward*, were stories of real people whose problems and victories became an inspiration to a wide circle of readers.

Mrs. Henry frequently returned year after year to places where she had conducted institutes and evangelistic services. For eight consecutive years she was called to Manistee, Michigan, where she spent a period of from two weeks to two months in the spring, when the woodmen would come down from the lumber region to spend the money they had earned in the winter camps.

The work was successful and gratifying from all calculable means of estimation. A large number were enrolled year by year for Bible study, pledges were signed, and a new building, Union Hall, was erected from the contributions of the people. But on her third visit

Mrs. Henry began to realize that somehow the effect was being nullified by some strong influence she could not perceive. Many men who earnestly began a new life during the annual meetings did not seem to maintain the experience through the year, and repeatedly fell into their former habits of vice.

Gradually Mrs. Henry put together bits of information fallen from the tongues of young men whom she visited, and guessed that the key to the puzzle did not lie in the saloon, as she had thought. "If it weren't for Old Mag . . ." some burly, rough-handed lumberjack would admit ruefully. Again and again the same name was mentioned, and the vision conjured up in the woman's mind was that of an old hag of evil countenance and ill-begotten figure, a veritable witch of Endor, who could by her necromancy weave a spell about the feet of these men, and take them away from their best efforts until hope and desire for right were gone.

"Have you ever made any attempts to restore Old Mag?" she questioned one of the leading women of the union.

"No!" the answer came from prim, pursed lips. "I think if you should see her once you would never ask that question."

The following year, when again the men mumbled of Old Mag, Mrs. Henry felt strongly that she should make an effort to see her.

She spoke of it frequently to her associates, but was silenced by their positive disapproval. The case was hopeless, they said, and interference would only involve them in trouble. Mrs. Henry's stay in Manistee was very brief that year, and she had to leave before she was able to carry out her resolve. Many times during her absence she regretted the neglect, and returned the following year with the thought foremost in her mind to ferret out this matter.

She hadn't removed her cloak and bonnet at the home of Mrs. R., the union president, who always entertained her, before she said, "I am going to find Old Mag."

Mrs. R. said, "I've heard that Old Mag has been very ill for a long time. Her evil ways have finally brought down her own punishment, and they say she is dying."

"I must go to see her without delay." Mrs. Henry was immediately concerned. "I am so sorry that I have not insisted upon this before."

"Yes," the other admitted slowly, "since I knew she was ill I have often thought that someone should visit her, but the house where she is staying is in such a disreputable part of town, I've been afraid to go over there."

"I am confident that God will take care of us, and I feel that I must go."

"You must not go alone," Mrs. R. said. "I do not know if my husband will consent that I should go, but we will pray about it."

That evening Mrs. Henry brought up the subject at the dinner table and told her host that she would consider herself unworthy of the great truth that had been given her if she made no effort to find and save this woman.

"I am willing to go alone," she assured him.

After considerable reflection and pacing around alone in his studio, Mr. R. decided it would not look well for Mrs. Henry to go alone, and stated that it was only right that his wife should accompany her. Her official position and social standing would be a protection to both of them. Hence he ordered the family carriage made ready for their use.

They drove through the worst quarters of the village, a ragtail of shacks on the edge of town. They were directed to a house next to a saloon, back in a field toward the woods. The women left the carriage and picked their way across the uneven ground.

A large slatternly woman answered their knock at the door.

"Mag?" she said, looking them over suspiciously. "Around there," she said, pointing to a small annex at the rear of the house.

Again they knocked, and were admitted by a tall country-woman with a kindly face.

The bed took up most of the space in that bare and tiny room, and the eyes of the visitors went at once to the face upon the pillow. Rarely had they seen a face of such surprising young beauty, although bearing the marks of serious illness. A mass of dark, curly hair was spread out against the whiteness of the linen, and the dark eyes stared questioningly from one to the other as the women entered the room. They came to rest on the white ribbons, and a strange light came into them as she understood from this symbol the purpose of the visit.

Standing beside the bed, Mrs. R. spoke first, "This is Mrs. Henry, who is doing a good work in our city, and hearing that you were sick, insisted upon coming to see you; and so I have brought her with me. I have wanted to come myself many times, but have not been able to do so until now."

Mrs. Henry picked up the white, frail hand lying on the thread-bare coverlet, and returning the steady gaze, seated herself beside the girl. After a moment the girl spoke, "What made you come?"

"Because I knew you needed me, or rather that you needed to hear what I have to say to you. I bring you good news."

"Good news!" she repeated, unbelieving.

"Yes," Mrs. Henry said cheerfully, "good news."

A little color came into the pale face, and the eyes again moved from one face to the other wonderingly.

"I bring you good news from a far country," Mrs. Henry explained, "from a dear Friend who loves you." She paused for a moment. "And this is the news I bring: 'For God so loved the world, that he gave his only begotten Son, that whosoever believeth in him should not perish, but have everlasting life.' 'This is a faithful saying, and worthy of all acceptation, that Christ came into the world to save sinners; of whom I am chief.' 'Come now, and let us reason together, said the Lord: though your sins be as scarlet, they shall be as white as snow; though they be red like crimson, they shall be as wool.' 'Whosoever . . .'"

The girl made an impatient gesture with her hand, "Oh, stop. That is not for me!"

"Yes, it is for you, every word of it."

"No, no, not for me," she said with more sadness than defiance. "I lost my chance for that long ago. I know what it all means. I heard all these things years ago."

"Where did you hear them?" Mrs. Henry's voice dropped very low.

"Oh, I heard them at home."

"At home! Where was your home? Who were your father and mother?"

It was a long time before the girl answered. She closed her eyes and lay as if asleep, with hardly a sign of the emotions that were stirring within her. Then she looked up at Mrs. Henry as if trying to find some trace of hypocrisy or condescension. What she saw must have satisfied her, for she said: "I will tell you the saddest story you have ever heard. My father is a minister in the city of _____ , a Presbyterian minister. My mother is one of the sweetest of Christian women. She never had any fault but one, that I can remember, and that was that she loved and trusted me, her only child, as I did not deserve to be trusted.

"As we were in a wealthy church, and lived among wealthy people, she wanted me to have every advantage, and thought it would be to my advantage to marry a wealthy man; and so, while I was young, without much thought upon my own part, I was married to a very wealthy bachelor. I did not know at all what it was to love my husband. He petted me, made a plaything of me, gave me everything that money could buy that a child such as I could wish for. He gave me everything but the ability to love him, and that he could not give. When I had been married about a year I became acquainted with a young man whom I soon learned to love, and that was my ruin. We eloped and went to California. There he abandoned me, and I began a life of sin.

"While I was with him I was not conscious of sinning. My love for him was a pure love, as pure, I believe, as any could ever have been for any man. It was the love I should have had for my husband. But from that time on my course was downward. I went from one grade of degradation to another until I came here, an abandoned woman.

"I have known you, Mrs. Henry, ever since you began to come here with your work. I recognized you. It was not necessary for your friend to introduce you. I have seen you as you have gone to and fro about your work. I have heard of the things you have said to the men, and sometimes I have longed to have you say the same things

199

to me. And then the devil would come in, and would make me determined to destroy just as much of your work as possible.

"I had to destroy your work, because if these men became converted, and remained constant and true, what would become of me? My life was of no use among good people any longer. I must have bad people around me, or starve. So you see, you and I have been fighting each other all these years that you have been coming to Manistee.

"But now I am where I cannot fight any longer. I have got to die before long, and I must die as I have lived. I thank you for coming, but do not come anymore."

Mrs. Henry had been holding her hand during this painful recital, and sat facing her, watching her, her own heart beating so loud it shook her body. She felt that there was more that she should know, so she said softly, "Have you never heard from your father or mother? Have you never written to them? Do they know where you are?"

There was a long silence. But at length she said:

"There is another part of my story, sadder than the rest of it. I did not intend to tell you that, but I think I will tell all there is to it once. After I was abandoned, I did write to my mother. In my homesickness and distress I craved a letter from her. I felt that I must come into communication with her in some way, and with my father; but after I had written the letter I determined to conceal my whereabouts so entirely that they could not trace me. I did so. I do not know, in fact, whether they ever attempted to trace me or not. I think they would have done so if they could have found me, and taken me home. They are that kind of people. I am sure my father is, for he believes the gospel he preaches.

"But I hid myself. After I had come East, before I had got quite so low as I was when I came here, I made up my mind that I would look upon my father and mother again if possible. So I made a trip to _____ and watched for them. I haunted the vicinity of the house, but did not see either of them. I became terribly afraid that I should be discovered.

"It was Saturday, and I felt that it would not do for me to remain

200

any longer than Monday. I had looked in the church directory, and found that my father was still pastor of the same church, and I made up my mind that I would attend church on Sunday evening, wearing a veil so that I would not be recognized, and then leave town.

"Several times that Sunday I was tempted to go home and tell my story, and see if there was any salvation for me. But I was distrustful of myself, and felt that I could not survive the ordeal of seeing the sorrow and perhaps the repudiation that would come into their faces. I was not quite sure whether they would receive me. And then I remembered that if they should, it would not be possible for them to keep me and live in the same circle, and it would be necessary for my father to choose between me and his church, if I returned. Then I began to fear that my desire to be better might actually cause me to do this reckless thing, and I actually prayed that God would give me courage to stand out against the desire of my own heart, from returning to my father and mother, and to a better life.

"Wasn't that a strange thing to pray for? But I think that God understood it, and my prayer was answered, whether He did it or not, because the day passed, and the time came for the evening service, and I had my ticket bought for the train that would leave about ten.

"I came very near failing, however, in my whole plan, because as I sat in a dark corner under the gallery in the old church, with my veil drawn aside so that I could get one good look at my father as he came from the study and ascended the pulpit stairs, he came out, an old man, bowed, with his hair as white as snow. I began to tremble, and as he went up the stair to the pulpit and turned, I got a good view of his face, and almost screamed outright.

"I gave one more glance, covered my mouth with my hand, and turned and fled. I ran until I happened to think that I might be noticed by the police, and possibly arrested. I hastened at once to the depot, waited for the train, and as soon as it came in I sprang aboard, and came back to my doom."

The soft voice fell into silence as the girl sank back into the pillows with exhaustion and closed her eyes. Mrs. Henry had been holding one of her hands, and Mrs. R. the other as the tale unfolded, their hearts stirred with compassion. Now Mrs. Henry said to her:

"One thing is sure: we are not going to leave you to any doom! I believe that God has sent us here for a purpose." And she told of the many years she had thought about Mag, and how she had inquired about her the instant of her arrival, before she had removed her cloak. "I know that this all means that God wants to save you, and you can let Him do it."

But Mag shook her head feebly, whispering, "There is no salvation for me."

The women realized that the telling of the story had been a terrific drain on her strength and emotions, and that this was not the time for continued conversation. They bade her goodbye and promised to return the next day.

"I wish you would come," said Mag, "for you have done me good, and I would like to see you again. But as for trying to save me, forget about that—I know it is too late."

The following day the women returned with pillows and robes, determined to take the girl out for a little drive. With the help of the large woman who was taking care of Mag, they carefully lifted her into the carriage and tucked the robes about her. The men in the saloon came out the door and stared curiously at the strange event.

After returning to the room Mrs. Henry took her Bible in hand and without comment read some of the precious promises to the weary and sinful hearts of earth.

"Those are all familiar," Mag said. "I have heard Father preach sermons from these texts, but I would like to have you sing."

"What shall I sing?" Mrs. Henry asked.

"Oh," she said, "sing whatever comes into your mind."

Mrs. Henry sang, "There Is a Fountain Filled With Blood," and as Mag lay on the bed with her eyes closed, the first tears came and began to run down upon the pillow.

"Now I want to tell you our plan," said Mrs. Henry; "we would like to take you away from this place, and take care of you, and make you as happy and comfortable as possible. It may be that you will get well if you have proper care. One of our good sisters of the WCTU will take you into her home. This has already been arranged. Just as soon as you consent we will take you in the carriage to her home."

And so Maggie spent the last months of her life in a lovely home, surrounded with every comfort, and cared for as a sister or a daughter might have been. And there she found the Saviour and became confident of acceptance with God, and when she passed away she had the assurance of a part in the resurrection of Christ.

Chapter Twenty-six

TWENTY YEARS

Twenty years of speaking and traveling! Twenty years of riding trains and buses; of catching streetcars late at night; of strange hotels, and hard beds, and separation from her children, and living out of a suitcase. Twenty years of public presentations, sometimes daily for weeks at a time. Sometimes twice or thrice daily.

Her message, her manner, her diction were adapted to the caliber of her hearers. She was equally at ease and as effective when standing before a group of shivering half-drunk down-and-outers in a small mission hall on Main Street as she was before a large audience of 3,000 people.

On one occasion, early in her work, she spoke to the parents and teachers on the Northwestern University campus, at the invitation of Frances Willard. Many in her audience of 1,200 were distinguished in theology and philanthropy. She addressed them earnestly and eloquently without notes. Oliver Willard, the editor of the Chicago *Post*, described this address as "one of the most beautiful pieces of word painting" to which he had ever listened, supposed that "Mrs. Henry must have spent a great deal of time on it, and used it often very effectively."

As a matter of fact, the message that she presented on this occasion was almost impromptu. She had arrived at the university on Saturday night, after six hours of traveling, and was very weary and tired. She had brought along the manuscript of a number of different talks and lectures, but as she realized the nature of her audience, felt that not one was suitable. Weary and tired, she felt overwhelmed with the situation. In her diary she tells of her dilemma:

"In the morning I began to think of the situation and realized that I could not break the Sabbath. I had never in my life done any work which could be called a violation of Sabbathkeeping, and I certainly could not begin now. I felt myself entirely dependent upon the inspiration from God to meet this emergency, and I could not begin by breaking what I believed to be His law. . . .

"So I went to church with Miss Willard in the morning, remaining until after the short session of Sunday school, and returning just in time for dinner. There would be only a very short time between the hour of dinner and the time of the gathering for the afternoon mass meeting. After we had seated ourselves at the table the burden of the whole situation came upon me with crushing force. I felt heartsick, unable to remain."

She asked Miss Willard to excuse her and went to her room, and as had been her lifelong habit when any burden came upon her heavily, threw herself upon the floor and prayed. When Miss Willard came for her to go to church, she rose and went without fear. Out of the storehouse of her mind she was able to bring forth "treasures new and old" for the inspiration of her hearers. From that time on, she never used notes on the platform.

Twenty years of speaking tours, institutes, chautauquas, and camp meetings! In between the trips to points in distant states, to the west, the south, the east, and the north, she spent periods of time in the slums of Chicago, working all day among the poor and sick, bringing physical and spiritual comfort.

And what of her family—of Mary and Alfred and Arthur—what were they doing all these years, and how were they faring?

Mrs. Henry had always been thankful that she had not yielded to the demands of well-meaning friends, early in her widowhood, that she give up her children to other homes. Her stubbornness on this point had almost caused a rift between her and her brother Hylas, who was at that time United States consul in Dresden. He had no patience or sympathy with what he considered a "wild attempt" on her part to be independent. He demanded that she divide up the children with James Henry's relatives in East Homer. Other friends and relatives had been equally positive that she would not be able to provide for them.

The matter had been decided in her mind, as all the problems of life had been, by prayer and the opening providences of God. In spite of all the good reasons suggested by others that it would be better to break up her home, she was convinced, after careful thought and prayer, that it was not God's will. But she could not make the others see it, and they were practically taking the decision and the children out of her hands. Alfred Hart, who through the years took upon himself the responsibilities of a self-appointed guardian, had gone so far as to make most of the arrangements, and upon a certain day had persuaded Mrs. Henry to go with him to meet the people and settle the affair.

Upon arriving at the house, and having a few minutes to wait, Mr. Hart said, "Sara, I think I will give you your mail." He handed her three letters.

In the first was a check from Bishop Vincent. With it was a note saying he had received the money for a lecture, and was sending it to her, for he knew that she must have some extra expenses, and advised her to find some quiet little corner where she could make a home for her children, and bring them up, as only she could do.

She read the letter and passed it on to her friend.

The next envelope contained a much larger draft from Mrs. Vincent, from her home in Plainfield, New Jersey, and a note saying, "You will be making a nest for yourself and your children where you can live together, and you will need a great many things which you will not feel like buying at present with money that you have yourself earned. I send this draft that you may provide yourself with the comforts which you will need but cannot afford."

After she read this note she passed it on for the others to read, and opened a third.

This was from the Methodist Book Concern in New York, saying in substance, "We have been looking for the continuation of the work which you began at our request. We are very anxious for these books, and will make you this proposition . . ."

She passed this to Mr. Hart and the others who had now joined them. Mr. Hart began to walk rapidly up and down the room, and after a moment turned to Mrs. Henry and said, "Sara, if I had your faith, added to my physical powers, I would turn the world upside down!"

To Mrs. Henry it was a vindication of her faith that God would point the way, for with the prospect of an outlet for her writing, she felt confident that she could provide for herself and her children.

"If you will get your horse and buggy," she said to Alfred Hart, "and take me out to find a house, we shall find one that will come within my means, in which I can begin to live with my children."

"But," he protested, "we have looked everywhere."

"We have not looked today," she said with a smile.

They found a humble little cottage in Rockford, where they spent a number of happy years. There were times during the early years of her public work when she allowed the children to spend short periods of time in other homes when she was absent, but as they became older and had learned self-reliance, they maintained the home while she was away. These leave-takings were always heartbreaking for both mother and children, and the reunions correspondingly joyous and thrilling.

In spite of necessary absences of the mother from the home, this household was a well-knit unit, possessing the keenest family affection and loyalties. Each bore his or her share of the responsibilities. Sarepta's own experiences as a young housekeeper had made her resolve that her daughter should be trained in everything that a woman ought to know. Mary was the cook and housekeeper. When she was 12 she made all the bread and cakes and cookies for the family, and Alfred, 2 years younger, helped with the kneading and baking.

It was always a hardship for the mother to leave home. Many and many a time her little daughter would find her, on the evening before she was to start on some trip, sobbing and crying as if her heart would break. When asked what had happened, "Nothing, nothing," she would answer, "only I cannot bear to leave my children. I cannot bear to go away." And while she was away her thoughts were constantly reverting to her dear ones at home. She delighted to select interesting gifts or dainty tokens to take home with her on her return or send in the mail pretty mementos of her experiences. Frequent telegrams brought assurance to the children that they were not out of mind. Once during a cold snap Mary was quite indignant to receive a telegram saying, "Be sure to keep the folding doors shut." She wrote her mother immediately saying that they had not thought of warming the parlor for a week, and were trying to thaw out the Christmas turkey on the old-fashioned base burner in the sitting room.

The home in Rockford where the children grew up was simple and bare of all but the necessities of life, but they were nonetheless happy because of it. Mrs. Henry thought it was a wonderful thing that she was able to make a home for her children and to provide them with food and clothing and to send them to school.

As the years went by, however, their circumstances improved. After all the early years of struggle and work, Mrs. Henry learned to her surprise that as a soldier's widow she was entitled to a pension, which came to about $2,000 in back pay. She was as delighted as a child with a new toy to be thus enabled to buy a little cottage of her own. She cut archways, changed doors, painted and papered, built a veranda, and took infinite pleasure in fitting up this cozy little nest.

This was in Evanston, Illinois, where they lived for a number of years. The children went to preparatory school, and also attended college at Northwestern University. And so Sarepta saw fulfilled the dream she had had years before that her daughter would attend the very college where she had wished to go herself.

It was while they were living at Evanston that Mrs. Henry was connected with the South Halstead Mission in Chicago. It would take many hundreds of pages to tell the stories of all the poor people who came into the circle of her care and inspiration at this time.

Every evening, after the long day was done, Mrs. Henry took the streetcar home for the night. The mission was in a rough area, and sometimes she was forced to show the conductor that her pocket had been cut off on the way to the car, and her money stolen.

One night she came home in great suffering, complaining of a terrible illness. Somewhere in going about in the slums, she had come in contact with two dread diseases, malignant diphtheria and erysipelas, both of which made an attack upon her at the same time. Her head and face were so badly swollen with the erysipelas that her mouth could not be opened to attend to her throat. For weeks she took her nourishment through a straw. Fannie Bolton, one of Mary's school friends, came into the home to care for the invalid. Mrs. Henry's affection went out to her at once, and from then on she would have no other nurse.

No one expected that she would live, and for three weeks she existed in a strange delirious world, doing and saying strange things. But finally her extraordinary vitality, Fannie's faithful nursing, and the care of a Christian physician pulled her through.

As soon as she was able she resumed her evangelistic work, going away for short trips, but spending more time at home engaged in literary work. She wrote *The Voice of the Home* at this time, a book that was a great publishing success and popular with the public.

Those who had known the girl Sarepta were amazed at the vigor and activity of her advancing years. Was this the consumptive maiden "with one foot in the grave," this woman of indomitable spirit who could do the work of several preachers? There were some who feared she was engaging in a too-strenuous program, and thought she should be forcibly compelled to give up her public work. But no one could compel or persuade her to any course of action. She knew no voice but that of her own conviction. And although there were frequent enforced rest periods, she continued her traveling, speaking, teaching, and writing. She especially enjoyed camp meetings, because they gave her an opportunity to combine outdoor life, which she dearly loved, with religious services.

In August of 1882 she was attending the camp meeting at Lake

Bluff when she was suddenly taken ill. At home, Mary was just putting some bread in the oven when she received a telegram from Miss Willard, telling her to meet her mother at a certain train with a physician and a carriage. This time the trouble was a nervous breakdown. In half an hour Mary was on the train for Lake Bluff, where she found her mother receiving the best of care from Dr. Burret, a lady physician, and a number of kind friends.

Mrs. Henry was brought home on a cot, and it was months before she was able to sit up, and almost a year before she left the house.

It was a hard year for the little family, and the boys left school and went to work in Chicago. Alfred was messenger boy in a bank, and Arthur ran errands for the publishers, Fleming H. Revell. Mary continued in college, while superintending the housework with the help of a hired girl. The three children experienced then what most people learn later in life—the horrors of debt, sickness, bills, creditors. During the year Mrs. Henry was able to do some writing and received $300 for one of her books, which relieved the situation.

The next winter she suffered a fall from a bus, which caused a severe spinal injury, and she was very ill again, and was not expected to survive. But she prayed to God to remove her weakness and disabilities, and the next day rose from her bed and declared herself better, and set about her writing.

In the autumn of 1884 she went to Nebraska for an evangelistic tour very similar to the work she had done in Michigan. If the story of those months in Republican Valley had been written, they would have shown the power of God through her ministry as vividly as did any experience of her earlier years. Whole towns were swept of every evil resort. Hundreds of people turned from a life of sin and worldliness to become earnest followers of Christ. Here, as in every place that she visited, she formed the warmest attachments with those to whom her unselfish and devoted life had been a revelation. A few years later she returned to Nebraska and spent two years, filling engagements all through the state, going as far west as Cheyenne, Wyoming. She made her home in Bloomington, a little town of 5 or 600 inhabitants, and Mary taught in a small Methodist college, while Arthur regained his health. Alfred was beginning his work in the ministry at West Point, Nebraska.

It was during these years in Nebraska that Mrs. Henry made her first contact with a group of people whom she thought had practically ruined the work in Republican Valley "because confusion and perplexity had resulted from their teaching."

She tells of this in a little tract, published in 1897, *The Way, the Truth, and the Life*, page 13:

"During this time I twice came in conflict with those who were teaching what I believed to be error, seriously interfering with the work which I was seeking to establish. This teaching was so revolutionary and exacting, that looking upon it as I did, I could consider it in no other way than as mischievous in character. With my whole heart given to the work to which God had called me, and for which He had endowed me with peculiar strength, physically, and wonderfully helped me spiritually—absorbed, earnest, persistent, as I was—I was in a condition which made it very necessary that I should not be left to reckon Truth as error, and so take a position and begin a warfare against it.

"I had come to a place through which I was not prepared to go with safety to my own peace. I had only one criterion by which to judge these new things and those who taught them; I had but one name by which to call them. They were known as Seventh-day Adventists; I called them 'Mischief-makers.'"

But Mrs. Henry was not to come in open conflict with these strange people at this time. She was sent east to Pennsylvania, and it was 10 years before she had further contact with them.

THE NAME

"God's name is Love.
He wrote His name in stars; and from the shining throng,
And from the heavens, there rolled a swelling tide of song.
The earth, which from the Hand Divine to motion sprung,
And quivering 'mid the hosts of heaven in floods of glory hung.
Had not an eye to read the Name; for praises, had no tongue.

Whirlwind of the Lord

> "God's name is Love.
> He wrote His name again in every changing hue,
> And set it high upon the clouds, a promise great as true.
> Men saw the ensign, but forgot the wondrous name it bore;
> The earth beneath the archway swept, forgetful as before,
> And yet God kept the hues, and wrote that one name o'er and o'er.
>
> "God's name is Love.
> He wrote it yet again all o'er the meadows fair,
> In grass, and rose, and lily-bells, that man might read it there.
> His sweetest, tenderest name He beaded with the dew,
> And called the winds to publish it each breaking morn anew.
> Man saw and heard, but in his heart the Name he never knew.
>
> "God's name is Love.
> And when each chosen sign of earth, or sea, or sky
> Had been employed to fix and hold man's restless eye,
> From out His heart of love God drew a wondrous plan,
> By which to seize the wandering gaze, and touch the heart of man.
> He wrote His name in blood, on Calvary's rugged hill,
> And heaven was veiled, and all the earth with awe grew still.
> The dead stepped from their graves to see and read the wondrous sign,
> And man, with heart grown tender, owned the Signature Divine."

—MRS. S.M.I. HENRY

Part Three

TRUTH
MARCHES ON

*B*ut he knoweth the way that I take: when he hath tried me, I shall come forth as gold" (Job 23:10). "The path of the just is as the shining light, that shineth more and more unto the perfect day" (Prov. 4:18).

Chapter Twenty-seven

WHO
KNOWETH
THE WAY?

T here seem to be a chosen few in every generation who experience a special hand-in-hand
walk with God. They receive His guidance in the small as well as the
major crises of life; they are conscious of His direction at the cross-
roads; they never doubt that the complex maze of human affairs will
be disentangled by the divine hand, so that His purpose for their individual lives may be worked out. Others who struggle with problems of unanswered prayer, and who never seem to receive the
clear-cut guidance in practical problems that they ask for, are inclined to regard these simple children of faith with cynicism, doubt,
good-humored tolerance, or admiration, according to their religious
background and experience.

We know that God is no respecter of persons—can the answer
be that these favored few are respecters of God more than others?

Horatio Irish had been such a person, claiming at all times God's
personal supervision in all his affairs. And Sarepta Myrenda Irish
Henry, like her father, had taken her heavenly Father's care for her
as much for granted as the sunshine and the rain. She never could
forget how the villagers at Pecatonica had provided for their pastor
friend when illness had made it impossible for him to continue his
missionary work; nor how the almost crushing weight of difficulties

215

of her early widowhood had been lifted in answer to prayer. Money had come in the mail just when it was needed, manuscripts had been accepted, and checks from unexpected sources arrived at strategic times. Time and time again the way had been pointed by unmistakable guidance in her public service. But all these things were as nothing to the evidence of God's power in her ministry. She had seen audiences turned to live better lives by the Word she preached, and had witnessed uncounted victories in the experience of those for whom she prayed.

Such triumphs as she had had in her public work, and the success that came in her speaking, writing, and traveling might have resulted in building up spiritual arrogance. Certainly as her Bible became more and more worn and marked from her constant study and use, she did not become any less sure of her convictions and knowledge.

After her work in Nebraska, Mrs. Henry entered a period when she was forced to submit, slowly but steadily, to chronic invalidism. Her gallant spirit continued to keep her on her feet long after others would have given up. She continued her work, teaching at camp meetings, assemblies, and chautauquas, convinced that she was performing a God-given work, and so determined to resist the inclination to lighten her load. Later on, seeing this as all in the providence of God, she said:

"The strong support of the hand of God, that had so wonderfully kept me in physical strength and vigor, was removed. God did not make me ill; but he declined any longer to use his power to keep me well, as he had heretofore done in a very marked manner. He left me to shift for myself until I should learn many things I must know, and could learn only by such experiences as awaited me."[1]

After the Chautauqua Assembly in New York in 1889, where she had taken charge of the women's department, she was compelled to cancel engagements as they came due, and in January 1890 went to a sanatorium for treatment. For a time she seemed to improve, so

---

[1] *The Way, the Truth, the Life*, p. 16.

that again she returned to the field, but had to abandon it after a short time. Her illness became worse every year, with shorter periods of convalescence.

But during the winter of 1894-1895, she was so much stronger that she took charge of the Bethesda Mission on Clark Street in Chicago. She was especially effective in this type of work. There was something about her that inspired the immediate confidence of rough and suspicious men; something too that touched their hearts, made them think of their mothers, and stirred old memories and ambitions.

She knew just how to conduct a service in the slums. This was nothing that had been learned in a school of methods. It was instinctive and spontaneous. Never was it necessary to call in a policeman to restore order or remove a man who was disturbing the peace. She probably would have dismissed the policeman if he had undertaken to enter in his official capacity. It was her fixed principle that no man should be suppressed by force. No matter how drunk or quarrelsome he might be, she had the power to subdue him. The secret lay in her absolute love and respect for even the lowest human soul, partly too in her courage and faith in dealing with those who were regarded by many Christian workers as dangerous and hopeless. She respected their little idiosyncrasies, neither laughing at or chiding them. One man used to come in regularly every night, march down the aisle with a military step, halt in front of the desk, and give her a military salute, then wheel about and march down to his seat. She always took this proceeding as a matter of course, acknowledging the salute by a pleasant look or word. If any man became really excited, or undertook to quarrel with others in the audience, she would give him something to do—ask him to open a window, close the draft in the stove, or perform some similar service, thus distracting his mind. If he became incorrigible, she would announce a hymn, and they would keep on singing until he quieted down.

Mary sometimes went with her to these evening services, and she recalls one occasion:

"One bitter cold night I shall never forget. Mother always went down early, and began a song service while the men were coming in. At 6:00 a cup of tea, covered by a slice of bread, was passed to each man. If there were enough, a second cup and slice would be passed. No one ever refused this plain refreshment.

"As I watched those men that evening, it seemed impossible that some of them could drink from those rough tin cups, and devour so eagerly coarse thick bread without any butter. One man, very decently dressed, with manly and even scholarly features, attracted my attention. Surely he was not going to eat that food! But he did. He made a great effort not to appear eager, but could not conceal his famished condition.

"While the men were eating, the workers sang. At half past six my mother rose, and, in her simple, cheery way, said that she was now going to pray. She would like to have the men join her in this prayer.

"'Now,' she said, 'I want to know how many men in this room have everything in the world that you want? Please raise your hand.' This absurd idea sent a murmur of amusement through the audience. 'Now,' she said again, 'I see no hands, so I conclude that you all want something. How many of you here would like a job?'

"A score of hands went up in response to her inquiry.

"'How many of you would like to have me pray that you may get this job?'

"A few signified their interest in this. Then she went on to talk to them a moment about the promises and love of God, and then she prayed—a strong, tender, sympathetic petition for these men— these homeless, sinful, wicked, discouraged, unfortunate men—that they might find the one great Friend who could help them in their extremity, that they might give their hearts to Him, that He might give them work and food, and the comfort of His peace.

"After that they themselves were asked to speak. This was the strangest part of the service. One tall, muscular Irishman told how he had been a bar tender in a neighboring saloon. But in this mission he had given his heart to God. Two days and two nights he had walked the streets, with not a morsel of food to eat, and no place to sleep, but he would never go back and 'work for the devil'; and now Mrs. Henry had found him a job that would keep him from starving and he was the happiest man in Chicago.

"Another, a fine-looking young Scotchman, with refined, intellectual features, said that he had been a hard drinker, and had lost a good position. He had fallen very low, until at last the shame of all he had become so overwhelmed him that he had fully made up his mind to put an end to his wretched life. On his way to do the deed, with the revolver in his pocket, he had passed the door of the mission, heard familiar old hymns, stopped to listen a moment, entered, and found Jesus.

"And so it went. Wonderful testimonies were given. A few asked for prayers. Some made a beginning in a Christian life. . . .

"Not later than nine o'clock the service closed. My mother lingered to give a word of counsel here and there, and to distribute a few lodging tickets to the most needy. She never could keep more than her car fare in her pocket to take her home. Would she save money in this city of starving and shelterless people?—It would be a crime.

"The tall Irishman and the young Scotchman always accompanied her to Wabash Avenue, where she took the car, while they walked home. Several times she had her pocket picked during this short walk. But there was never anything in her purse but receipts and the five cents."[2]

During this same winter she conducted the noon meeting at Willard Hall in Chicago. One cold day as she was on her way to the temple to lead this meeting, she fell unconscious on the pavement, and was discovered a few minutes later by Mrs. Carse. She was carried into the corridor of Willard Hall, revived, and sent to her home in a carriage. She supposed that she had simply been overcome by the cold, and went about her work as usual. But in a few days she had another attack in the house, fainting away while passing from one room to another. A physician was called, who pronounced the disease "mitral insufficiency," with serious heart involvement.

Alfred was sent for, and found his mother so low that she could not speak. Mary arrived the next day, and for weeks they watched at the bedside, thinking that every night must be her last. When she

---

[2] Mary Henry Rossiter, *My Mother's Life,* pp. 289-292.

finally did rally, her physicians began to concede that she might live for several months, but certainly not more than a year.

When she had regained sufficient strength to take stock of herself, and to think things over, even Mrs. Henry had to admit to herself that she could never expect to resume her active work again. But her whole being cried out against it, and she protested, "I cannot be laid aside this way."

"Now, Mrs. Henry," said Mr. F_____ , the medical student who had occupied one of the rooms in her cottage and who had attended her with untiring devotion, "how do you know the Lord doesn't want you to keep still a while, and learn a lot of quiet graces—patience and the happy art of waiting—maybe?"

It really did seem that the Lord wanted her to keep still for a while, but why?

She could never doubt that God had blessed her in the work she had been doing for the past 20 years. He had led her, and guided her through many strange providences, and His Spirit had been poured out upon her hearers. Always He had given her physical strength to accomplish what her heart constrained her to do. Even with occasional periods of illness, she had been capable of greater physical endurance than any of those who were associated with her.

Was God asking her to spend the rest of her life in a program of invalidism, her days composed of pills and pillows, trays and treatments, crumpled sheets and crumbs in the bed? Could she harness her ambitious spirit within four walls, and leaning contentedly against the cushions let others wait upon her and push her around in a wheelchair? Her family tried to assure her that she might live a long time in this fashion, and that for their sakes she should be reconciled. But Sarepta was not reconciled, and she rebelled against what she believed to be the direct work of Satan.

There are times when it is difficult to decide whether adversities are the weapons of the devil to prevent us from accomplishing the Lord's work or are the chastening of the Lord to refine the character. Usually subsequent events remove the veil that shrouds the issue, and a work of cleansing is accomplished during the period of questioning and heart searching.

In the year that followed her heart attack Mrs. Henry gradually became weaker, and her general condition more hopeless. She was not afraid to die, but to live and be a burden of helplessness and expense she could not stand. It was a time of bitter mental conflict, because of the unshaken conviction that her work for God was not finished. Later on she was to speak of this period with confidence:

"I now stand in awe before the revelation of God's providential care over me from this point. He knew that I had, because of this, my ignorance, which counted Truth as error, come into a condition which, if allowed to develop, would . . . become a burden of untold regret. Consequently He, like the Father that He is, set to work to save me from myself. He knew that I honestly loved Him and all truth. He also knew that because of my absorption in my work, my habit of incessant activity, as well as positiveness in convictions, it would require a 'process' to bring me out of the danger into which I had fallen."[3]

_____

[3] *The Way, the Truth, the Life,* p. 15.

Chapter Twenty-eight

THE PATH
OF THE JUST

Truth that yesterday was mine
...Is vaster truth today;
Its face hath aspect more divine
...Its kingship fuller sway;
For truth must grow as ages roll,
...And God looms larger in the soul.

The invalid had looked at the quaintly lettered motto on the wall so many times that it seemed to mock her. "In quietness and confidence shall be thy strength." Confidence she had always had in abundance, but quietness was a difficult lesson to learn. Mrs. Henry was trying, however, to adjust herself to an invalid life, to be quiet enough to avoid further setbacks, and to live simply enough so that she could almost take care of herself.

She had converted one corner of her room into a cozy little kitchen, not more than six feet square, but so arranged that it was a marvel of economy in space. She had a tiny refrigerator and a little gas stove. This corner was shut off from the rest of the room by a tall Japanese screen. She had simplified her diet so that she lived almost entirely on fruit, zwieback, and nuts. She kept a few plants that

222

thrived and bloomed. She slept on a cot near the window, which she raised every night at least six inches, no matter what the mercury might be. Her room was the front parlor of the house, and more than once the landlady was called up in the dead of night by a policeman, who, seeing the window open in such inclement weather, could not possibly think of any cause but burglars. Her landlady was the same Mrs. Scribner whose business she had bought out three years before—a lovely, sincere woman, who was devotedly attached to her, and who did everything possible to add to her comfort.

The little room was a mecca for visitors—Miss Willard, Bishop Vincent, hosts of WCTU women, and many of the reformed men who treasured the memory of her influence, men and women of all classes of society who had been helped by her work.

She had bought a wheelchair, and hired a boy to take her to church every Sunday. However, she had to be very careful to avoid any unusual exertion. A little overwork or excitement would invariably bring on a period of prostration. She was never able to get up in the morning until she had taken her cup of hot water and some heart stimulant prescribed by her physician.

Underneath the apparent reconcilement to the protocol of invalidism was growing the thought that maybe her illness was owing to some nervous disorder with which her heart sympathized, instead of being organically affected. Perhaps the trouble was merely functional! If she could get some doctor to confirm it, she would not hesitate to defy it, and overcome it by sheer force of will.

She had been thinking specifically of Dr. J. H. Kellogg, whose work in connection with the Battle Creek Sanitarium was well known at that time. Mrs. Henry was also acquainted with his health reform work in connection with a sanitarium in Chicago, and with a mission not far from the Bethesda Mission. His approach to the subject of health was the same as hers to temperance: The body is the temple of the Holy Spirit, and cleanliness of body is as important as purity of heart. The follower of Christ can do no less than to offer his or her best. The conviction that she must see Dr. Kellogg deepened through the year until the summer of 1896, when it seemed best, not only to her, but to her children, for her to enter the Battle Creek Sanitarium.

On Friday afternoon, August 31, 1896, Mrs. Henry and her daughter Mary arrived at the little station in Battle Creek, where they were met by a "bright-faced young man," who stowed them away in his carriage and put the wheelchair up in front with him. Both women had been solemn on the trip, as they faced the soon-coming separation and the uncertainties of the future.

Neither of them had met Dr. Kellogg, but knew him simply as a progressive physician, a philanthropist, and a friend of the WCTU. His wife was a very prominent member. They did not know then that he was a vegetarian, or especially opposed to the use of drugs. They had heard rumors of the queer diet he advocated, and one of Mrs. Henry's roomers at the house on Vernon Street had remarked to Mary, "You may depend on it, Miss Henry, that when your mother gets to Battle Creek, they will find out that 'tisn't her heart at all that ails her, but her stomach!"

They understood vaguely that the sanitarium was a Seventh-day Adventist institution, but this fact had had no bearing on their choice, no more than if it had been a Catholic or a Jewish hospital. Now as they were on their way, Mary laughingly remarked to her mother, "You'd better watch these people; they might convert you!" She would have been dismayed had she thought the prophecy likely to come true.

However, Mrs. Henry, half laughing, half indignant, replied, "It's not likely that anyone of my age and convictions should change her views."

Mrs. Henry was a woman of very decided opinions. Her religious convictions were strongly based on the Bible, which she knew verse by verse from cover to cover. It was very true that no one would be able to convince her of anything not contained therein. Her viewpoint, by reason of her disposition, training, and work, had been largely focused on the great principles of salvation and not matters of doctrine.

Not only was Mrs. Henry a woman of strong convictions, but

she had formed the lifelong habit of obedience to the will of God, and in all her work for the salvation of others this principle had been stressed, as she had pointed the way to Christ. Another characteristic that appeared now in this crisis of her life was her disregard for conventions or customs or circumstances if they conflicted with her knowledge of right.

The next morning after their arrival at the sanitarium, Mrs. Henry was visited by "a sweet woman physician," Dr. Lauretta Kress, who arranged for a nurse to give her some treatment. Dr. Kress took Mary through the treatment rooms, which were not in operation, "it being the Sabbath," and explained some of the special treatments that would be used in the care of the patient and assured the anxious girl that her mother would be tenderly cared for.

During rest hour Mary took her mother in her wheelchair out to the veranda. Mrs. Henry's keen eyes had already made note of a special atmosphere that seemed to pervade the place.

"You know," she said, "I think this is going to be a delightful place. Everything is so restful, and I really begin to feel the Sabbath atmosphere. Of course, I shall not think of doing anything to infringe upon the Sabbath of these people. I can keep my own and theirs too."

A few days after her arrival Dr. Kellogg came to see her. She was still too weak to undergo a thorough examination, or even engage in conversation except for a few words. She could sit up for only brief periods, and walk but a very few steps. Dr. Kellogg could not answer her yet as to whether her trouble was organic or functional, but he cheered her slightly by saying, "I think you will grow stronger."

And he dispensed with all the drugs she had been taking to stimulate her heart, and ordered methods of hydrotherapy instead.

"The first result," she said, "was that I dropped into a very low condition of strength, but under the treatments I did begin to improve in health. The superiority of natural methods of treating disease over the ordinary process of medication was fully demonstrated in my case during the first six weeks, at the end of which time I had a thorough examination by Dr. Kellogg."

The result was a great disappointment, since he confirmed the diagnosis of her Chicago physicians, that she had what appeared to be an incurable organic heart condition. Mrs. Henry felt then that the last hope of taking up her work must be abandoned.

In spite of this great disappointment, she was so interested in her new surroundings that she found herself inevitably adopting a cheerful and happy attitude. Life had always been a great adventure, people and their problems had always fascinated her, and now she was about to embark on the greatest adventure of all. She tells of it in the following:

"I had from the first greatly enjoyed the spiritual atmosphere of this place. I had been so long shut away from all but the most quiet worship, that the services to which I was taken in my chair were a feast to my soul. I especially appreciated the Bible studies, which were in a peculiar way adapted to those who were in need of consolation. Nothing in conversation or teaching could by any candid mind be considered aggressively doctrinal; to brand it as proselyting would be to reveal the existence of a very sensitive theological nerve. The 'peculiar views' of this people were never thrust into notice. . . . Of course the Sabbath is kept, and in such a manner as to commend it to, and command the respect of, the most unbelieving who are honest. The *prejudiced* mind, of course, respects nothing.

"Under these circumstances I settled down into a very restful and happy life. I seemed to grow away from the burden and anxiety of the past years, although the question of why I had been so laid aside was still unsolved. I determined, however, that I would no longer be made unhappy by these perplexities. I would accept the inevitable, and leave everything with my Heavenly Father to adjust.

"Among the guests at the sanitarium were many congenial spirits—WCTU women, Christian men and women of different denominations—with whom I had delightful association. A little company of these women very frequently gathered in my room in the evening. I was unable to talk much; but I enjoyed them as they would sit around on my bed, recounting experiences in various lines of Christian work.

"Such was my life at the sanitarium until about the middle of

November, when, one evening some of these friends came into my room to ask me that memorable question as to the authority upon which the observance of Sunday rested. . . .

"They represented a number of different denominations— Methodist, Congregational, Presbyterian—and they had become stirred up on the subject, not by reading or interference, but from the Sabbathkeeping of the institution.

"They came to me as a Bible teacher, because they thought I could help them out in their difficulty. I supposed that I could do so very easily; but when I began to state the reasons as I knew them, I was chagrined to find how they fell flat from my lips, like the words of men. I was simply giving secondhand tradition, and felt how unsatisfactory it was to myself, and began to cast about for something from the Bible.

"My memory immediately seized upon the New Testament's statements concerning the Sabbath and the first day of the week. The history as given in the Gospels and in the Acts flashed upon me. The statement of Christ concerning those who should 'break one of these least commandments,' and 'teach men so,' came to my mind. This transpired in a process so rapid that no one could have noticed or understood what was passing in my thoughts. But the result was to make me hesitate in what was evidently a matter of awakened conviction. I would become conscience for no one.

"Those who had come to talk with me were old enough and intelligent enough to study for themselves, and take their own share of responsibility. I felt that I must decline to answer. In fact, I found that I had no answer to give.

"When they were gone and I was alone, I thought, 'What if these had been converted under your own work? Suppose they were your own children for whom you are responsible? What would you say to them?'

"I determined that since I had nothing to say, I would go through the Scriptures which touch this subject until I should find a reply. I never thought of going out of God's Word for such a reply. Accordingly, the next day, as soon as I was at liberty, I took my old

Bible and began to read the first passages in Genesis. But my strength was small, my Bible was heavy, and I soon found it was too wearisome to search the Scriptures.

"Besides, the thought kept coming, 'Why search and labor for what you already have?' I knew what the Word said already. I looked at my Bible, which is worn to rags, as it lay beside me, and it answered me with reproach. It shows all through the marks of long use. I could not disguise from myself the fact that I had a hoard of hidden truth laid away, and I felt a sudden sense of responsibility not unmingled with humiliation. I wondered that I could have been so slow to understand.

"The next morning as I met the chaplain, I said to him, 'Why do you not have both sides of the Sabbath question here in some convenient form for us to read? People have come to me who want to know about it, and I would like to read it myself. I certainly think you ought to give us both sides.'

"'I don't know but what that would be a good thing,' he agreed.

"The next morning he brought me what he described as both sides of the question, in a pamphlet which he was sure would meet my want. I took the book eagerly, thinking that I would read and circulate it. But when I came to look it through I discovered it was purely controversial. I have always looked upon religious controversy as vicious. Candid discussion I consider legitimate, but for controversy I have no use. I am, in fact, afraid of it, for it always arouses in me a spirit which does not conduce to enlightenment. I laid the book down with the keenest disappointment for myself and those to whom I had thought to pass it on.

"While I was lying on my couch under the shadow of this disappointment, a friend of past years—herself an Adventist—came in. I told her of this, which had become a real annoyance, vexing me greatly. She took the book, and said, 'If you are interested in this subject, what you want is a history of the Sabbath.'

"'Certainly,' I replied, 'that will be the book for me. Take this one away. Tell the chaplain I want nothing controversial.'

"I did not see her for days. I waited with considerable interest and no little wonder. Once or twice the thought occurred, 'These people are very slow to furnish one with anything to read.' My mind was not idle, however. Never before had I been left with a question to dispose of out of which I could get no satisfaction for myself or anyone else.

"I have always believed Satan to be a real being, and know well enough that he was busy with me during those days.

"'It is very foolish to give this subject any thought. When you leave here, you will not know which day to keep. You can't go on keeping the seventh day and Sunday always. . . . You are wasting spiritual strength that you need for other things. . . . If you were convinced that the seventh day is the Sabbath, you would not be able to keep it, associated as you are.'

"Such were some of the vexing thoughts that came to me during those days, and which I constantly thrust aside as utterly unworthy; I had recognized their source.

"One morning after worship, I again met the chaplain, and said to him, 'I am having a very hard time to get hold of anything to read on this Sabbath question.'

"'Did you not get the book I sent you, the *History of the Sabbath?*' he asked.

"'I have not had anything but that *Great Controversy*, which I returned.'

"'Well,' he said, 'I will get you another copy.'

"This he fetched from his office—a large volume, which was almost more than I could take from his hand. Evidently literature on this subject was not intended for invalids! I said to myself it would be impossible for me even to make a beginning of this book. I could not get into any position where I could hold it long enough to read a full page.

"While I was lying with the book beside me, discouraged by my efforts to use it, the same friend to whom I have referred came in with a duplicate copy under her arm, and a handful of leaflets.

"She said, 'I have brought you this volume, *History of the Sabbath*, but I know it is too heavy so I have also brought these leaflets. They

contain the gist of the matter, mostly the Scriptures. If you are interested to look them through, they will be easy to handle.' I thanked
her, laid them aside, and we talked of other and lighter matters.

"That evening, when I was alone and quiet in my room, I concluded to begin to read these leaflets. I took up one which seemed to
be a compilation of excerpts from the Fathers; then another which
contained simply the Bible references to the Sabbath and the first day
of the week, in the order in which they appear in the Scriptures, without comment. This I studied for some time, while the same conviction
recurred as when I first began to look up the passages in my Bible, that
I was simply walking over familiar ground, with no purpose whatever,
unless it were to gain time before taking the final step, which would
lead me out of the old into the unknown and unexpected.

"I laid the leaflet down, and turned the scriptures over in my
mind. One after another there came to me statements in the New
Testament, the old, sweet beautiful words which, precious as they
were in themselves, must necessarily fall under criticism if they were
compelled to stand as sponsors for a Sunday sabbath.

"The necessary attitude of the apostles toward the Sabbath and
the first day of the week came plainly to my mind. Considering that
John, the latest of the apostolic historians, wrote about forty years
after the ascension of Christ, and that he made a very clear distinction between the Sabbath and the first day of the week, I could not
but see that he, as well as his yoke fellows in the gospel, must have
kept the seventh day as the Sabbath, according to the law which
Christ came, not to abrogate, but to fulfill.

"Further, considering the bitterness with which Jews persecuted
every infringement of the traditions which among them passed for
law, certainly, if the followers of the hated Jesus had tried to create
another Sabbath, it would have been a cause of accusation, and they
would have brought as much force as they could control to bear
against it. Things must have happened which would have been
recorded in the Acts of the Apostles, the Epistles, and the histories
of those days. Such an innovation could not have been passed over
in utter silence.

"I had supposed all my life that the Sabbath day had been changed from the seventh to the first day of the week by divine authority. I remembered, however, that in a pastoral letter issued by some of the fathers of my own church a number of years ago, the statement was made that the 'Sabbath as given through Moses on Sinai had never been abrogated.' Why, then, have we not kept it all the time? was the query which startled me.

"Then began a mental search for such fragments of church history as I might be able to rake out of the dust of memory. I saw that we had been led on by the same power which first changed the day away back in early times, that the responsible agents had gone to their account, leaving to innocent generations a legacy of error, which God had evidently condoned because of honest service and true love which had been given, in place of actual obedience to the law which had been covered from their eyes; but that in some way I did not understand, the vision of this later generation had been opened to recognize the long-neglected commandment, so that these modern 'fathers' had been compelled in honor toward God and the church to declare the fact that the 'Sabbath as given through Moses on Sinai had never been abrogated.' The more I thought, the more I became convinced that they were right!

"The thought came that if the Sabbath day had been changed, it was a great misfortune. I could not believe that if Christ had done it, it would have been passed over in silence; and I knew that if He did not, no apostle or any other man had authority to do it.

"As I sat in my wheelchair, with my eyes closed, looking deeper into the Bible than I could have done with it open before me, there came again and again suggestions which I knew were not from the Spirit of truth—of such nature that I became thoroughly aroused to the fact that I had entered an almost mortal conflict.

"'You will never decide in favor of the seventh day. You will never do it. You could not stand to this position if you were to take it. If your soul's salvation depends upon this, then your soul is lost.' These were some of the suggestions. Immediately I said, 'My soul is not lost! It is in God's keeping. I will do what He makes clear to me as right.'

231

"I never before came face to face with a more solemn moment than that which followed this mental declaration. I had nothing to help me. I seemed utterly alone. But my faith in God held me steady. I lifted my soul in prayer, and laid the case before Him. I said: 'You know, my heavenly Father, all about this matter. You know me and mine, the truth, and all the difficulties. Now help me to see clearly. I will decide this question here and now. It must be decided now and forever.'

"Those who have passed through any similar experience will not be surprised that I received a direct answer to my prayer in an illumination on the Word of God, which made decision easy, especially since long ago I had formed the habit of obedience to recognized truth or duty. This experience was more like that through which I passed when I was called into the temperance work in 1874, than anything else which has ever come to me. I said, in reply to the light which shone upon me, 'That settles the question forever. From this time I keep the Sabbath, the Lord's own day, which He appointed from the beginning.'

"I had no sooner decided than the real conflict began. Up to this time all temptation had been of a quiet nature—simply suggestions which were easily put aside. But now began a genuine battle with harassing suggestions of difficulties—petty, small, mean difficulties—which like the prick of a thistle in the hands of a mischievous tormentor, had in them a vast resource of annoyance."

Mrs. Henry saw that she would have a wakeful night, and determined that the way to end the conflict was to express her decision to someone else, thus making retreat impossible. She rang for a callboy and requested Dr. Kress to come to her. A great affection had grown up between the two women, as of a mother and daughter, but not a word had been spoken between them upon this subject.

Dr. Kress entered the room and sat by the invalid's bed. It was much more difficult to speak than Mrs. Henry had anticipated, and for a long time it seemed that her tongue was tied. Dr. Kress waited in silence, sensing that her patient had something important to communicate but was unable to speak.

Shall I tell her now? There is still time to retreat. I could keep it to myself; quietly observe the Sabbath, and Sunday, and say nothing to anyone, and so avoid a great deal of trouble. Why should I, in my shut-in life, be compelled to make so great a change as this involves? So Sarepta reasoned within herself.

But the answer from her own soul was inevitable and could not be reasoned away:

"God has accepted Sunday service all my life, because it was honest. He would never do that again. I had suddenly come into knowledge which would have compelled me to keep the seventh day as the Sabbath whether it had ever been so kept by any Christian or not, if I would be at peace with God. He and I had lived together so long I could not endure a separation now. Cost what it would, I would speak—and I did."

She describes the inspiration that came to her in this new experience in the following words:

"It seemed that a high wall which had bounded my horizon on one side of my life way, but of which I had had no knowledge, had suddenly been opened by the swinging of a wide gate, and I saw through into a vast field of beauty and delights, of the existence of which I had never dreamed, but for which my soul was unconsciously hungry. I not only *saw* but *entered*, and am enriched as I had never hoped to be, because I did not know enough to have such hope. I thought I knew my Bible, but I find so much now to learn that I am as eager for years in which to study it as though I had only just begun." [1]

Mrs. Henry had thought that the remainder of her life must be endured as patiently as possible, and was trying to be reconciled and happy under great difficulties. But now she felt that life had become so large and full and opulent that difficulties did not count.

She understood now why she had been shut out from her work, and shut in alone with God and her own soul. Although she realized a great change in all her future relations with her work and friends, she accepted the Sabbath with all that it involved.

---

[1] *How the Sabbath Came to Me*, p. 29.

She said:

"At first I had no thought of changing my church relations; but I could not occupy equivocal ground, and when I saw the inconsistency of continuing in a church which regarded Sunday as the Sabbath, after I had found that it was no more sacred than any other day, I could do no other than to sever the old relations, and unite with the people who were walking in what I had discovered as truth. It was not easy; the ties which bound me to the associations formed in my earliest childhood were very strong. Everything connected with my work seemed to appeal to me to refrain from taking this step. Yet I knew that it was the only right course for me, difficult as it was made to appear. There was one obstacle in my way which for a time seemed insurmountable; I had been baptized in infancy; I could not but believe it to have been a valid baptism; yet if I made this change, I must be immersed. If I could have quietly passed in the letter which I received from my old church, nothing else being required, I could have seen my way clear at once. . . .

"My father had taught me, . . . from my earliest recollection, of the significance of my baptism, . . . [when] he and my mother had solemnly consecrated me to God. . . . At an early age I solemnly ratified this baptismal covenant; and later, . . . the ties with which it bound me to the church, had held me during a short but perilous period; and how could I now renounce it, since God had certainly seen fit to use it?"[2]

Although baptism by immersion meant nothing to Mrs. Henry at that time, except the door into the church of which she desired to be a part, so great was her love and admiration for the people "among whom Jehovah had planted His standard for this latter day rally," and so great the respect and confidence she had gained for them as she had studied them and their methods in church councils, as well as in their daily service, that she felt willing to go through any ceremonial that they used, if she might come in and be one of them. Accordingly, all plans were made for her baptism.

---

[2] *The Way, the Truth, the Life*, pp. 29, 30.

The evening before the rite was to be administered, she went over the subject in her Bible, and especially read and studied the sixth chapter of Romans. For the first time the reason for the ordinance unfolded to her searching mind with such clarity that she wondered that she had never seen it before. She felt better prepared to take the solemn step.

But the next morning, during the sermon by G. A. Irwin, then president of the General Conference, more doubts and misgivings arose in her mind. What if someone should consider her receiving this ordinance as a repudiation of her former life and experience? As it seemed to her:

"It would be a denial of Christ, who had been so much in my life. In him I had been dead to the world for years. I could not even be 'coming out of Babylon,' as some of my correspondents had intimated, for I had never lived in Babylon. I had been a member of the body of Christ, that invisible church of which he is the Head, and whose members are found in every denomination as well as outside of any. I had been fighting the devil in my own heart and in the world for years. One might as well expect the Armenians to renounce the Turks, as for me to 'renounce the devil and all his works,' as it is expressed in the baptismal covenant, to which I had been accustomed. Then what could this baptism mean, more than simply an open door to me?

"Burdened with this query, perplexed, struggling against many tormenting questions, and in utter gloom, I stood at last upon the verge of the pool, waiting to take the final step; and then suddenly the light of God burst upon the darkness. I saw the rite as it is, and Christ himself in it. That pool was a grave, and he almost a tangible presence was going with me to this burial. This truth was as new to me in its application and my appreciation of it as the Sabbath had been. I was overwhelmed by it, so that I forgot everything else. This was the most solemn moment of my life. I went down into that sepulcher, fully conscious of what it meant to be buried with Christ. I had been dead to the world; it was time that I was buried! And in that burial I received a manifestation of God for which I praise him

235

with my whole being, and which was, I believe the beginning of healing to my whole body. I arose from it filled with a resurrection light; and the only adequate utterance of my soul would have been, 'O death, where is thy sting? O grave, where is thy victory?' "[3]

[3] *Ibid.,* pp. 36, 37.

THE SABBATH

"When the busy work of the week was done,
  With the last faint glow of the setting sun,
  The Sabbath stole softly into my room,
  Her garment sweet with a strange perfume.

"'Twas the breath of Eden, before a leaf
  Had fallen to hint that life was brief—
  Before the dews of that garden fair
  Had woven a cloud for the light to wear.

"In changeless calm on her quiet breast
  Was folded Jehovah's perfect rest;
  And her hands were filled with gifts, to prove
  The truth of that Prince whose name is Love.

"A sweet old charm about her clung,
  Of the time when the days of earth were young,
  Before their shadows had dreamed of fears
  Or ever their nights were wet with tears.

"A something prophetic was in her face;
  And my chamber became a holy place
  As she opened to me an ancient book,
  And a wondrous truth from its casket took:

"A Word, *with whose entering cometh light,*
And a faith that far transcendeth sight—
The answering of a thousand prayers,
And the peaceful ending to strifes and cares.

"Blest day of days! thy deepest shades
Are shot with a light that never fades;
Thou holdest in every briefest hour
The hiding of Great Jehovah's power.

"And to thee is given the golden key
That unlocks the secret of things to be,
That keepeth the wealth of the ages sure
For the children of light—the loving and pure."

—MRS. S.M.I. HENRY
(Sanitarium, Battle Creek, Dec. 18, 1896)

Chapter Twenty-nine

THE SHINING LIGHT

*M*rs. Henry was certain that she felt a definite increase in strength after her baptism. That flash of insight that had come to her as she entered the pool was so wonderful and illuminating that she felt a moral responsibility to share it with others, especially those who were present at the service. She knew that there were many who wondered by what strange reasoning she had thought that such a ceremony was necessary for one who had been preaching the gospel for 30 years. It was only right that they should know. She was sure that God would give her the strength to speak.

She told the chaplain her desire, and he arranged for her to speak to the patients and sanitarium staff on Sabbath morning. She had privately determined to stand while she spoke, but after informing Dr. Kress of her intention was persuaded to remain in her chair. Every day a new enthusiasm for living filled her with ambition and courage far ahead of her bodily resources, and led her to renewed efforts to demonstrate progress toward recovery. It was still impossible for her to lift her left arm for dressing her hair, on account of a partial stroke of paralysis suffered in 1895. When she awoke in the morning she was so prostrated that it was almost more than she could do to press the button of the electric bell that was laid in her hand. At an early hour a nurse arrived to prepare her for breakfast and morning worship. A few times she had attempted to leave her chair in the corridor and sit in a dining chair during the meal, but this had never been successful. The left side was so weak from this partial paralysis that she could not sit without support of the chair arm.

All efforts to exercise in any way, even to speak, were greatly curtailed by the peculiar and unpredictable leaps and starts of her heart. Even when lying quietly in her bed, Mrs. Henry was never free from that constant threatening murmur. But in spite of all these discouraging factors, she could not quite quell that feeling of new life.

And when, as occasionally happened, other patients came to her to ask her to pray for their recovery, she began to be ashamed of her wheelchair. She began to walk a little. She would push her chair before her a short distance until the short breathing made it necessary to stop and rest.

A week after her baptism her mental exuberance surmounted her own good judgment and the cautions of her doctor, and without asking Dr. Kress's permission, and contrary to the remonstrance of her nurse, Mrs. Henry walked in to her breakfast in the dining room and took a seat at the table. Very soon, however, she became so weak, prostrate in fact, that she had to be taken to her room and put to bed. She was much discouraged and filled with the same old unrest and depression from which she had suffered so long. She wouldn't send for Dr. Kress, because she knew she had brought it all on herself, so grimly forced herself to take the consequences.

On Monday when Dr. Kress called, it was with a sense of relief that she told her what she had done and with what unfortunate aftereffects.

"Don't you realize," the young doctor said reprovingly, "that you must not overdo? Your heart is just a worn-out leaky old pump, and when you exert yourself beyond a minimum you become cold and weak." She recalled the experiences of the previous winter, when Mrs. Henry had been so greatly helped and blessed physically, and told her that she should be satisfied and contented.

"You can do a great deal in your chair. Your condition is such

239

that it would be an absolute miracle for you to be healed. God can do it, but He only."

"Perhaps if I had faith that God would heal me—"

"There is a point where faith may become presumption," Dr. Kress reminded her, "and you want to avoid that. So much has already been done for you, and you can do so much good work just as you are, that I would advise you to be quiet and contented, without making any further efforts to walk."

Quietly convinced, Mrs. Henry promised that she would make no more attempts, but would settle down to live quietly in her chair, and cause no further anxiety if she could avoid it.

She tells of her own experience:

"After she had left me, I sat and thought the situation over prayerfully, and concluded that nothing was left for me but to think no more about it; to forget myself and my chair, and remember only the exceeding mercy of my Heavenly Father. The fact that He had so remarkably made use of the opportunity which my illness afforded, to bring me into the light of this blessed truth, had given a sacred significance to all those shut-in years which sanctified them; and since it was the removal of His hand of power that had lost me my physical strength, I must certainly be willing, if I trusted His love, to wait until He should choose to lift me up; and if He should not ever choose to do this, one thing comforted me: The responsibility of strength was no longer mine, but His; I was free. It was only mine to lie still, be glad in Him, and shine my little space full of His reflecting light. . . .

"On Tuesday morning a young friend came to say that her case had been pronounced incurable by her physicians. She said, 'I have tried faithfully everything that has been prescribed for me. I have been honest in my use of all, and nothing remains for me but to try the prayer of faith. I have been thinking of this for a good while, and have decided that it is the thing to do. There is to be a service of prayer for me in the chapel this evening. Will you come and pray for me?' The thought flashed into my mind, How inconsistent! But I immediately repelled it, saying to myself, It is not inconsistent; I am

240

doing the very best I can do, and that is always consistent. So I promised, and at the appointed time was taken to the chapel. Several of the physicians and the elders of the church, with another patient besides my young friend and myself, were present. The scripture was read, and the instructions given by James for the healing of the sick were observed, and prayer offered. I did not feel like voicing a prayer; my heart was almost too heavy. After several had prayed, I bethought me of my promise, and at once began to pray for my young friend. Almost immediately the suggestion was forced into my mind that it was my privilege to pray for myself. In all the prayers I had not been mentioned. I was not there to be prayed for. I was there as one of the helpers. I realized how peculiar was my position—neither a subject of prayer, nor apparently in a condition which made it seem consistent that I pray for others. But I had been assured that it was my privilege to pray for myself. . . .

"What should I pray for? I had given up asking to be healed. However, I began, but instead of prayer, it was only earnest questioning of the Lord. Could it be possible? Was it according to his word, or was it presumption for me to think of being healed? This was my burden.

"As soon as I began my questioning, the others began earnestly to plead my case before the Lord. I have an indistinct remembrance of prayers offered by Brother A. T. Jones, and Father Prescott, who placed the oil upon my forehead. My questioning became desperate in its earnestness. I supposed I had given it up forever; but now all my soul was aroused to know if deliverance was possible for me, and at last the answer came clear and positive that it was God's will that I should be made well; that he intended to heal me; but that it must be *done then and there, if ever.* I must step out on this assurance of his regardless of anything that had been said to me, or that any one might think concerning my attempt. Dr. Kress was kneeling at my side. I sat in my wheel-chair. I remembered her anxiety, and reaching over, I took hold of her hand, and said, 'Dr. Kress, will you release me? will you give me up? will you let me go?' She returned my clasp with a strong pressure, and, after a moment, answered, 'I will; I will.' I immediately felt that I was cut loose. I can describe it in no other way. A tide of strength rushed in upon me. I knew that the work was done. I think that every person in the room recognized that the Spirit of healing had come upon me. I leaped from my chair, saying, 'Dr. Kress, I will never go back into that chair again,' and started to walk from the chapel. I do not remember the incidents of that walk to my room. I know that Dr. Kress accompanied me, and that I felt strong and free, with a peculiar sense of vigor. I have been told that I walked with a strong, elastic step, like that of a young woman. . . .

"After a while, I found myself in the room alone, preparing to re-tire, facing this startling suggestion, 'What if, when you lie down to go to sleep, you shall hear that same old saw going?' (The murmur at the apex of the heart had sounded like a small saw going through a board.) I was appalled. What if I should hear it? For an instant it seemed that the foundations were being removed. If I could not be-lieve the testimony I had had of the power of God, I could believe nothing. I had had many blessed experiences with God, but nothing that had ever touched my life had brought the same realization of his presence as had this, which had lifted me bodily out of the very weakness of death; and O, if it should not be real and true! It was, however, but an instant before I recognized this as temptation, and its source. Quickly I answered aloud: 'I know you! My Heavenly Father would never have made that suggestion to me. It does not make any difference if I do hear it. I know what has happened. You could make me believe I heard that sound, whether I did or not, if I should give you a chance; but I will not give you a chance. I will not lie in any position where I may hear my heart beat.'

"So, as I laid down in bed, I turned entirely onto the right side. After a while, however, as I became drowsy, I naturally turned into the usual position for sleeping, but, suddenly aroused, I found my-self wide-awake and listening for that 'old saw:' *not a murmur!* my heart was beating as steadily and strongly as it ever had done in my life. I placed my hand against it, lying over onto the hand and count-ing the beats. There had been heretofore, upon lying down, turning over, or making any muscular effort, after the first tumult of beats which could not be counted, a gradual settling down to three beats, and skip of the fourth with a heavy, trembling throb, or jerk. I had had a peculiar interest in watching this phenomenon. It had come to be a sort of gauge of the various degrees of fatigue with which I closed the day. But now there was no tumult, no quivering, no skipping, no murmur; all was quiet, natural, steady, and strong.

"I leave you to imagine my joy, and the sense of triumph over my enemy; also the next morning's awakening—strength instead of weakness which I had known so long. . . . *It was true* that he had 'borne our sicknesses'—that he 'healeth our diseases.' . . .

"I surprised the girls in the bath room by appearing on foot for my early morning treatment; and my nurse, when she came at seven, by being dressed, even to my hair. The weak left arm and side were as strong as the others. I was altogether new. I walked down the stairway to the parlor, being stopped by a great many people who marveled to see me on my feet. I had countless questions to answer, and received wondering, timid, congratulations from all sides. Soon after I had seated myself in my usual place at the end of the piano, a lady arose, crossed the room to me, and said, 'Why, Mrs. Henry, you are not in your chair! and how you look!' 'How do I look?' 'You look like the morning star!' I could not describe the thrill which went through me at this from her, but I answered as calmly as I could, 'I *feel* like the Morning Star; at least I am related to Him.'

"It had been decided by the chaplain and myself that it was best for me to intercept flying and sensational rumors by making a statement of what had happened, giving the plain truth at this hour of worship. Accordingly, I stood at the desk and told the story, all my sensations being of strength and vigor instead of any nervous hints of weakness. I could scarcely believe that I had ever been ill; I still seemed to have just awakened from a dream. When I returned from breakfast to my room, having walked in and out, up and down, like any well woman, I was exceedingly tired, not with the old sense of exhaustion, but a natural weariness, such as I had not known in years. I threw myself down on the couch to rest. Almost immediately that feeling of natural weariness began to change into the old form of exhaustion, and accompanying it was a severe pain in the cardiac region, which grew rapidly intense. I could not account for it, and was for an instant staggered; then I remembered my enemy, and springing up, I said, 'This is the work of Satan, and I will not tolerate it.' I have always believed in a personal devil, and knew that he had been following me all through this experience, and understood this as one more effort to throw me into confusion, and cause me to lose confidence in God. So I said, 'This is altogether unnecessary. If this is going to be practiced on me, I will go to work;' and I began moving about, picking up things in my room. The pain continued and increased, while the sense of exhaustion became so great that it seemed I would be obliged to surrender; but I persisted. Meanwhile I had many callers. With each one I was obliged to go over the experience. I ignored the pain and present sense of illness. Every time I related the story, and came to the point where I could have made some complaint of present weakness, I was strongly tempted to do so, but resisted, ignoring it entirely, and each time felt that I had attained a victory and gained strength. . . .

"I do not know how long I was under the lash of that pain. It was long enough to put me to a very grim test; but not for an instant did I yield. I can see how, if I had, I should have lost all. I kept busy, going here and there . . . and ignoring the pain; and after a while I found myself free. I had conquered in the name of Him who had assured victory, and have since had no return of that persecution. It probably lasted four or five hours." [1]

The following Friday Dr. Kellogg made a thorough examination of Mrs. Henry, and issued a statement, the essential facts of which are given here:

"Last August, when Sister Henry arrived here, I made a careful examination of her case. She was bedridden, extremely weak, spoke in a very faint, low voice, and could utter but a few words at a time. She had general dropsy, her pulse was almost imperceptible, and

---

[1] *The Way, the Truth, the Life*, pp. 43-55.

irregular. The heart was extremely weak, and dilated to twice its normal size. . . .

"Yesterday I examined her again, and found no symptoms of dropsy. She no longer needs the wheel-chair. I found her able to talk freely, and to walk quite rapidly up and down stairs, and to engage in other vigorous exercises without any evidence whatever of cardiac insufficiency or weakness, or any shortness of breath or blueness of the lips, and no symptom whatever of any heart disturbance. The pulse is regular and strong, and normal in frequency, and the sphygmographic tracing shows a pulse perfectly normal for a person fifty-eight years of age. . . .

"(Signed) J. H. KELLOGG, M.D."[2]

---

[2] *Ibid.*, pp. 56, 57.

Chapter Thirty

SHE SHARED HER FAITH

*A*few days later Mrs. Henry spoke in the Battle Creek Tabernacle to an audience of 2,500 people. A new radiance shone from her face as she stood before the large assembly and talked for an hour with perfect ease. From that day she resumed her former active life. The month of June she spent in Chicago, by invitation of the WCTU, taking charge of the noon meeting in Willard Hall and doing other mission work.

No one was more astonished at the turn of events than her daughter Mary. In November she had received a letter that stated various reasons that the seventh day should be observed as the Sabbath, and her mother added, "I have always believed in the soon coming of Christ, so I suppose that in all essential points I am really one of these people." Mary read it again. "What does it mean?" she said to herself. "Does it really mean that she is going to join the Adventists?" She could not believe it. She knew how positive her mother had always been in her convictions. "Oh, why didn't I bring her home?" she bemoaned.

Then in April she had received a still more surprising communication. A typewritten letter came, informing her that her mother had been healed by prayer, and a little note in her mother's handwriting telling of the event, and announcing that she had already felt "the evangelistic impulse moving within" and might consider it her duty to go out once more into the evangelistic field. This announcement was like a voice from the tomb.

Mary wrote at once begging her mother to be careful, and above all not to say anything in public about being healed by faith. Every day for a week after that she fully expected to receive a telegram stating that her mother had fallen dead. Before long she received a detailed account of the whole event.

When she arrived to take her mother from the sanitarium she found her going happily everywhere with the vigor of a young woman. Mrs. Henry spent more energy and accomplished more work in a day than many people do in a week. She enjoyed wheeling the patients around in their wheelchairs, remembering the kindness she had received from others.

It was the last straw, as far as Mary was concerned, when her mother decided to learn to ride her daughter's bicycle. But it was not for long because Mary vigorously discouraged the idea. Riding a bicycle at her age! Ridiculous! She wouldn't allow her mother to be made a laughingstock. It gives some index, however, of the flow of vitality and energy that filled Mrs. Henry with continual delight. Her cup was full to the brim and running over, and she wanted to hold it out to others. In her sincerity and simplicity she was convinced that all she needed to do was to offer it to others to find a delighted and wholesale acceptance on the part of the Christian men and women with whom and for whom she had worked in the previous 30 years.

Emerson has said, "With consistency a great soul has simply nothing to do." And yet consistency is generally demanded of people in prominent position by their contemporaries. Any deviation from the established pattern brings a storm of criticism. History shows many great figures who have not hesitated to change the pattern of their lives if a change in viewpoint required a change in policy. They were not afraid to be thought inconsistent.

Saul of Tarsus was just as conscientious before he saw the vision of Christ as he was afterward. But he would not have been if he had continued on the same path. Luther stepped out of the comfortable pattern of conformity to brave the blast that arose when a new viewpoint demanded a change of course. The passage of time generally lulls the criticism and magnifies the heroism of such courage.

Even today when a person in prominent position makes a dramatic change of faith the press usually favors the event with sympathetic publicity. Some magazine will publish the individual's own story as a newsworthy event, and will give opportunity for him or her to express in his or her own words the reason for making such a change. It is accepted by the public with interest and admiration if not agreement with the opinions expressed.

Why the same thing does not occur when a person in public life becomes a Seventh-day Adventist is not clear, for manifestly if the world acclaims those who merely make a change in church affiliation it takes even greater courage and faith to join a group whose pattern of life is as separate from the world as that of the early Christians. But when Mrs. Henry joined the Adventists, the news brought consternation to her friends and associates instead of admiration.

She was unprepared for the storm that broke upon her. Her life had been ruled by one purpose, "to grow in grace, and in the knowledge of our Lord and Saviour, Jesus Christ," and to show others the way of life. She attributed this same ruling purpose to every other Christian. It never occurred to her that they would not listen with eagerness and interest to what she had to say.

She fully believed that if the Methodist Church and the WCTU could once look at Bible teaching free from the centuries-old interpretation of the Fathers, they would come in a body to share her belief.

During the days of inquiry and mental conflict as she had studied the matter of Sundaykeeping or Sabbathkeeping, Mrs. Henry had written to some of her oldest and best friends, leaders in her own church, for help in answering the question "Why, as a church, do we keep Sunday?" Their replies were tested in the light of God's Word, and only served to aid in convincing her that the new light was the true light. Soon after her healing, before she left the sanitarium, a flood of inquiries had come in from old friends and acquaintances asking about the new light and the healing. These she had answered in a straightforward manner, simply telling her experience, or answering without argument the questions put to her. She wrote:

"It will be impossible for me to give the full pound of experience which you and so many others require of me, without also giving at least one drop of the blood of that peculiar truth with which it is filled, and which must flow at the first incision. There may be protest and outcry from those who do not like blood; but I sincerely hope that you who have asked the experience will receive it as given."[1]

To explain her position and answer some of the questions that had come to her, she wrote the story of her experience in a small leaflet, *How the Sabbath Came to Me,* and made a great effort to have it reach all who might possibly have come under the influence of her former teaching.

One minister had written, "Christ never spoke a word in favor of it [the seventh day]." She answered:

"The silence is one of the very things that startled me. It hedges the seventh day about with all the force of an actual repetition of the commandment. If he had found that the Sabbath had been forgotten, would he not have spoken? . . . That day which was hallowed from the beginning, and proclaimed amid the thunders of Sinai, could not be abrogated by *silence.* The voice that changed it must have spoken in unmistakable terms."[2]

Another wrote, "It is clear to me that, for some reason, the people who were nearest to Christ, made the change." She answered thus:

"Here, then, is a marvel. . . . It is not known in human affairs that any lesser authority can change or invalidate any law that was ever made. Think of the legislature of the State of Illinois undertaking to change the most trifling act of the Congress of the United States! . . . It seems to me that something like that caused us four years of bloody war. . . . Christ, in his prenatal majesty, was the Creator of all things . . . (John 1:1-3); and . . . made the Sabbath for man in the beginning.

---

[1] *The Way, the Truth, the Life,* pp. 6, 7.
[2] *Ibid.,* pp. 31, 32.

He was, from the first, the Lord of the Sabbath. That being so, *he* could have changed it to any day, or wiped it out entirely, if he had chosen to do so; but with him ends forever the right to meddle with it."[3]

Another claimed that "Sunday is the Christian Sabbath as truly as Saturday was the Jewish rest day."

To this she replied:

"The seventh day was not a Jewish rest day. It was the Lord's Sabbath day from the beginning, and by him given to man more than two thousand years before there was a Jew. . . . Not for a moment did Christ tolerate the class idea which separates man from man, race from race; but it crept in as the 'mind of Christ' was thrust out. He said: 'The Sabbath [speaking of the seventh day] was made for man.' He did not say 'for the Jews,' but 'for man.'[4]

"Was not the old Sabbath one of the ordinances mentioned in Leviticus 23, and which were 'nailed to the cross'?" To this she answered:

"A clear distinction is made between the *ordinances* of the ceremonial law and the moral Law proclaimed by God himself. The ordinances referred to the sacrificial service which would come to an end in Christ. The Law was for all time. The decalogue was not a series of ten separated laws, but one Law of 10 inseparable specifications."[5]

"How can we know that the day has been preserved? Was it not lost in the long interval between the fall of man and the proclamation on Sinai?" To this question she replied:

"It may have been lost to man but not to God. . . . It was also he who proclaimed it with the other commandments to Israel. He would make no mistake in the calendar. . . . Christ found it remembered when he came. . . . They so loaded the fourth commandment . . . with man-made conditions, that it became a burden and an offense. . . . Christ therefore rebuked their traditional observance of it, but never once hinted that it or any other part of the

---

[3] *Ibid.,* pp. 33, 34.
[4] *Ibid.,* p. 36.
[5] *Ibid.,* p. 39.

Law had been placed among the ordinances that were to be canceled by his sacrifice of himself." [6]

These and many other questions regarding the Sabbath were answered by her in the same clear, forceful way. She showed how unconsciously the church had accepted the traditions of men for the Word of God. "If the teachings of the Fathers can satisfy you," she said, "God will leave you with the Fathers in the end."

She felt that the Sabbath was "the pivotal point upon which the destiny of the organic church must turn," and was the clue to all understanding of Bible truth.

"Much that is closed to the Bible reader . . . becomes plain as day to a very ordinary mind, when you start with the true Sabbath clue in your hand. To take hold of this truth is, in Bible reading, like seizing the right end of the thread if you would open a machine-sewed seam. Begin at the wrong end, and you must cut every stitch, and your thread is in fragments; find the right end, and the seam falls open, the thread comes whole in your hand, leaving no refuse." [7]

Regarding her healing, she received scores of letters, with a variety of views. One minister discounted the experience by saying, "I have heard of people who have been healed before, and I have buried some of them." To this she answered, "I suppose that somebody buried all those whom Christ healed, but they had been healed just the same. I may die and be buried, but I am alive and well today."

Another minister wrote, "If you are healed, don't ascribe it to the fact that you have become a Seventh-day Adventist."

She answered, "I might have become a Seventh-day Adventist and not been healed; but I could not have been healed if I had refused to follow the leading of my Lord in one single step of the way."

The story of her healing was published in the leaflet *The Way, the Truth, the Life.*

The summer after her healing, the officers of the WCTU re-

---

[6] *Ibid.*, pp. 39, 40.
[7] *Ibid.*, p. 35.

quested Mrs. Henry to resume her former position as national evangelist. Realizing that some complications might follow in view of the change in her religious views, Mrs. Henry held her acceptance in abeyance until they could study her leaflet, *How the Sabbath Came to Me,* which she had sent out for the express purpose of acquainting them with her beliefs. With many "kind and sisterly utterances" she was assured that her religious beliefs would in no way interfere with the work they knew she could do, nor affect her relationship with the organization. She was very happy with this response, and in the fall of 1897 resumed her work as national evangelist of the organization.

On the other hand, the circulation of the leaflets brought a storm of criticism and debate that caused her a great deal of grief. One of the hardest things to bear in this connection was the criticism she had unwittingly brought down upon the sanitarium, which she so dearly loved. There were many who charged that they had taken advantage of her weakened state to sway her from her real convictions. She was stout to protest that there had been no influences brought to bear aside from the sweet happy atmosphere of the place, and the life of Christ as presented by the staff and workers.

However, she felt that the Adventist brethren needed a deeper appreciation of the sincerity of Christians in other denominations. In a letter to an Adventist brother she wrote:

"I could not stay in my old church because the Spirit of God led me out into this one. . . . The point is this: *Every man must walk in the light as God has given it to him.* Whatever light we have must have a chance to shine, but it is not for any one to go in advance of the Holy Spirit in promulgating the doctrine. *We are not teachers of doctrine,* but witnesses to the truth."[8]

Mrs. Henry had always been a witness for truth, and now as her vision comprehended a broader meaning to the plan of salvation, she was filled with greater urgency to complete the work that God had commissioned His disciples to do. She recognized that she had made

---

[8] *My Mother's Life,* pp. 315, 316.

some mistakes in the past, and had taught points of doctrine that she now saw were not upheld by the Scriptures. She was not the type to waste time in regrets over the past or in looking on her previous work as a failure. She was not denying her faith; she had simply enlarged it.

Chapter Thirty-one

A GIANT
TELESCOPE

*T*here was one question that was asked Mrs. Henry more often than any other when she became an Adventist, for which she did not have a ready answer. What did she think of Mrs. White and her writings? Did she accept what was called the "Spirit of prophecy"?

Like many other intellectuals, Mrs. Henry was very conservative about accepting anything without thorough investigation and study. Unlike many intellectuals, she had an absolute gauge and a standard by which to test any teaching or manifestation of spiritual power— the Bible. "To the law and to the testimony: if they speak not according to this word, it is because there is no light in them" (Isa. 8:20). Prophecies of the last days stated plainly that one of the gifts of the church would be the Spirit of prophecy (Joel 2:28-32). The last church was characterized as possessing the commandments of God and the "testimony of Jesus" (Rev. 12:17). The testimony of Jesus is "the spirit of prophecy" (Rev. 19:10).

Mrs. Henry studied these things. Still she was not satisfied.

However, she knew that outside the denomination many stories regarding Mrs. White and her writings were being circulated that were not true. She was quick to defend against any such misrepresentation. Everything she learned regarding Mrs. White's character and writings was in harmony with the spirit of Christ. This she was assured of.

She had not read extensively in the writings, but she said:

"I had read only a few paragraphs from these writings, but to everything that I had read or heard I found a chord in my heart ready to respond; nothing seemed strange or new; it was always like a stave or bar from some old song; a repetition or resetting of some truth which I had known and loved long before; hence I had found nothing which could lead to any controversy."[1]

But what if I should find some point in these writings with which I cannot agree? she thought. *What would I do with it? Must I surrender my own judgment to this authority?* She had always pledged unquestioning obedience to the Bible. She granted that the Testimonies might be good, sound, and helpful. "But are they sufficient authority to silence controversy?"

These questions became such a burden on her mind that when she attended the Chicago Medical Missionary Training School, she asked the brethren to join her in a season of prayer that the Spirit of God might enlighten her mind in this respect. The answer came in a remarkable manner. While bowed in prayer, a bright light seemed to shine upon her and opened her eyes. She tells of it:

"The manifestation of the power of the Spirit of God was as clear as sunlight; and in that light I saw the Testimony as simply a lens through which to look at the truth. It at once grew from a *lens* to a telescope—a perfect, beautiful telescope, subject to all telescopic conditions and limitations—directed toward the field of the heavens—that field, the Bible. Clouds may intervene between it and a heaven full of stars—clouds of unbelief, of contention; Satan may blow tempests all about it; it may be blurred by the breath of our own selfishness; the dust of superstition may gather upon it; we may meddle with it, and turn it aside from the field; it may be pointed away toward empty space; it may be turned end for end, so that everything is so diminished that we can recognize nothing. We may

---

[1] *The Gospel of Health,* January 1898.

change the focus so that everything is distorted out of all harmonious proportions, and made hideous; it may be so shortened that nothing but a great piece of opaque glass shall appear to our gaze. If the lens is mistaken for the *field,* we can receive but a very narrow conception of the most magnificent spectacle with which the heavens ever invited our gaze; but in its proper office as a medium of enlarged and clearer vision—*as a telescope*—the Testimony has a wonderfully beautiful and holy office.

"Everything depends upon our relation to it and the use which we make of it. In itself it is only a glass through which to look, but in the hand of the divine Protector, properly mounted, set at a right angle, and adjusted to the eye of the observer, with a field clear of clouds, it will reveal *truth* such as will quicken the blood, gladden the heart, and open a wide door of expectation. It will reduce nebulae to constellations; far-away points of light to planets, and to suns burning with glory.

"The failure has been to understand what the Testimonies are and how to use them. They are not the heavens palpitating with countless orbs of truth, but they do lead the eye and give it power to penetrate the glories of the mysterious living word of God.

"This has been the most beautiful experience which has ever been granted me; it grows on me from day to day. . . . I have often tried to imagine how Galileo's heart must have throbbed and his whole soul filled, even before he obtained one glimpse—and now I think I know."[2]

---

[2] *Ibid.*

Chapter Thirty-two

HANDS ACROSS THE PACIFIC

Mrs. Henry stepped forth from the doors of the Battle Creek Sanitarium with new energy, courage, and ambition—a self-appointed defender of the faith. She knew only too well how misunderstood the people were whose banner she now carried and how much she might do to disarm prejudice and build up confidence in them and their work. Her position of prominence and influence would open doors for her to present in an extensive way the truth as she saw it. There were problems to face too, and battles to fight. Sarepta Irish Henry did not like battles, for she had come from a long line of Quaker stock. She had always been careful to avoid controversy and disagreement and dispute. This she would continue to do, but never again would the path be so smooth.

The cause for which she had labored so long and arduously and which had grown into a powerful force in the nation would always be close to her heart and interest. But now she was ready to pour her heart and strength into a cause she knew to be greater. It was greater, as the whole is greater than the part. It was a cause that included all the noble causes for which men had lived and died; civil and religious liberty, temperance, personal freedom. It went beyond any single one of these because it was lined up with God's great plan for the universe, stretching back before the creation of the world, and looking far ahead to the end of sin and death when Christ would establish His eternal kingdom. There was greater urgency to forward the gospel in all the earth in view of the realization of the soon appearing of Christ, as shown by the prophecies of Daniel and the Revelation.

The church to which she was ready to offer the devotion and experience of her riper years welcomed her with open arms and loving hearts and happy recognition of her talent. With great consideration for her health and respect for her special qualifications, the leaders arranged for the harnessing of her abilities to the greatest advantage: speaking, writing, traveling to camp meetings, counseling. At the same time she continued her work for the WCTU.

Ellen G. White, who was pioneering the work in Australia at the time, and endeavoring to build up the college at Avondale, rejoiced with the leaders of the denomination at the news of Mrs. Henry's healing and acceptance of the Advent faith, and sent a letter of greeting and encouragement:

"I am so pleased, and gratified, and thankful that the Lord has raised you up from sickness to do His work," she wrote. "I am more rejoiced than I can express."[1]

"I would be very much pleased could I be seated by your side and converse with you in regard to the incidents of your experience. I have an earnest desire to meet you. It is not impossible that, even in this life, we shall see each other face to face. When I learn of the gracious dealings of God with you, I feel very grateful to my heavenly Father that the light of the truth for this time is shining into the chambers of your mind and into the soul temple. *Across the broad waters of the Pacific, we can clasp hands in faith and sweet fellowship.*"[2]

This was the beginning of a most tender and beautiful friendship. Although the two women were separated by thousands of miles, and limited to communication on paper only, yet there was formed a special bond of love and appreciation that reveals the humility, the sincerity, the womanliness of both.

---

[1] *Review and Herald* Supplement, Dec. 6, 1898.
[2] Letter written by E. G. White from Sunnyside, Cooranbong, N.S.W., Jan. 2, 1898.

Probably there was no other woman so qualified by experience and nature to understand the burdens that were resting on Ellen White at this time. Repeated over and over in Mrs. Henry's letters is this golden thread of sympathy and concern.

"I have felt myself drawn out to you . . . in the most earnest sympathy." [3]

"In the night . . . I suddenly became wide awake, with you in my mind, and found my heart going out to you with unspeakable sympathy. I felt as though I wanted to fly to you and comfort you. It seemed to me that I saw you as a burdened woman, with a burden that was too heavy to bear; and I longed to take it off of you. I found myself weeping bitterly, which is very unusual for me. I am not a woman given to tears. . . . My whole being seemed to reach out toward you as might have been if you had been my own mother, and I were separated from you, and homesick, and longing to see you and comfort you. . . .

"It is impossible for me to tell you how my heart goes out to you. I would be more glad to see you and talk to you than I can express." [4]

And Mrs. White, on her part, showed her affection through the many personal, handwritten letters, and the timely words of encouragement and counsel. Although far removed from the scenes of Mrs. Henry's activities and adventures for God, Mrs. White followed every detail with keen interest and appreciation. In a letter from Cooranbong dated January 2, 1898, Mrs. White requested permission to reprint the leaflet *How the Sabbath Came to Me* for circulation in Australia. Then she added a postscript saying that her son Willie felt that the urgency to have this message in the hands of the people was so great that they should not wait for an answer, feeling assured that there would be no question about it. Replying to this request in a letter dated February 18, 1898, Mrs. Henry assured Mrs. White that she was gratified that they had not waited to hear from her before printing the tract. "From this time on," she said, "please

---

[3]February 18, 1898.
[4]October 23, 1898.

remember that anything that comes from my pen is for our work in any way that it can be used. You are to appropriate anything without any apology or waiting to ask permission." Such a spirit is unusual among authors, even authors of religious works.

There was a timeliness to the messages that Mrs. White sent to Mrs. Henry that is interesting and significant to note. "I cannot tell you what a channel of strength and light your communications have come to be to me," wrote Mrs. Henry. "It has always transpired that your letters have come at some crisis in my work, just in time to give me needed help."[5]

And there were crises.

One of Mrs. Henry's first objectives after becoming an Adventist was to try to change the position of the WCTU in regard to Sunday legislation. She realized that she had been one of the strongest supporters of the Sabbath Observance Department, and had done all she could to make it function in a practical way. Her purpose, to help the oppressed "sweaters" in the factories who were denied all religious opportunities by being forced into a seven-day working week, had been righteous, she knew. But the department had grown to be a political power, pledged to the support of Sunday laws, allied with the National Reform Association, which was already wielding a heavy hand in some states against those who desired to keep the seventh-day Sabbath and keep open shops on Sunday.

Many women in the Seventh-day Adventist and Seventh Day Baptist churches, who were wholeheartedly pushing the cause of temperance, felt that they could not conscientiously belong to an organization that promoted legislation that was causing hardship, and in some cases, persecution to their own members. Mrs. Henry felt herself in an equivocal position, torn between her loyalty to the union and her realization of trends in the movement that she could not support.

The national convention was to be held in Buffalo in the fall of 1897, and looking ahead to that time, Mrs. Henry prepared a

---

[5] Victoria, British Columbia, Oct. 11, 1899.

memorial in regard to the Sabbath Observance Department, asking that it be abolished or modified so as to eliminate its legislative and compulsory features. She conceived of a strikingly unique manner of presenting this, involving a gigantic amount of work that only one of her inexhaustible push would have carried through.

Soon after Mrs. Henry's healing, the General Conference had chosen Miss Grace Durland to assist her in her literary work, and accompany her on her trips, serving as traveling companion and secretary. Miss Durland was a sprightly, talented young woman of 18 who had just completed some special private courses in shorthand in Battle Creek, and who was working as stenographer in the editorial rooms of the Review and Herald. She entered enthusiastically into all the projects that Mrs. Henry was so courageously attempting. Mrs. Henry depended heavily on her to make train connections, buy the tickets, see that the baggage was delivered to the proper places at the right time, take down in shorthand all her sermons and addresses, and transcribe her notes into articles and chapters for books. Miss Durland was resourceful and ready for anything, but she did have some strange assignments.

Their headquarters during the national convention at Buffalo was at the home of a dear friend of Mrs. Henry's who lived in Niagara Falls, just across the river on the Canadian side. They arrived early to get a good night's rest before the bustle and activities of the conference.

Miss Durland was sleeping soundly the next morning, when, very early, while it was yet dark, Mrs. Henry still in robe and slippers, came to her bedroom and awakened her.

"Grace," she said, "wake up! I want you to dress as quickly as possible and go across and down to the convention headquarters in Buffalo. I want you to find the ball, and see that it's ready in the wings of the auditorium when I will need it."

Grace rubbed her eyes and looked up sleepily, hardly comprehending. Then gradually the idea percolated. *Me? Go over alone? Why I don't even know how to get there,* she thought. But as she roused a little she remembered her role as managing agent. It was her business to know how to get there, and she remembered she had been doing all right finding her way about in new cities. She throttled her misgivings, agreed to the task, dressed, and was soon on her way to keep the assignment.

The "ball" had been her problem child from first to last. It was a huge affair as tall as herself that had been brought all the way from Washington. It was composed entirely of signatures to Mrs. Henry's memorial regarding the Sabbath Observance Department, pasted carefully one by one onto long strips of white cheesecloth and rolled into a huge snowball—13,000 signatures from Sabbathkeeping women! Obtaining them represented a monumental amount of work in personal correspondence.

Miss Durland arrived at the hall, located the ball still in its crate, removed it, and took up a position offstage where she would be ready to roll it onto the platform at the psychological moment.

Mrs. Henry's presentation of her cause with the dramatic entrance of the "ball" was the sensation of the session. At the close, the delegates flocked around her, assuring her of their sympathy and desire to cooperate, but also endeavoring to dissuade her from her purpose, which they felt was a matter of small importance. She was overanxious concerning the matter, they said.

This was a crushing blow to Mrs. Henry after all her hard work, but she was not ready to give up. She returned to Battle Creek and continued her campaign by correspondence. She was helped greatly in this by many women from both the Adventist and Seventh Day Baptist churches. Regarding this follow-up work, she wrote Ellen White, "Much prejudice has already been destroyed, as well as many false notions regarding the Seventh-day Adventists."[6]

It would have been so much easier if she had not changed the formula of her life. Although many of her friends and coworkers assured her that she was "just as acceptable to them as a Seventh-day Adventist as she was as a Methodist," yet in her relationships she was conscious of a slightly concealed irritation and disappointment on the part of many. She said:

---

[6] February 18, 1898.

"Many of the women wonder why I cannot still be among them just as I was when a Methodist, why this truth should make a difference, why they should always have to remember when they see me that this difference has come between us. Apparently they cannot see that it is because the Spirit of God is convincing them of the truth."[7]

She had no heart in her for differences. According to her own statement, she had "no fighting qualities." But she always stood for principles. She could not yield principles, and would be strong to defend them. She wrote in regard to the coming convention:

"That day as Brother Jones and I talked together it was made clear that this was the one thing which the Lord had given me to do—to stand as a defense against many things which were unnecessarily brought against Seventh-day Adventist faith and people, and that my work for the WCTU should prevent much which might come in the nature of antagonism almost amounting to persecution."[8]

It turned out that her work at this time accomplished a double objective: she influenced a large number of women of the WCTU to understand better the work of the Adventists, and many to take up membership in the church, and she led hundreds of Adventist women to come into the union and work for the cause of temperance.

Many of the state presidents of the WCTU were won to signing the memorial, and followed up their interest by inviting Mrs. Henry to present her cause to the state conventions. In a letter to Ellen White, dated October 23, 1898, Mrs. Henry wrote:

"In May I was invited to attend the Wisconsin State convention as national evangelist. I went, and had charge of all the consecration services and devotional exercises. The Spirit of God came in from the beginning in a wonderful manner. As a result, without one word of discussion or a dissenting vote, the Sabbath Observance Department was abolished for the State of Wisconsin. This was done without a suggestion from me at that time, and resulted solely from

[7] Letter to Mrs. White, Oct. 23, 1898.
[8] *Ibid.*

the correspondence that I had had with the women, and the memorial that I had sent them after the last national convention."

Soon after this Mrs. Henry was invited to the Iowa state convention, where she hoped to accomplish the same thing. She was asked to go before the executive committee to present her plea for the abolition of the Sabbath Observance Department, but was obliged to leave the city before any action was taken in the matter. Later she was disappointed to learn that it had been crowded out after she left, and no vote had been taken. She said she was heartsick at this, and began to dread the coming national convention that was to be in St. Paul. She had premonitions that "something certainly would happen this coming national convention which would change the whole current of events, and perhaps my own lifework."[9]

But she felt that she must go, that her witness was necessary. Conversations with the denominational leaders A. T. Jones and A. E. Sutherland and others confirmed her determination and gave her confidence in knowing they were praying for her success.

Just at this time, when it seemed that her future work in the WCTU might be curtailed, she received a letter from Mrs. White containing a proposal to enter a new field of work. The presenting of this plan, which will be discussed in a following chapter, seemed to Mrs. Henry to be "a very remarkable coincidence."

A few weeks later, accompanied by Mary, and Grace Durland, Mrs. Henry boarded the train for St. Paul, where she hoped to put through a change in the constitution that would make impossible the incorporation of denominational differences in the work of the union. They had a pleasant journey together, making themselves at home on the coach in a way that is no longer seen in a modern train. Mrs. Henry took with her a little alcohol burner and granite cup, and plenty of supplies of food for use on the train. She would prepare malted nuts for the refreshment of the girls, and then she and Miss Durland would retire to another seat and work on dictation.

She was unable to present her cause at the convention, however,

---

[9] *Ibid.*

on account of other matters absorbing the attention at the time. Miss Willard had recently passed away, and the women were under a burden of sorrow that made any further disturbance most untimely. Disappointed, convinced of the inconsistency of belonging to the organization if the Sabbath Observance ordinance was retained, she felt that she could no longer remain with them. After a long struggle she sent in her resignation as national evangelist, and appeared for the first time in 25 years without her white ribbon.

The national officers, however, refused to accept her resignation. Many of them wrote, urgently protesting her action, and reminding her that not very long before she herself had been one of the most earnest friends of the Sabbath Observance Department just as it stood in the constitution. They promised that at the next convention she should have an opportunity to present her cause. Many of the leaders pledged her their strong support. Another crisis had come in her life, and another letter of encouragement from Ellen White strengthened her resolution.

In a handwritten letter to Mrs. White dated January 15, 1899, Mrs. Henry said:

"I must not let the next mail go without at least a line to tell you how directly from the Lord your last letter came to me—just in time to prevent the final act that would have separated me from the WCTU. . . . I cannot tell you what a comfort your letter was to me and to many others because of the light it threw on what had come to be a great problem to us in the WCTU, but I will explain later."

Thus persuaded that the great sacrifice was not required of her, she put on once more the little white ribbon without which her costume did not seem complete.

On March 24, 1899, Mrs. White wrote to Mrs. Henry, "I am so glad, my sister, that you did not sever your connection from the WCTU. Hold your place. Speak the words given you by God, and the Lord will certainly work through you."

In October of the following year Mrs. Henry carried her cause to the national convention at Seattle, Washington. Again she was filled with dread and uncertainty. She realized the discussion, disagreement, and argument that her resolution was bound to excite. Perhaps she should be content to carry out her assigned part—preparing for and leading the evangelistic conferences—and avoid presenting the debatable issue. It was a great temptation, for "I am a woman of peace," she said. "The sound of discussion has always been so painful that I could not endure to be mixed up in it."

A day or two before the opening of the conference she had almost decided that she would have very little to do outside the regular convention, and would hope that the matter of the resolution could be decided at a regular session of the executive committee.

In spite of her reluctance to being the center of a controversy, she was deeply conscious that the principle involved was more important than any of the other women realized. It was not merely a matter of assisting a few Seventh-day Adventists who had come into conflict with Sunday laws. It represented a trend toward religious intolerance, which she felt was contrary to the principles of the WCTU. She had been one of the founders. She had a special concern to help guide the movement.

She and Grace Durland spent three days in the home of Grace's parents in Victoria before continuing on to Seattle to attend the convention. Here a letter reached her from Ellen G. White, quite surprisingly, for nothing had been written to apprise Mrs. White of the crisis that was facing her friend and sister. She wrote: "God has called upon you to make your appeal, to show that you are worthy of the sacred trust which He has in His providence conferred upon you. . . . Having adopted a right principle of action, reverence and obey it." [10]

Any inclination toward appeasement disappeared. Her course was now decided. She would present her resolution. But, "of course, my face was still set toward peace," she said, "even if I had to contend for it!"

The first hurdle was the committee on resolutions. The members were furnished with copies of the resolution, as were also many of the officers and leaders. The resolution read, in part:

---

[10] September 13, 1899.

"*Resolved,* That our plan of work shall be so changed as to remove from its departments everything that tends to sectarian controversy, or which can in any sense be made to interfere with perfect liberty of conscience as regards the days which shall be given to worship, rest, or labor, or which can be used to give aid or comfort to any who through ignorance, prejudice, or malice would enact, or so enforce civil law as to interfere with the religious convictions of any and all people."

At the end of the first day Mrs. Hoffman, the recording secretary of the national union, and a pledged supporter of the proposed change, informed Mrs. Henry that the resolution had been thrown out of the committee.

The next move was to request the privilege of presenting the resolution in person from the floor of the convention. This was granted, and a special orders session was arranged for Wednesday morning.

Mrs. Henry realized the strength of the opposition. Many of the women had told her directly that they would speak against it with all the strength they had. Some had written letters of abuse. One woman wrote, "You, of course, cannot consistently remain among us, and think of flapping your Second Advent wings at our sessions. . . . We want you never to claim any influence with us."[11]

The opposition was more or less organized and spearheaded by Dr. Wilbur F. Crafts, of the National Reform Association, who was attending the convention regardless of the fact that he was not a member entitled to vote. Since Mrs. Henry had passed out copies of the resolution, it was quite well known, and the women were primed to speak against it.

On Tuesday night Mrs. Henry awoke suddenly in the middle of the night and felt impressed that she should rewrite her resolution, modifying some of its provisions. This she did and returned to sleep.

On awakening, her courage for the day was strengthened by the receipt of a telegram from G. A. Irwin, president of the General Conference. He said, "Read 1 Samuel 10:7 and Isaiah 41:10: 'And

---

[11] From stenographic report of the session by Miss Grace Durland.

let it be, when these signs are come unto thee, that thou do as occasion serve thee; for God is with thee.' 'Fear thou not; for I am with thee: Be not dismayed; for I am thy God.'"

Arriving at the convention hall, she located Mrs. Hoffman and showed her what she had prepared. Mrs. Hoffman said, "No, nothing that you have will do. These women are wedded to that Sabbath Observance Department. I wish that something on this question would go through. There is nothing in the world so terrible to come into our organization as religious intolerance. But you have nothing there that will even be given a hearing."

Mrs. Henry decided to trim down her resolution still further. Retiring to a quiet corner she wrote:

"Resolved, That as a National Woman's Christian Temperance Union we protest against any such interpretation or use of any lines of work as shall give aid or comfort to those who through ignorance, prejudice, or malice, would enact or enforce such laws as can be made to serve the purpose of persecution, or in any manner interfere with the most perfect liberty of conscience concerning days, or the manner of their observance."

This resolution Mrs. Henry read from the floor of the convention, and moved its adoption. The motion was immediately seconded, and a vigorous discussion began. Mrs. Henry was allowed three minutes to speak for her own resolution. She said in part:

"Madame President and sisters of the convention: The glory of the Woman's Christian Temperance Union has ever been that it was a channel of light, that it has always been open toward the throne of God for illumination, open always toward the darkest corners of the earth for the dispensing of the light which it should receive from the throne.

"I have faith and confidence in our organization, and in the manner in which it came into existence, and in the spirit which has wrought through us from the beginning until now. I believe we are still open toward the throne to receive light, open to communicate to those who are down in the depths any light which comes to us, and that whenever we come to see in any line of our work that which does in any way interfere with this open channel, which does prevent the dissemination of light, that we will at least take it into careful consideration.

"I stand before you this morning to make an appeal for a large class of Christian workers in our organization—a number growing larger and larger every month; for from among the ranks of the people who observe the seventh day of the week as the Sabbath there has come into the WCTU in the last year a large number of workers, good and true, many of them giving time and energies to the teaching of the ignorant in the very principles for which the WCTU stands.

"In some cases these workers have met with a strange interference in their work, an interference of a character so malignant as to be nothing less than persecution; and I feel that I would be unjust to the WCTU, as well as to my fellow laborers, did I not bring these matters to your notice, and make an appeal to you for the help which you can give. I know that our women would not countenance persecution; nor could we be a persecuting organization. I know our women do not understand the use that is being made of our Sabbath Observance Department, and that the department itself does not at all presuppose any such use as is made of it."

In spite of Mrs. Henry's eloquence, and many strong speeches supporting the resolution, many clung to their position that to make any change in the Sabbath Observance Department would be taking a step backward. Finally, the following substitute for the original resolution was adopted:

"*Resolved,* That we favor the amendment of all State Sunday laws which do not contain the usual exemption for those who keep the Sabbath day."

On the whole the proponents of the change felt that it was a victory and that gains had been made. The discussion had brought out the latent sympathy for justice and equal rights, and an awakening to the fact that liberty of conscience was actually in danger in the WCTU.

Mrs. Henry conducted the closing evangelistic service of the convention, speaking from the ninety-third psalm, directing the mediation to the power of God, who is "mightier than the noise of many waters," and who can keep the hearts of His children steady with love and confidence toward one another, even when they disagree on what seems some vital point. Her words, like a steady musical current, were full of comfort and spiritual uplift to the group of women who were weary with discussion and disagreement.

Chapter Thirty-three

CALLING
ALL WOMEN

*T*he campaign to remove the Sabbath Observance Department from the WCTU was only one of Mrs. Henry's interests and activities during these busy years.

In a letter to Mrs. White dated October 23, 1898, Mrs. Henry makes this report:

"I have been traveling almost constantly since the first of May. Have attended eleven camp meetings, besides the Wisconsin and Iowa State conventions, the General Conference of the Seventh Day Baptist denomination, where I went by their invitation; and spent one week at College View, Nebraska, working in behalf of the students and church members."

On this same trip she was invited by the secretary of the faculty of the university at Harriman, Tennessee, to give a series of lectures to the 500 teachers at the teachers' institute.

These events were only incidental, however, to her last and greatest project. The idea had come to her about the time that she was beginning to feel that it might be necessary for her to resign from her position as national evangelist. It was a plan for the mobilization of a vast force to do the work of God. The women of the Adventist Church! What tremendous power and influence might be theirs! Properly organized, trained, and directed, they could do a work equal, if not superior, to that of the WCTU. The more this thought stirred in her mind, the more excited she became.

Mrs. Henry had been working with a very consecrated and superior group of women—women of education, means, and Christian character. They were tireless, energetic, enthusiastic, and hardworking. By comparison, it seemed that many of the Seventh-day Adventist women were more or less apathetic, unambitious, and provincial in their outlook. They had received wonderful counsel and instruction, they were earnest and devoted, but actually they knew little of their own mission and possibilities in the church. If she could only lead them on to do a work greater than that of the WCTU! Her eyes had been opened to see the need, and she felt so small and inadequate to do what should be done. She said, "I have longed to go down into the slums and take up the work that I used to do, but of course, my years are against me in that, and I seem to have other work pressed upon me to such an extent that I cannot do it. But now I see a way by which I may reach out by hundreds of hands where I could by myself only have used two!" Every waking moment her mind was busily at work making plans and envisioning a wide scope of united service for the women of the church.

As she went about to various camp meetings and became better acquainted with the women, the value of such a plan as she had been considering grew in her mind. And so, when a letter reached her at Rockford, Illinois, from Mrs. White, suggesting that she do this very thing, it seemed "a remarkable coincidence."

Mrs. White said:

"SISTER HENRY:

". . . I have thought, with your experience, under the supervision of God, you could exert your influence to set in operation lines of work where women could unite together to work for the Lord.

"There certainly should be a larger number of women engaged in the work of ministering to suffering humanity, uplifting, educating them how to believe—simply believe—in Jesus Christ our Saviour. . . .

"I am pained because our sisters in America are not more of them doing the work they might do for the Lord Jesus. . . . Many women love to talk. Why can't they talk the words of Christ to perishing souls? The more closely we are related to Christ, the more surely the heart will know the wretchedness of souls who do not know God. . . .

"Believing the teachings of Christ, that through you, the human agency, He communicated His light, His truth, you are the frail instrument through whom the hidden power of God does work, that His strength may be perfected and made glorious in your weakness.

"(Signed) MRS. E. G. WHITE."[1]

Now that her idea had become a specific assignment, and she felt she had the green light to go ahead, Mrs. Henry began enthusiastically to work out her dreams in a practical way.

It was right in line with the passion of her life, THE HOME. It must be remembered that the great work she had done for the temperance cause had grown out of her determination to make the nation safe for the home—her home, all Christian homes. She had been privileged, as few others, to observe the needs of the home, and the causes of success and failure in the home. She realized the relation of the home to every good or evil in the world. She said:

"In its relation to the church, the home is as the heart to the body, and the mother in the home is its life center. What the mother is, so is the home. What the home is, as a rule, so is the husband and father in his strength or in his weakness. What the home is, what the mother and father are, such are the children in their certainty to fall under the power of temptation. It cannot be otherwise without some special manifestation from the Spirit of God. It is therefore necessary that a work should be done in the home such as has never been attempted.

"It must go from our women to all the homes the world over. And when each woman among our people shall come to appreciate her opportunity, and rejoice in it, realizing not the burdens she must bear, but the abundant strength that is given with which to carry them, seeing not the danger from the lions in the way, but how they

---

[1] *Review and Herald* Supplement, Dec. 6, 1898.

quail and fawn before the courage of even a weak woman's mighty faith; then shall our ministry go abroad in their work, strong, refreshed, victorious."[2]

The plan she formulated was so broad and comprehensive in its scope that only one of indomitable purpose would have attempted to carry it out. In it she visualized the womanhood of the church united in study and purpose and self-sacrifice, devoted to a practical demonstration of the power of the Christian home. It was to be, in effect, a woman ministry, not an organized body of women preachers, but a systematic service for mutual help. It had many of the aspects of a vast correspondence school, really a form of adult education.

Study cards were prepared: one for the worker, and one for the learner. The worker, by signing the card, pledged "to be so instructed in all truth, to be so led and used by the power of the Holy Spirit, to be so taught a true woman's ministry in my own home, among my neighbors, and in my own immediate social circle, that I may be prepared to labor for suffering humanity, and to help in uplifting the fallen, and educating the ignorant to believe, simply believe—in Jesus Christ our Saviour: for the first glance of any soul must be Jesus Christ. Then, if he follows the Lamb of God, as he remains a learner, he will have an intelligent knowledge of what is truth."

The pledge of the learner was "to study to know the principles which constitute Christ's character as they are set forth in His Word, and to live them out practically in the common affairs of everyday life."

A system of correspondence was devised by which women who needed help in any way in their home life, in dealing with spiritual, moral, or domestic questions might write to those who were qualified by experience to give instruction, and who would answer by personal letters.

This plan meant the undertaking of an overwhelming amount of correspondence, and in the year 1899 Mrs. Henry received hundreds of heartbreaking letters from women seeking her counsel, comfort, and advice about their problems. She took their problems and sor-

---

[2]*A Woman-Ministry*, p. 13.

rows into her heart and made them her own. Sometimes they so touched her tender sympathy that they became intensely real and personal, and made her ill.

If there is one quality above another in Mrs. Henry's character that makes this story worth recording, it is just this extreme sensitivity to the burdens of others. When men in her reform club in Rockford were in temptation or out of work or in danger of losing what they had gained, she bore them in her heart for days, hardly eating or sleeping, and agonizing upon her bed at night. This same concern was now given to the large body of women, her sisters in the Seventh-day Adventist Church for whom she had such exalted aspirations.

It was not her intention, however, to take this whole load on her shoulders, but one of the main objectives of this new department in the General Conference was to operate as a sort of agency whereby those who had questions and needs could be put in touch with those who had solutions and helpful experience to offer.

Mrs. Henry did a monument of work at this time, answering personally hundreds of letters and speaking before many assemblies. From the response she was assured that the work that was begun was filling a vital place in the denomination. She speaks of this in letters to her friend Ellen White:

"I have for some time been wanting to write to you and tell you how the women's work is going on, for I know that many things in it would gladden your heart, although, of course, there are other things that might give you many sad hours. . . . I have never before realized the situations quite so sad as some that appear in these letters, and this gives me to understand how truly the Lord moved in opening up this line of work for our women.

"Already we begin to see results in the conversion of souls. These conversions have been principally among the husbands of our sisters."[3]

"The work is going forward among our women with great power. They are eager to take hold, and the letters which I receive reveal how great was the need that they should be set to work."[4]

---

[3] Battle Creek, Michigan, June 16, 1899.
[4] Battle Creek, Michigan, Jan. 15, 1899.

From the volume of notes of her addresses and letters, a brief selection has been made of her thoughts on a few vital questions that were put to her, and that mothers of today are still asking.

"What Can I Do?"

"Many women have written me saying, 'I want to do something. I realize the need in the community, and I would like to do something to extend the truth. But what can I do? How can I do it?' or 'I received your letter, but you did not tell me what to do, or just how to proceed.'

"No, I do not tell any woman what or how to do. I do not know enough. The only thing that any of us can safely do for another is help her by a living testimony, to see what we must BE; and when we come, by the power and light of the Holy Spirit, to be what we ought to be, there will be no trouble about the doing.

"The world has a right to expect more from us than from any other people. The world's preparation day is nearly passed; its momentous hours have been frittered away; the sun hangs low in the west; the last Sabbath of earth is almost here; the gospel proclamation must begin to run and fly; at last the King's business *truly* requires haste; and it is our work as women to send forth messengers fully equipped for their holy errand. And if she will, every mother may speak with as many tongues, run with as many feet, and work with as many hands as she has children.

"It is especially the mission of Seventh-day Adventists to make the consecrated life beautiful in the eyes of a beauty-loving world. Your home must be made so attractive because of the manifestation of the Spirit that is in it, because of the beauty of love and faith, because of the aroma of heaven, that it will hold the children and youth against all the show and glitter of a vain world.

"This must be done. It is our only resource in preserving our children against the day of the Lord."

"Why Is It That My Children Do Not Obey Me?"

"The child in the home deals by the father, mother, and the

principles they represent, precisely as father and mother deal by the heavenly Father and the principles He represents. The only deviation from this rule is found in the personal repentance and conversion of the child. This may seem like a hard thing to say, but it is so awfully true that it must be said, no matter how hard it may strike home. The time may come when your child will see where you have failed, and correct himself by the light of the Holy Spirit, and in so doing give you a little taste of the judgment day in your own soul. Pray God that it may be so, and not too late."

"Hard to Manage"

"A sister said to me, 'What is the matter with Seventh-day Adventist children? They are the hardest in the world to manage.' I have heard that said again and again, and it is true.

"There is good reason. Seventh-day Adventists are a peculiar people. They are all hard to manage. And for this, *be thankful.* Any man or woman who is not hard to manage is sure sooner or later to become somebody's tool. All that is needed to make the tool is to find somebody who has a little larger ability, a little more wit to take hold of the manageable man, and make him over, and use him as he will.

"There is a sentiment that it is a Christian grace to be easily managed, and people have tried to cultivate a manageable spirit with the result that Seventh-day Adventists, their homes, their children, as well as all that goes to make them are a necessity in the economy of God. They have a strange place to fill in the earth. Their homes must be unlike any other. Take two people such as will make good Seventh-day Adventists, let them come together in the making of a home, and they must have an experience such as no others can have in so relating themselves to each other that any home life at all will be possible. Before a home is possible those who compose it must come to know that divine principle of unity which is never found excepting through the manifestation of the Spirit.

"The husband in this home, recognizing the life which he lives in his flesh is altogether by the power of the Holy Spirit, settling every question for himself alone as if he and God alone in the world—will be a hard man for his wife to 'wind around her finger.' And she should be glad to have it so, for if she could wind him, another woman might. Let her thank God that no other brain, not even hers, can think for him.

"And the same thing must be true of the wife. Her relation to God must be settled upon the same basis. The same divine intelligence that is accessible to man is open to woman, that it knows just as well how to teach and lead a woman as a man. No man knows any woman well enough to cut out a lifework for her to make up.

"When two people have come together according to this plan, each adjusting his individuality to the same Spirit, although they may be filled with the material out of which dissension might be manufactured, they must live at peace in the unity of the Spirit. This is the true basis of the home. Without it there can be no home such as God intended to establish in the earth for a testimony of His Spirit.

"The children that are born into such a home of two such people, must be unmanageable until they have elected and surrendered themselves to control. They can be taught, cultivated, grown, but as God in the beginning had planned, they will be free. God must have willing service that a son yields a father, from a loving, free, deliberate preference to serve.

"God wants out of you a child like himself, of free and independent action, instead of a tool such as he can pick up and use as a stick. This is one feature of the image in which man was created. Your home is to be made a place in which this image of God shall be reproduced in every child that comes into it.

"The child in your home with this wonderful legacy of power may be so taught in principles, and established in truth that he shall make the wise choice, and by his own election become not only willing, but an unchangeable servant of God; and it is the mother's grandest office to preside over and direct the processes by which this end shall be attained. . . ."

Principle, Rather Than Emotion, the Best Influence

"One mother said to me, 'I have wept my eyes almost out over my boy, but it does no good. He has got so that just as soon as he sees I am going to cry, he will take his hat and get out of the house.'

"And who can blame him? That sort of influence is not of God. Character can not be built by tears and pleading, but only by the principles of truth. The only power to which the child should yield is the power of the Word and the Spirit that is life.

"A father or mother will sometimes say to this or that Christian friend, or to the minister, 'I wish you would try to exert a personal influence over my child.' But nothing has made God more trouble than the possibilities bound up in a strong personal influence brought to bear upon the individual who at last must give an account of himself. Personal influence must always go by spasmodic periods. Many a mother has defeated the work that God wanted her to do in her children because she has depended upon that, instead of the patient teaching of principle.

"There are so-called Christian people who would apparently be glad of any influence that would lead a child into any sort of a show of Christian living, if only there might be avoided the disgrace of a public revelation of wickedness. They would not care so much for anything that could be kept covered. They reason that if the boy can only be kept in church, if he can only be kept to a profession of faith, be kept from outbreaking sin, he is all right.

"It often happens, when a child has done something that the mother has seen as wrong, that she has used command, pleading, and tears, living all the time herself in direct violation of the special principle involved, and still hoping by these flimsy devices of her influence to restrain him from an openly evil course and the public disgrace that it might involve."[5]

---

[5] Selected from *A Woman-Ministry*.

Chapter Thirty-four

"MORE AND MORE UNTO THE PERFECT DAY"

One beautiful Sabbath afternoon Mrs. Henry and her daughter Mary were sitting together on the lawn by the sanitarium, enjoying the loveliness of the summer day, watching the birds and listening to their songs. They had been silent for some time, and then the mother, with an expression of great peace on her face, turned to her daughter and said, "I have been thinking of the difference between myself now and years ago. Once it would have spoiled my Sabbath to see men working on the road. Now I hardly notice them. My Sabbath is within."

Mary had not noticed them, either, but there they were, a score or more of dusty laborers, mingling the sound of hammer and spade with the carol of birds and the singing of hymns. As they watched the shadows deepen and the sun go down, Mary thought, *It is because my mother has made the supreme sacrifice that she has infinite peace. Like Abraham of old, she went up with her all to the altar. And God blessed her and multiplied her strength.*

God had indeed multiplied her strength, and though her last years were marked by a beautiful serenity of spirit, her energies seemed to be gathering momentum. Every moment was occupied. She seemed indefatigable. A summary of her activities reveals a tremendous output of work—tracts, letters, addresses, books, and an

extensive trip. It was almost as if she had some premonition that time
was running out for her, and there was so much that she wanted to
do. Those who were closest to her, however, think that she did not
have the least intimation that her work was almost over. The impelling purpose was her feeling that "the coming of the Lord
draweth nigh," and the "King's business requires haste."

She neglected nothing that she knew of to maintain her health.
She lived entirely upon zwieback, granose, legumes, nut foods, and
fruit. If she were going to give an address soon after a meal, or had
an unusually hard day's work in mind, she would eat nothing but
fruit for dinner or breakfast, or both. She always slept in a cold room,
with the window halfway up. Every morning she took a cold
shower or plunge bath, priding herself on getting into the water in
winter as cold as it came from the pipes. When at home, she always
went to bed about 8:00, and rose at 5:00. Her heart was examined
several times during the years of 1898 and 1899, and always seemed
perfectly normal for her age.

On July 12, 1899, Mrs. Henry and Miss Durland left Mary's
home in Battle Creek for a six-month evangelistic trip through the
South and West. Her youngest son, Arthur, came from New York
to have a short visit with her before her departure. They went away
in high spirits, full of enthusiasm for what was to be Mrs. Henry's
most memorable itinerary.

Miss Durland, now Mrs. Mace, of Takoma Park, Maryland, recalls some interesting sidelights on the trip. She says:

"We traveled constantly for six months, taking in meetings in the
Central States and on to various parts of California. We carried large
portmanteaus filled with health foods in bottles and cans—almond
butter, malted nuts, protose, bromose, and all the other oses and but-
ters. We were equipped with a little alcohol lamp or stove, and had
our meals in fine style wherever we were. I still remember how heavy
were the containers of food, and how difficult it was to get a meal
properly served when the train was rolling and everything sliding
about. But we did it, and Mrs. Henry thrived on the meals. I had to
use an old-fashioned Remington typewriter, which was like a thresh-

ing machine compared with the typewriters of the present day.

"Because I could not check the typewriter or handle it with all the other baggage, I checked it in a trunk, wrapping it in a red flannel blanket, and padding the corners in the trunk in order that my beloved machine would come through without injury. We usually traveled in day coaches for economy's sake. But one particular time, I remember, Dr. J. H. Kellogg chanced to be on the same train and discovered that Mrs. Henry and her secretary were in the day coach. Suddenly the porter arrived and bundled us, bag and baggage, into the Pullman, where, he said, it would be more comfortable. And sure enough it was luxury, but short-lived luxury, for we soon reached our destination."

Mrs. Mace smiles as she looks back on her experience as she first began her traveling career. She says:

"It takes time and resourcefulness to know just how to make train connections and get baggage delivered to the proper place at the right time. . . . Not the least of my unhappy and rather amusing recollections was my traveling attire. I surely lacked a guide in choosing my outfit, but lacking such an asset, I chose my own apparel. I remember starting out on a long trip for the first time wearing an inexpensive dark green flannel suit, and a yellow straw hat of wide brim and ribbons and bows. It was a real picture hat, entirely inappropriate for traveling, both as to size, shape, and color. I remember thinking that when I made my first appearance at the depot Mrs. Henry looked me over somewhat unapprovingly, but she did not make any unfavorable remarks. She simply trusted circumstances to bring about the needed discipline in dress, and sure enough they did. It was not long before we were caught in a drenching rain, for which I was not prepared, and soon my traveling attire wilted, shrunk, and creased, while my yellow hat looked like a market basket. As quickly as possible, I secured permission to go to the nearest shopping district and picked out a small black hat, ornamented only by a long black quill. When I returned in triumph with my purchase, Mrs. Henry smiled and seemed very much pleased, and said I had chosen a very becoming hat for traveling."

They visited the South first, touching points in Tennessee, Arkansas, Texas, then on to Missouri, Colorado, Utah, Washington, California, Oregon, British Columbia, returning to Seattle for the National WCTU Convention, stopping at her son Alfred's home in Salt Lake City both going and returning, and finally reaching home again the tenth of December. Everywhere she was strong, alert, observing.

Her impressions of the South were expressed in a letter to her daughter:

"If those who are indifferent to the Southern work could make this trip, and even from the shifting standpoint of the moving train observe the half-clothed men, women, and children, black and white, squatting before the cabins, perched upon fences, lounging everywhere empty-handed, gazing with brutish interest at the train, there would surely be an increased interest in this direction.

"The question would come to my mind, Do those people never do anything? If they had been standing with tools in their hands, as if they had been at work, it would have relieved the situation, but I do not remember having seen one of all this wayside-cabin class, either black or white, who appeared to have any further interest in life than would have been manifested by a herd of cattle chewing their cud; except once, when a woman was seen walking briskly through a company of lounging men as if she were really going somewhere with something on her mind."

One stop-off at camp meeting remains especially vivid in Mrs. Mace's mind:

"One time we were at camp meeting, and a little oil heater had been provided as a protection for Mrs. Henry against dampness and chill, supposed to be lighted early in the morning. One particular morning Mrs. Henry awakened before I did, and thinking not to disturb me, she got out of bed and lighted the stove, then went back to sleep. In the meantime the flame rolled up and the smoke poured out, covering everything inside the tent. By the time we came to our senses we found ourselves and our clothing and everything else covered with long strips of soot and smoke. It was a funny experience to remember, but not so funny at the time. But dear Mrs. Henry did not scold or complain, but took right hold with me to begin to clean up. What a time we had getting our complexions back to normal! That was to me a lesson in patience and Christian charity which I have never forgotten."

Everywhere on the trip she met those whom she had blessed with her counsel, prayers, and evangelistic fire, as well as colaborers and old friends. At Spokane she met Bishop Vincent, who was holding a conference of Scandinavian ministers. It was a great comfort and pleasure to be invited by this friend of her youth to "speak a few words of greeting and counsel" to the conference. In Victoria, British Columbia, she gave her two lectures of former years, "What Is the Boy Worth?" and "Why So Many Children of the Church Go to Ruin." Here also she met another old friend, of 25 years' acquaintance, who was at that time United States consul at Victoria. This gentleman with his wife invited her to dinner, and gave her the most delightful reception. Again, in Portland, Oregon, and in St. Helena, California, she had in her audience friends and acquaintances of former years.

Upon the return trip she spoke Sunday morning in her son Alfred's church in Salt Lake City, taking as her theme the "Ministry of the Home." The last time she had left her son's home she had been taken away in a chair, supposedly a confirmed invalid. Now, five years later, she stood in perfect health before a large congregation, "a sweet-faced old lady, with a most pleasing manner on the platform, and a voice like a silver bell," as one of the newspapers expressed it. The same paper said, "From the first word of her discourse to the last she held the close attention of every hearer."

Mrs. Mace speaks from memory of her impression of Mrs. Henry's appearance at this time:

"Mrs. Henry's eyes were so clear and brilliant as to never be forgotten. I can see her now—a frail little woman standing in the pulpit, wearing a black dress, with a white lace kerchief fastened in the folds about the neck and extending down to the waist like a vest; her pince-nez glasses riding a rather protruding long nose, and her gray hair precisely parted over the forehead and twisted into a knot at the nape of the neck; and the charm of her personality displayed in a smile such as I have never seen since. Mrs. Henry was too wonderful a character to describe in cold type. One would have to be associated with her really to understand the worth of her character."

In a postscript to the letter that Mrs. Henry wrote to Mrs. White on November 8, 1899, in which she described her trip, Miss Durland made this comment regarding newspaper publicity: "I add this note to Mrs. Henry's letter to say that her work is always received with the greatest interest at every place where she goes. The newspapers are very liberal in their notices of her work, often giving a good sketch of her life, and a very complete synopsis of her lectures."

Home again after the long trip, Mrs. Henry summed it up as follows:

"I was absent from home five months; traveled over nine thousand miles; have spoken two hundred and fourteen times; was subject to nearly all conditions of living and climate which would test the strength of the most robust, and yet have returned in good working order. I would not hesitate to start at once on another tour if circumstances required. After one day of rest I have taken up the work which is waiting for me in my office, without any sense of especial weariness, and with a consciousness of strength and courage for all that is before me. For all of this I am profoundly grateful to Him who evidently planned the journey, and led me all the way; for I have received many tokens of the fact that each stage of it had been divinely ordered."

It was good to be home and to turn from public responsibilities to private enjoyments in the bosom of her family. Mrs. Henry was living now with Mary, who had married and with her husband and little son was living on Van Buren Street in Battle Creek, Michigan. Mary's husband, Dr. Rossiter, was a member of the staff of the Battle Creek Sanitarium, and taught in the medical school. Mary was editor of the *Good Health Magazine*.

The last days of the nineteenth century were rapidly running out like the sands of the hourglass, and as the holiday season drew near, celebrations to welcome the dawn of the twentieth century were being planned all over the country.

All unconscious that the sands of her life were also running low, Mrs. Henry joined in the preparations for an unusually festive and happy Christmas. She invited Arthur and his wife and little daughter Dorothy to join the Rossiters for the holidays. Alfred and his family were too far away to be present. Mrs. Henry had always made birthdays and holidays occasions of great merriment and glee for her children, observing year by year certain time-honored family traditions in their celebration.

Now she helped Mary as they brought out the box of tinsel and trimmings and prepared to deck the rooms for Christmas. A large crepe-paper bell hung in the hall, and festoons of twisted tinsel and crepe-paper crisscrossed the ceilings. There was no tree, but mistletoe and pine boughs adorned the mantels, and Christmas candles imparted the necessary aroma to complete the requirements for the seasonal atmosphere.

On Christmas Eve the stockings were "hung by the chimney with care," and later surreptitiously filled by the different members of the family, each acting for Saint Nick. Long after others had succumbed to weariness and gone to bed, Mrs. Henry was still "spooking around," as Mary put it, tucking in a last gift to the stockings on the mantel.

The opening on Christmas morning revealed the mother's love and thoughtfulness for her children as she had traveled far and wide, gleaning here and there a choice treasure to bring surprise to their eyes on Christmas Day—tiny white dresses for the baby, pieces of silk, rare colored photographs, a Japanese lacquered box, and many other articles.

The mother claimed the special privilege of cooking the dinner, wishing to demonstrate her new principles of diet. All morning she busied herself in the kitchen and pantry, cutting, slicing, chopping, mixing, and when the dinner was served, the large turkey of former years was conspicuous by its absence. But no one minded, for the healthful delicacies that had appeared in its place made a very satisfactory substitute.

Three days after the turn of the century Mrs. Henry started off to attend a special session of leaders of the General Conference in Graysville, Tennessee. She had been so happy with her children and grandchildren that she was unusually reluctant to leave.

"Why must you go?" pleaded Mary.

"Because I have promised. Besides, you cannot understand what a rest and treat it is to me to hear some voice in Bible teaching beside my own."

She took her little grandson in her arms for a moment, and bade the waiting group goodbye as usual, stepped out to the carriage in her usual brisk manner, and was rolled away to the station.

On Tuesday morning, January 12, Mary received a letter from her mother saying she had succumbed to an attack of la grippe with pneumonia complications. "I feel that I have done wrong in that I have not taken periods of rest, and have promised the Lord that I will take at least one week every three months, whether I feel that I need it or not; and more if I do need it."

Enclosed with the letter was an importunate note to Dr. Rossiter, requesting him to come without delay to bring the invalid home. The doctor left that afternoon, but the disease had progressed too rapidly for her to return home. She died Tuesday afternoon, January 16, 1900. Many asked whether it was a return of her old heart trouble, but the doctor confirmed her statement that it was simple pneumonia and nothing else. She was reconciled to go in the assurance that she had "fought a good fight; she had kept the faith," and she was confident that there was a crown of life laid up for her which her Lord and Master would give to her at the resurrection.

She was laid to rest beside her father and mother and twin babies in the little cemetery at Pecatonica, Illinois, in the beautiful spot she had herself chosen 40 years before as the resting place of her dear father. Here she waits the touch of the Life-giver, who has promised, "I am the resurrection, and the life; he that believeth in me, though he were dead, yet shall he live."

A TRIBUTE BY
BISHOP VINCENT

I knew Mrs. S.M.I. Henry in her early womanhood, when she was a student at the old Rock River Seminary at Mount Morris, in Illinois. I have known her through all the years since then—wife, mother, friend, writer, worker. She was a loyal wife, a faithful mother, an unfaltering friend, a gifted writer, an indefatigable worker. As the base of all this, and as the crown of all, and as the sweet strength of all, she was a Christian—simplehearted, devout, righteous, sympathetic, consistent, unselfish, honest, full of charity. As I reread this list of adjectives and weigh them, my sober judgment demands that they remain on record.

As a girl Sarepta Irish was guileless and gentle. She was the embodiment of generosity.

She was an idealist and a dreamer. She was born a poet, and some of her work in this realm is exceptionally fine. On the other hand, she has written many practical papers, and several volumes of real value to parents and to reformers.

She was a good mother, and at times under most adverse circumstances fulfilled her duties and bore her burdens. Her children in varied spheres are an honor to her, and pronounce her name with reverent affection.

She had her share of suffering, but the faith that made her strong in her struggle for the common mercies of life, and for the education of her children, transformed her into the heroic saint in the years of pain and feebleness. She was a model of submission and patience; she never lost the child-like grasp of her Father's hand.

Of her change of religious profession I say nothing. I do not understand it. But she did, and that is enough for me. She was, under her later confession, just what she was through all the years before—a sweet, consistent, unselfish Christian.

The church with which she spent her latest years is to be congratulated for the service she rendered, and for the memory of goodness and serenity she bequeaths to it.

I saw her last in the state of Washington, where, at an annual conference over which I presided last autumn, she presented the cause to which she was so deeply devoted—that of the Woman's Christian Temperance Union. Her face was thin, her profile clean cut; lines of thought and earnest purpose were drawn across her brow, and her eyes were full of light. She never seemed to me to be so strong and gentle and consecrated as at that moment.

I am glad that my last vision of her, as a sweet memory, is a kind of prophecy of what I expect to see in her beyond the river!

Her death ended the earthly part of a pure and lofty life.

A TRIBUTE BY
FRANCES E. WILLARD

*U*nder the sway of a Christian civilization the tendency is toward individuality of character, and as a natural sequence, of vocation also. Hence this is the age of specialists and experts. "This One Thing I Do" must be the motto of that man or woman who would condense into a year results one thought sufficient for a lifetime. Perhaps no field of labor illustrates this practical truth more clearly than our well-beloved WCTU. Since we emerged from the nebulous period, and sought specific work through superintendencies, national, state, and local, the change has been as from a picture in Berlin wools to a clear-cut steel engraving. Among those who, though their gifts would have made them successful in almost any field, showed their wisdom by the careful cultivation of one, Mrs. S.M.I. Henry, for years our superintendent of the National Department of Evangelist Work, stands prominent.

Long before either of us had asked concerning the blessed cause of temperance, "Is all this anything to me?" I had read with great interest the poems of Sarepta M. Irish, in the *Ladies Repository*. The same love for humanity and loyalty to its best Friend, that characterized her earliest lines, shines in her temperance addresses, books, poems, and daily life.

She had nothing but the promise of God behind her pen as the means of an education, and the Lord and her friends know much better than she does how she got along. She was paid liberally for her pen work, however, and thereby enabled to spend two years at school. She had many convictions that she ought to enter the foreign missionary field, and had there been agencies at work then that are now so successful, she would doubtless have done this. At her study table she worked out the problem of daily bread with her pen.

The crusade found her at this study table, and she was called out of the quiet she had always known before. She was a most timid woman. No one ever expected her to do anything in public, but under the pressure of a conviction that had to be answered, she made the call for Christian women to come together, and became the mouthpiece of a WCTU, March 27, 1873.

She made her first public address in State Street Baptist Church, Rockford, during the crusade, to an audience that overflowed into the street, and with as little embarrassment as she has ever experienced. A reform club was organized the year after she began her work.

Mrs. Henry was one of our most effective speakers at the capital of Illinois when we presented the great Home Protection Petition. She made the memorable plea from the point of view of a widow with fatherless children, and asked the same power to protect them from the dram shops that their father would have possessed had he not given his life for his country. Her lecture on "What Is the Boy Worth?" is a masterly presentation of the most vital question of the hour, and has been given with telling effect in scores of towns and cities. Mrs. Henry's book *Pledge and Cross* has had the largest sale of any book of its kind, and conveys the very essence of the gospel temperance crusade. The Temperance Training Institute is a very happy invention of Mrs. Henry, by which normal Sunday school methods are applied to the elucidation of our work and the spiritual side is strongly emphasized. Mrs. Henry is also superintendent of our National Training School for Temperance Workers.*

---

*A condensation of the sketch by Frances E. Willard in *Woman and Temperance* (1883), pp. 184–192.